CONFESSIONS OF A RELUCTANT HATER

AND OTHER ESSAYS

SECOND, EXPANDED EDITION

by

GREG JOHNSON

Counter-Currents Publishing Ltd.
San Francisco
2016

Cover image:
Domenico Ghirlandaio
Saint Jerome in his Study, 1480
Church of Ognissanti, Florence

Cover design by
Kevin I. Slaughter

Published in the United States by
COUNTER-CURRENTS PUBLISHING LTD.
P.O. Box 22638
San Francisco, CA 94122
USA
http://www.counter-currents.com/

ISBNs
Hardcover Edition: 978-1-940933-41-2
Paperback Edition: 978-1-940933-42-9
Electronic Edition: 978-1-940933-43-6

Library of Congress Cataloging-in-Publication Data

Names: Johnson, Greg, 1971-
Title: Confessions of a reluctant hater and other essays / by Greg Johnson.
Description: Second, Expanded Edition. | San Francisco : Counter-Currents
  Publishing Ltd., [2016] | Includes bibliographical references and index.
Identifiers: LCCN 2016004902 (print) | LCCN 2016021998 (ebook) | ISBN
  9781940933412 (Hardcover : alk. paper) | ISBN 9781940933429 (Paperback :
  alk. paper) | ISBN 9781940933436 (Electronic Edition) | ISBN 9781940933436
  (E-book)
Subjects: LCSH: Whites--Race identity--United States. | Whites--United
  States--History. | Race awareness--United States. | United States--Race
  relations.
Classification: LCC E184.A1 J57 2016 (print) | LCC E184.A1 (ebook) | DDC
  305.800973--dc23
LC record available at https://lccn.loc.gov/2016004902

CONTENTS

PREFACE

This is my first book. It is not the first book that I had imagined for myself long ago when I aspired to an academic career. Then, I envisioned my first book as a scholarly tome published by a university press for an audience of a few dozen experts and a few hundred research libraries. That career and that book were not to be.

Indeed, two days ago, I had not imagined this book at all. Then I received a suggestion from Mark Hovhannes, a reader of the Counter-Currents/*North American New Right* blog, that I collect together some of my more introductory and topical essays and reviews, pieces that might be useful for people just beginning to explore White Nationalism. I opened the file where I list all of my writings, and after a few minutes of tinkering, the table of contents fell together almost on its own.

This is a humble effort, particularly when judged in the light of my vanity and my ambitions. But still, I offer it to the world in the hope that it might, in some small and unforeseeable ways, contribute to something immeasurably greater: the establishment of a White Republic in North America.

I wish to thank Michael Polignano, Alex Kurtagić, James J. O'Meara, Mark Hovhannes, and our meticulous proof-reader "White Republican," as well as the editors of *The Occidental Observer*, *The Occidental Quarterly*, *TOQ Online*, *Western Voices World News*, and the *Vanguard News Network*, where some of these pieces originally appeared. I also wish to thank those online commentators, most of them anonymous, who helped me to improve my arguments and develop my thinking.

San Francisco, December 7, 2010

This second edition has been improved by being reset, by Kevin Slaughter's cover design, and by the addition of 24 more pieces and an index.

Budapest, October 14, 2015

To R.
I wish I could offer you something greater.

CONFESSIONS OF A
RELUCTANT HATER

I wrote the following essay in June 2005. I circulated it around the internet under the pen name Michael Meehan.

Racism, properly understood, is the acknowledgement of the reality of objective, biological differences between the races, differences that are so profound that racial mingling inevitably causes hatred and violence, thus racial separation is the best way to preserve all races.

Racism, properly understood, is also the recognition that it is perfectly healthy and normal and right to love what is one's own more than what belongs to others. It is natural, normal, and right to show preferences to one's self, one's family, one's friends, one's homeland, one's nation, and one's race.

Why is so healthy, rational, and enlightened an outlook as racism smeared as "hate"? To prefer one's family to the neighbors is not hate. To prefer one's friends to strangers is not hate. To prefer one's homeland to a foreign country is not hate. I prefer whites to other races, but *that fact alone* does not mean that I hate other races.

Preference does not mean hatred, but merely an inequality of loves. I love New Mexico, but I love California more. And I perfectly understand why a New Mexican might feel exactly the opposite.

I will grant that some people are attracted to the White Nationalist movement simply because, for whatever psychopathological reasons, they are filled with hate, and they think that the movement will offer them a place to express their hate openly. But angry, hate-filled people are attracted to all causes. Every cause has an enemy, who is marked as an appropriate object of hate. Thus every cause will attract angry, sick people looking for an outlet for their aggression. I know from personal experience that anti-racists are typically a venomous, aggressive, hate-filled lot.

I suspect, moreover, that some marginal, psychopathic people are attracted to White Nationalism precisely because anti-racists have fostered the impression that we are all crazy. But I also suspect that far more psychopathic haters are attracted to the cultural and political mainstream than to a marginal movement like White Nationalism, simply because the establishment offers no shortage of *socially acceptable* objects of hatred. It is, for instance, socially acceptable to hate white people, especially rural and Southern whites, White Nationalists, Arabs, Muslims, and other enemies of the Jews. So look for the majority of psychopathic haters in the ranks of the anti-racists, in the police forces, in the military, and in the mainstream conservative movement, especially among the warmongers.

But I must be frank. Although preferring one's own race does not *in itself* lead to hating other races, *I really do hate other races*. This is where my enemies will place the close quotes, when they lift my words out of context to smear me. What follows is the context, i.e., some necessary distinctions, qualifications, examples, and explanations.

First of all, I find it very difficult to say that I hate anyone or anything. It goes against my nature. If anything, I tend to be too sentimental and soft-hearted, too open to appeals to emotion. I fawn over children and dogs, and I find it especially hard to say no to women.

Second, I do not hate *all* other races. If tomorrow we discovered life on Mars, I know that I would prefer my race to the Martians. But I would not hate them. Likewise, I prefer my own race to the headhunters of Papua, the aborigines of Australia, the pygmies of the Congo, and the Bushmen of the Kalahari. But I do not hate them.

Why not?

Because I do not have to live with them. Because I am separate from them. Because, so far as I know, they do not negatively affect my life.

If, however, the Catholic Church, the federal government, or the Hebrew Immigrant Aid Society established a colony of Papuans, aborigines, pygmies, bushmen, or Martians on my block, and I had to live in close proximity with them—and, worse yet, subsidize them with my tax dollars—then I probably would start hating them.

Of course it would begin slowly. I might try to get to know them at first. I might bring them food as a housewarming gift—although nervously, because I would not know if it would upset their stomachs or violate some unknown food taboo. Since they would probably know little or no English and show little interest in learning, I might try to greet them with a few words of their native tongue—although nervously, because I would always fear that the pygmy word for "hello" would, to my ears, be undetectably similar to a cuss word. I would try my best to interpret their reactions, to determine how my friendly gestures were being received, but I would probably find them inscrutable and begin to feel uncomfortable around them. Then, as time revealed more and more of our racial and cultural differences, we would really start getting on one another's nerves.

A year ago, I would have placed Polynesians on the list of peoples I had nothing against. But I had no direct contact with them. Then several families from Samoa or Tonga moved in a few buildings down. I thought they were aesthetically unappealing: large, brown, Australoid-Mongoloid hybrids who easily run to flab. But they seemed pleasant enough at first. Then I started noticing certain annoying differences.

For instance, although their personal hygiene does not seem problematic—though I have not gotten close enough to confirm that—in other respects, they are unspeakably filthy people. For instance, they are fond of noisily socializing and eating together outdoors. This is bad enough, but days later, the ground is still littered not only with trash and toys, but also with discarded food. After their last cookout, their landlord had to pay Mexicans to clean up after them. After another cookout, I found a mound of rotting fish, crawling with flies and maggots, dumped in a neighbor's yard. Of course this kind of behavior would not be a problem in Tonga or Samoa, where it is probably accepted by everyone. But here it is disgusting and disrespectful, not to mention a potential health hazard.

Other behaviors are simply attempts to exploit white Americans, whom these Polynesians seem to regard with cordial contempt. It is hard not to be contemptuous of people whose commitment to "multiculturalism" means abandoning their own cultural standards whenever they conflict with foreign standards, no matter how barbarous and inferior. For instance, when the local Samoans or Tongans (or whatever) find the washing machines in their apartment building engaged, they simply come over and use the machines in my building. I do not know how they get in. I suspect that they have their abundant children lurk around and then prop open the door when someone leaves. Not only does this inconvenience people in my building who wish to do their laundry, it is a security hazard for doors to be propped open. Furthermore, once they gained access to the laundry room, the detergents I had left out without fear of theft by fellow whites were rapidly depleted. These Polynesians did not even care to hide their theft by pilfering a little at a time. Either they are incredibly stupid, or they think they can steal from whites with impunity.

Now these are minor problems, particularly compared with the plight of whites forced to live among blacks. But they illustrate how irritating diversity rapidly becomes. Furthermore, I can't honestly say that I hate Polynesians—not yet. But if I confronted them about their behavior and the response were ugly, I might very well end up hating them. (I have not confronted them because I am planning to move in the near future, because it would do no good, and because I have bigger fish to fry.) But hate them or not, I don't want to live around Polynesians, any Polynesians, ever again.

I do not deny that white people can be obnoxious. But I prefer obnoxious whites to obnoxious non-whites any day. Even the worst white people are easier to handle. At least I can appeal to common standards, and confronting them is not an international incident.

A third important qualification: it is possible to hate a group of people and yet not hate individual members. I am unfailingly polite in my dealings with individuals of other races. I have met likeable individual blacks, Jews, mestizos, and Orientals. I have even met non-whites who are capable of adopting white standards and customs and living harmoniously in a white society.

But I never lose sight of the fact that these likeable individuals are members of races with identities and interests different from my own, races that inevitably come into conflict with my own when we share the same territory.

An individual black, especially if nurtured by a white civilization, may turn out to be an intelligent and admirable scholar like Thomas Sowell. But a lot of blacks living together according to their own natures never rise above primitive savagery. The potential Thomas Sowells are nipped in the bud. And when large numbers of blacks are loosed on a white civilization, they inevitably drag it down to their level, as can be seen in Haiti, South Africa, and Detroit. There are just not enough good blacks in the black community to make any other outcome possible.

An individual Jew can make genuine contributions to white civilization. Gustav Mahler, for instance, was a first-rate composer. But a lot of Jews living amongst us according to their own natures and interests have been overwhelmingly destructive. Without the Jews, there would have been no Communism, which is the single deadliest folly in human history. (Christianity, another Jewish product, is not far behind.) Without the Jews, the United States would never have gotten into World War I. Without the Jews, there would have been no World War II. Without the Jews, the United States would not be at war with Iraq. Nor would the US government be planning wars with Syria and Iran. Nor would the US be pursuing a reckless anti-Russian foreign policy. If any of these adventures leads to World War III, a future historian will tell us that it would not have happened without the Jews either. Compared with these crimes, it seems almost petty to complain about the Jewish role in promoting every form of cultural ugliness, filth, and degeneracy. But there are just not enough good Jews in the Jewish community to make any other outcome possible.

By all means, treat individuals as individuals. But don't fall for the folly of individualism, which denies the reality of group identities, group interests, and group conflicts. Be on guard when an individualist waxes gooey and sentimental about the Gustav Mahlers and Thomas Sowells and then "concludes," by sheer assertion, that collective problems are non-existent or that collective solutions are immoral and out of the question.

Alex Linder once summed up this sort of individualism brilliantly: "Because the black race produced a Thomas Sowell, the white race must die." Because the Jews produced a Mahler, the race that produced Bach, Mozart, Beethoven, Brahms, and countless other geniuses must perish. After all, if whites were to secure our survival, that would be "collectivism." But individualism founders on the fact that groups are real. And collective problems require collective solutions.

I showed a draft of this essay to a friend who questioned the wisdom of giving our enemies a sentence like "*I really do hate other races*" to quote. My reply was: we White Nationalists claim that, as a general rule, the mixing of races inevitably causes hatred and conflict, so it is preposterous for us to pretend that we are immune to the effects of multiracialism. If White Nationalists who claim this are honest, then they are living refutations of their own claim that multiracial societies breed racial hatred.

I am living proof that multiracial societies cause racial hatred. But here is another line to quote: *I do not want to hate other races.* That is why I want to live in a homogeneously white society. Such a society would have plenty of problems, but racial hatred and conflict would not be among them.

Racism, properly understood, means recognizing biological differences between populations and preferring members of one's own group. Racism has no necessary connection to hatred or violence toward other races. In a racial nationalist utopia, all races would have separate, homogeneous homelands. All distinct tribes or nationalities would have separate homelands too.

Racial and cultural nationalism would not impede peaceful cooperation: the exchange of goods and ideas, tourism, international athletic competitions, artistic and cultural exchanges, studies abroad, etc. But nationalism would impede the hatred and violence that are inevitable when different races and peoples are forced to share the same territories and governments. Nationalism, consistently practiced, would even discourage the scourge of war between ethnostates, since true racial nationalists would neither seek to rule over other peoples nor stand in the way of the secession of separate ethnostates from multiracial, multiethnic states.

Multiracialism and multiculturalism do, however, have a necessary connection to hatred and violence toward other races. In theory, of course, the advocates of multiracial, multicultural societies are all about love, tolerance, and peace toward all men. (Except for racial and cultural nationalists, of course, for whom they have no love and tolerance, and against whom they are willing to wage wars of extermination.) But in practice, multiracial, multiethnic states do not work. They lead inevitably to hatred, intolerance, and bloodshed.

They even made a hater out of a nice guy like me.

Counter-Currents/*North American New Right*,
October 23, 2010

A NATION OF IMMIGRANTS?

One of the worst clichés of contemporary politics is "The United States is a nation of immigrants." The implicit argument is: "If we look back far enough in our family trees, we will find that all of our ancestors got off a boat. So doesn't it seem arbitrary and unfair to declare that America won't take any more immigrants? After all, what if they said that before your ancestors came here?"

The "nation of immigrants" cliché smuggles in the premise that all immigrants are basically equal, hence the unfairness of distinguishing between them. But not all immigrants are equal. As immigration advocates never tire of telling us, immigrants are a racially, culturally, and religiously "diverse" lot.

And that is a bad thing.

No society is improved by racial, cultural, and religious diversity. These merely become fault lines along which social frictions and upheavals regularly occur.

America would be improved by fewer blacks, Asians, mestizos, and Jews, not more of them.

But there is another kind of diversity that needs to be faced when talking about immigration. This kind of diversity can exist between two people of the same race, religion, and culture. It is a diversity of economic and political interests. Just because we are all immigrants or descended from immigrants, that does not imply that we all have *the same interests*.

Each new immigrant inevitably dilutes the political and economic power of the people who were here before. This is still true no matter how much a new immigrant may later contribute to society. When Nikola Tesla stepped off the boat, life became a little bit more competitive for engineers and inventors—even though Tesla's inventions eventually made everybody's life easier.

A favorite argument of immigration advocates is to seek out Italian, Polish, Irish, or other "ethnic" (i.e., non-"Anglo-Saxon") Americans, and say: "They wanted to keep you out too, you know, so how can you side with people who want to keep out Somalis and Haitians and Mexicans?" Of course, in doing so, immigration advocates tip their hand. They know diversity is a source of weakness among whites. It undermines our solidarity, and our enemies seek to exploit that.

To my ears, there is nothing more grating today than a white American talking about his "Anglo-Saxon" identity. It is grating for two reasons. First, most of them are Euro-mutts anyway. Second, pure Anglo-Saxons like me are the people who gave this country away in the first place, and if "we" are going to take it back, we are not going to do it alone. Perhaps, then, we should begin by shutting up, setting aside our old prejudices against fellow whites, and learning to work with the Irish and Italians and Poles who as a rule are far less hamstrung by "white" guilt, emotional repression, and reluctance to take their own side in a fight.

That said, I can still grant that the Anglo-Saxons of the past had good arguments for wanting to exclude other white ethnic groups. They knew that ethnic diversity was a source of social conflict and weakness, even when the diversity was among fellow whites. The same arguments are even more cogent today when applied to non-white immigration, since non-whites cannot be assimilated without the destruction of the white race and white civilization.

When it was founded, the United States was primarily an Anglo-Saxon society. If we really take seriously the idea that diversity weakens a society and homogeneity strengthens it, then we must conclude that the US should have striven to become even more homogeneously Anglo-Saxon. And that implies that if the US permitted immigration at all, it should have been only from Great Britain. That means no Irish, Germans, Poles, Swedes, Norwegians, Italians, Greeks, etc. need apply.

But immigrants from Europe are not like non-whites. The peoples of Europe have common racial and cultural roots that make it possible for Irishmen, Germans, Italians, and Frenchmen to all become Americans. Europeans can be assimilated. But non-whites can never become Americans, except in a purely legal sense. This means that immigration from the whole of Europe was not an unmitigated disaster for the United States.

But we must be objective enough to admit that it was a (mitigated) disaster nonetheless. Just because non-Anglo-Saxon immigrants were assimilable, that does not mean that they had *the same interests* as the Americans who were already here. Their arrival depressed wages, just as non-white immigration does today. Immigration aided the rise of an establishment of rootless, raceless men, just as non-white immigration does today. Immigration led to an increase in crime and violence, just as non-white immigration does today. Immigration diluted the political power of Anglo-Saxons, just as non-white immigration dilutes white political power today.

I do not deny that many immigrants who would have been excluded by this argument made enormous contributions to this country. But, by the same token, there is no way to calculate the Anglo-Saxon geniuses who may have been lost because of the social dislocations caused by immigration. Furthermore, it is possible to point out real contributions by Jews and other undesirables, but does that constitute an argument for letting them in? If the contributions of a Jonas Salk do not trump considerations of homogeneity, then why should the contributions of a Nikola Tesla?

How would the vastness of America have been settled without immigration? Where there's a will, there's a way. Without immigration to fill sweatshops and coolie gangs with the half-starved refuse of Europe and Asia, the capitalist class would have lost a significant advantage over the working class. Wages would have been higher and work weeks would have been shorter. And since the only way to add new workers would have been reproduction, the system would have encouraged large families and made sure the children were properly educated. Big business would have developed more slowly, if at all — which is fine.

America's large and prosperous working class would have developed much sooner, along with a large and prosperous middle class of farmers and shopkeepers. Both groups would have had the resources and the leisure to protect their rights and liberties from the plutocrats and do-gooders and warmongers.

America would have been a freer, less divided, more harmonious, and happier society.

Well, it was not to be.

Now white America is a mixture of people from all over Europe, slowly being submerged in a rising tide of mud.

If we are going to survive as a race, we have to unite as one. In this context, I understand why my fellow White Nationalists are hesitant to revisit old debates about immigration. How does it help the cause of white unity in today's America to look at failed arguments to exclude the Irish, the Slavs, and the Italians?

The Americans of the past wanted to hold onto their Anglo-Saxon identity, and they failed. With each new generation, there is more and more mixing between the descendants of different European immigrant groups. What is emerging is a generic white American, with a sense of his interests merely as a white. The linguistic and cultural divisions of the Old World are fast disappearing, and with them the ability of our enemies to exploit them.

This need not be seen as a loss. After all, there is still a France. There is still a Poland. There is still a Germany. And Americans will probably continue to celebrate Saint Patrick's Day and Oktoberfest. It will simply be the same crowd at both events.

But how is this a gain? America may be the place where we recreate the original unity of the white race before it was divided and pitted against itself. In order to preserve and advance this emerging (or re-emerging) white unity, we need to stop and then reverse the influx of non-whites into the United States.

Aside from barring non-whites, what sort of immigration policies would a White Nationalist America have? I would of course open our borders to persecuted whites in Rhodesia and South Africa. But does that apply across the board? Do we open our borders to persecuted Muslim Kurds and Afghans too? Some of them are not just white, but Nordic looking.

And how white is white? Most of the peoples of the Middle East, Central Asia, and South Asia have to be categorized as Caucasians. Even pure-blooded Dravidians of South India, unmixed either with the Aryans or with the Australoid aborigines, are Caucasian, even though their complexions are sometimes blacker than Negroes'. There is, in short, quite a lot of diversity within the Caucasian race.

But we should remember that in politics diversity brings weakness and homogeneity brings strength. Therefore, we should be quite hesitant to accept any immigrant simply because he or she is Caucasian in the broad sense.

Since the population and culture of white America is still primarily Northern European, I would like to see immigration policies that preserve and strengthen that element. If we value greater homogeneity, the quickest way there is to promote immigration from Northern Europe.

Then there is the issue of quality control. Obviously, the United States has no interest in importing stupid people. But should we really be encouraging smart people to come here either? Would it be proper for a White Nationalist America to compete with other white nations for their best minds? Shouldn't we be concerned to see all white nations prosperous and well governed? But that means that every white nation will need its own elite. So America should not be a "brain drain."

Of course if other white nations have backward and oppressive systems that waste their native talents, it seems only humane to allow talented people to move here. But shouldn't our first priority be to encourage such societies to improve themselves? And if they do, shouldn't we encourage the immigrants to return home to work for the advancement of their own people?

There is another, more fundamental question that must be raised before we discuss immigration policy: Why does a healthy nation need immigration at all?

It may be that immigration is not a social good, but a symptom of social ills. In America today, immigration serves to cushion the system from the consequences of its own failures. For instance, progress requires more and more intelligent people, yet intelligent Americans have disastrously dysgenic breeding patterns. Progress requires more and more educated people, yet America's educational system is ever worse. Instead of addressing these problems, we simply import brains from South and East Asia. But if America needs more brains, we should grow them here, not import them.

Immigration is really just a question of distribution. But distribution presupposes production. So the ultimate question is this: How do we put our house in order, take control of our own destiny, and produce more and better white children? Until we deal with that problem, the whole question of white immigration is moot.

"The Cat Lady," *Vanguard News Network*, April 2003

THE FIRST WORD:
CRAIG BODEKER'S
A CONVERSATION ABOUT RACE

A Conversation About Race
A Film by Craig Bodeker
Denver: New Century Productions, 2008

When a white person awakens to our race's peril, the first impulse—and the first duty—is to try to awaken others. But where to begin? Becoming a White Nationalist often takes years of experience, reflection, and reading. And one has to find one's courage along the way too. How does one condense all that into talking points? Big books like Wilmot Robertson's *The Dispossessed Majority* may well be the last word on these matters. But what is the first word? How do we begin the conversation? We live in an increasingly post-literate society, so for most people books are not the place to start, big books especially.

This is why I highly recommend Craig Bodeker's masterful 58-minute documentary *A Conversation About Race*. It is an ideal first step on the road to racial awakening.

Bodeker posted an advertisement on Craigslist in Denver under the heading "Ending Racism Now," then interviewed respondents on film. He also did "man on the street" interviews. The interviewees who made the final cut are a very diverse group. About half of them are black, including two blacks in interracial relationships. Most of the rest are white, with a couple of Hispanics or Amerindians thrown in.

The premise of Bodeker's film is that he is responding to Barack Obama's call for a national conversation about race.

His first question is about the pervasiveness of racism. His respondents all agree that racism is everywhere. He then focuses on the definition of racism, comparing what his sources say to definitions drawn from Wikipedia and standard dictionaries. Initially, I found this concern for definitions and piety toward dictionaries silly. But my objections vanished once I realized that

Bodeker was merely trying to show just how astonishingly vague people's understanding of racism is.

Some interviewees seemed to think that any form of distinction-making is racist, which probably explains why discrimination against women, homosexuals, and poor people was defined as racism, even when no racial distinctions were involved. Others regarded drawing generalizations about groups based on experience and using these generalizations to predict future experience as racism. Still others seemed to think that any judgment that one person or group is better than another is racist — although subsequent questioning yielded significant exceptions. When racism is defined at this level of generality, cognition itself — perception, generalization, induction, evaluation — becomes morally objectionable. On this account, to be a non-racist is to be brain-dead.

Because of the vagueness of the definitions, Bodeker asked for concrete examples of racism in daily life. Again, the answers are astonishing. Whites excoriated themselves as racist for noticing the existence of blacks and drawing generalizations about them based on experience. In short, for whites, racism is simply race-consciousness.

For blacks, however, day to day racism seems largely to be a form of self-consciousness, i.e., feeling conspicuous and out of place in white society. Blacks complained about whites staring at them, being overly friendly and solicitous, giving them compliments, not laughing at their jokes (although some blacks would probably describe laughing at their jokes as racist too), and being afraid of them (because of black criminality). That's it. No slurs, no lynchings, just feeling self-conscious.

I drew two lessons from this segment of the film.

First, if a large part of the black experience of racism amounts to feeling self-conscious in the presence of whites, how much of this is due to whites and how much is due to blacks themselves? Frankly, several of Bodeker's black informants seem to have chips on their shoulders, i.e., pre-existing grievances against whites that cause them to view even innocuous white behavior in a jaundiced manner. One might even say they have prejudices against whites.

Second, who are these overly friendly and solicitous whites who make blacks feel so self-conscious? Do these whites think of themselves as racists or as anti-racists? I would lay odds that 99 percent are liberal anti-racists, who think that simply by going out of their way to be *nice* they can charm sullen blacks into acting like white people, absolve themselves of the sin of racism, and demonstrate their good faith and intentions. It is ironic that such liberal solicitousness is the primary example of day to day racism cited by Bodeker's black interviewees. Presumably, whites who genuinely dislike blacks will *not* go out of their way to be nice to them, and so will not be perceived as racists.

Bodeker rightly dismisses his informants' definitions of racism as vague and their concrete examples as trivial. From that point on, his focus is not the definition of racism, but the double standards that govern its use. Bodeker shows that all people are "racists," to the extent the term has any meaning at all, but only white people are excoriated for it. The charge of "racism," therefore, functions merely as a club to intimidate whites into not looking out for our own ethnic interests. Thus, although *A Conversation About Race* can be viewed with profit by people of all races, whites clearly have the most to gain from it, and Bodeker frankly takes our own side and does not pretend to be impartial.

His first demonstration of the double standard is quite entertaining. He asks if blacks are better than whites at basketball, on the average. His interviewees do not hesitate to answer yes.[1] He then asks if whites are better at some things than blacks. (He asks one young white woman if white men are better at keeping jobs and paying bills than black men.) The reaction is very different. Not one of the respondents gives a simple yes. One white woman grants that it is conceivable that whites might be better than blacks at *something*, but claims she has no idea of what that would be. The double standard is breathtaking: the conventional

---

[1] J. B. Cash argues that this is not true, but that the college and professional basketball teams in the United States systematically discriminate against white players. See J. B. Cash, "The Racial Caste-System in Sports," *The Occidental Quarterly*, vol. 8, no. 2 (Fall 2009): 37–48. Also see his website, http://castefootball.us.

wisdom on race has no problem with the idea of racial superiority, as long as it is not whites who are superior.

Presumably since none of his informants could come up with a single example of something whites do better than blacks, Bodeker suggests one: whites perform better than blacks on intelligence tests. It was surprising to see how many interviewees explained this away on the grounds that such tests are created by white people and thus culturally biased toward them. Whites, in short, do better only because they stack the deck. Clearly, our enemies are doing a very good job of propagating their ideas.

Bodeker's follow-up question is brilliant: if white performance on intelligence tests is explained by cultural bias, then why do Asians outperform whites on the same tests? It is amusing to see the gibbering this elicits. Again, the double standard is remarkable: when whites outperform blacks on intelligence tests, this result needs to be explained away as cultural bias, not taken at face value; when Asians outperform whites, cultural bias is never suggested. Again, people have no problem with racial superiority, as long as it is not white superiority.

Another important segment of the film deals with black criminality. When asked whether whites are right to fear blacks, and whether blacks commit proportionately more crimes than whites, the white interviewees are reluctant to agree and tend to avoid the question by making excuses. The blacks, however, readily answered yes. I found this surprising and really rather admirable. Blacks also frankly admitted that other blacks intentionally intimidate whites. But they also made excuses for it, claiming that it is a response to white misdeeds.

Bodeker cites truly shocking interracial rape statistics: in the United States in 2005, 37,000 white women were raped by blacks, while in the same period "fewer than ten" black women were raped by whites. (The odd locution "fewer than ten" rather than a specific number leads me to think that the number could be zero, but that the statistical margin of error is ten.) Bodeker then makes another brilliant point: according to the conventional wisdom on racism, we are supposed to be worried if, on any given day, a white person somewhere in America is harboring racist attitudes toward blacks; but if one is concerned that, on the very same day, 100 white women are being raped by blacks, that is racism most foul.

Bodeker also deals with the question of collective racial guilt. He shows handily that blacks and whites are willing to impute collective racial guilt to whites for enslaving blacks and ethnically cleansing American Indians, even through many white Americans, like Craig Bodeker, are descended from people who never held slaves or fought Indians. Yet none of his interviewees were willing to give collective *credit* to whites for the good things about the United States, even though this society was founded by whites and for whites. Moreover, Bodeker points out that the same people who assign collective guilt to whites for black slavery and the ethnic cleansing of American Indians, tend to ascribe collective *innocence* to their putative victims, even though blacks also practiced slavery and American Indians also slaughtered one another for land. Finally, Bodeker points out that whites today are assigned collective guilt for what other whites did long ago, but if one suggested that blacks are collectively guilty of the crimes committed by blacks *today*, that would be branded racism.

Another double standard Bodeker explores concerns racial advocacy. In America today, Mexican mestizos, united under the banner of "La Raza," advocate the ethnic cleansing of whites from vast areas of the United States. This is not condemned as racism. Instead, that epithet is reserved for whites who object to their ethnic displacement. Bodeker points out the existence of black advocates like Jesse Jackson, but none of his interviewees can name a white advocate. When Bodeker asks a white woman about White Nationalists, she says she does not appreciate such groups, but pauses to say that she can relate to their sense of loss. Clearly any form of white advocacy would be branded racism.

Bodeker deals squarely with the long-term consequences of this double standard: white dispossession. If whites, and only whites, are intimidated by the charge of racism from protecting their own ethnic interests, while other ethnic groups are emboldened to pursue their interests at our expense, we will eventually lose what we have: our wealth, our power, our culture, our values, our country, and eventually our very existence, once we become a minority in the land our people created and scapegoats for the failures of the non-white majority.

When Bodeker asks his interviewees about the possibility of their own group being displaced by newcomers, the answers are remarkable. When a white woman is asked what she thinks about whites becoming a minority, the only alternative she can envision is outright white extinction through miscegenation, the creation of a completely homogeneous mongrel race. In short, if one wants to avoid the charge of being a racist, whites must meekly consent to subordination or extinction. Anything else would be immoral. From a biological point of view, such suicidal moralism is a sickness that might indeed doom our race to extinction. Do these people think that a warm feeling of moral superiority will survive their physical annihilation?

When Bodeker asked blacks about their displacement by immigrants from Mexico and Central America, however, their answers surprised me: "Send them back!" "Close the border, build a wall." "They're here bleeding our social services, using our hospitals, without contributing anything to our society." "They come here and don't even speak English. If we went to their country, we would have to adapt." "*Cinco dos adios.* They'd be gone. No problem. They'd be gone. Oh Lawd!" Say what you like about black IQ, these attitudes indicate that blacks may be better adapted for survival than we are. As Michael Polignano, who viewed the documentary with me, quipped, "Maybe it won't be so bad to have a black president after all!"

Clearly the prospects for a harmonious multicultural rainbow utopia are quite dim. More diversity just means more conflict and hatred.

Bodeker's powerful conclusion is the story of how he himself became a believer in the toxic doctrine of white guilt. He does not describe how he freed himself from it, but I am confident that for many years to come, white people will point to *A Conversation About Race* and say that their awakening began here.

It is interesting to study the faces of Bodeker's white interviewees, particularly a young woman named Tina and an older woman named Mary Ann: one can *see* their minds opening; one can *see* the cognitive dissonance between the facts and arguments offered by Bodeker and the conventional wisdom about racism.

A Conversation About Race is all the more impressive when one learns that this is Craig Bodeker's first film — the first, I hope, of many. It was created on a shoestring budget and put together almost entirely on a home computer. It does not look expensive and slick, but neither does it look cheap and amateurish. It is well-edited, well-paced, and consistently engaging, with simple, hip-sounding music. It is proof that while money is no substitute for good taste, good taste can often substitute for money.

Bodeker also has an appealing onscreen persona. He looks like the recovering liberal that he is, which allows a large target audience to relate to him. He comes across as self-assured but laid-back and non-threatening, personable but not glad-handling, serious but not forbidding. He is proof that one can talk about uncomfortable facts and defend radical positions as long as one is soft-spoken and reasonable. It is encouraging to see people of this caliber openly questioning the racial dogmas of our time. This is a talent to be encouraged and emulated.

I have two suggestions. First, I hope Bodeker makes the raw interviews available online. Not only would they be entertaining and informative, but it would also deflect any charges that the interviews were cherry-picked and edited to slant or change their meaning. This film is too important to allow anyone to sow doubts about its credibility. Second, how about *A Conversation About Diversity?*

You can order *A Conversation About Race* from Craig Bodeker's website.[2] The website also contains excerpts from the film, reviews, and interviews with Craig Bodeker.

The Occidental Quarterly, vol. 8, no. 4 (2008): 109–14

---

[2] http://www.aconversationaboutrace.com/

THE CONVERSATION CONTINUES:
MORE OF . . . A CONVERSATION ABOUT RACE

More of . . . A Conversation About Race
A Film by Craig Bodeker
Denver: New Century Productions, 2010

I can't praise Craig Bodeker's path-breaking 58-minute documentary *A Conversation About Race* too highly. As I explained in my original review, it is an excellent tool for getting white people to begin thinking about the most important issue of our time: the preservation of the white race.

In my review of *A Conversation About Race*, I suggested that Craig Bodeker make more of the raw interviews available. Bodeker's new DVD *More of . . . A Conversation About Race* is pretty much what I had in mind.

The original documentary is a stand-alone feature. The new DVD is not. It clocks in at 38 minutes and is one of those "bonus" discs containing deleted scenes, behind the scenes footage, and director interviews that are often packaged with movies.

Fans of *A Conversation About Race* need to see *More of . . . A Conversation About Race*. Bodeker left us wanting more, and now he has delivered.

But *More of . . .* is not essential for first-time viewers of *A Conversation About Race*, which can stand on its own and is probably more effective at only 58 minutes.

Film watchers tend to be naïve and filmmakers tend to be disingenuous about the power of editing to take people's words and use them to advance the filmmaker's agenda. Craig Bodeker is refreshingly honest about this.

In making *A Conversation About Race*, he chose clips that illustrate the incoherence of the conventional wisdom about race. Here he shows some of the material he left out, which allows us to get a fuller and fairer impression of his interviewees.

A lot of the material simply could not be used for technical reasons. Sometimes the interviewees stutter or gibber. One time the cameraman's cell phone rang, and Bodeker rebuked him for it, for apparently this was the fourth time it had happened. Sometimes there were small problems with focus or sound.

The most regrettable glitch was the crying baby that interrupted an interview with a young woman who appeared to be an American Indian. (Craig tells me she is from the Philippines.) The baby in her lap was blonde-haired and blue-eyed. (I thought she might have been a nanny.) She began like many of the interviewees by claiming that she thought that racism was all-pervasive, then the baby started crying, and nothing after that point made it into the first film. In the *More of . . .* DVD, she goes on to reveal that she had lived around whites her entire life and had never experienced any racism, save for the time when someone asked her if she was Chinese! The baby turned out to be her adopted child, and she was in an interracial marriage. Quite a story!

We get glimpses of how Bodeker set up and conducted the interviews. There were two kinds of interviews: impromptu man-on-the-street interviews and studio interviews.

At the end of one of the street interviews, he engages in shameless flattery to get his subject to sign the release necessary to use his interview. The standard procedure is to have the release signed before the interview, to prevent people from backing out afterwards if they do not like their performances.

In the studio interviews, Bodeker warns the interviewees that he is going to ask them questions that might make them angry. He apparently allowed them to read through a list of sample questions. At least some of them were asked to prepare a statement of their views on race.

Two sequences stand out as my favorites.

The first is a segment of Bodeker's interview with Ruben, a Mexican national who in *A Conversation About Race* appeals to his rights as an American citizen until Bodeker gets him to admit that he is not one. In *More of . . .* , Bodeker sets up the segment by telling us that Ruben got under his skin. In the segment, Bodeker is not just asking questions, he is pressing an argument. His passion is apparent, but I detect no anger, and to my surprise he manages to get Ruben to concede his point. Bodeker again demonstrates that one can persuade people of quite radical ideas as long as one is soft-spoken, reasonable, and does not allow oneself to be pigeonholed as a skinhead or one of "those people in Idaho."

My other favorite segment is a montage near the end called "Words of Wisdom" in which the interviewees make some very sensible and admirably candid remarks. Bodeker sets this segment up by saying that it is easy to use editing to poke fun at the views of his subjects. But he reminds us that the incoherence of their views reflects the incoherence of the received wisdom on racism. I liked his tone and message here, but unfortunately he undermines it in the earlier part of the DVD with some snide, sniping comments, for example putting one person's profession (actor) in "scare quotes" and making fun of the coinage "extinctuate" (it was a white person who came out with it, by the way).

The style of *More of . . .* differs from the original *A Conversation About Race*. The original is in black and white and has a minimalistic style. The new DVD is shot in color and includes flashier editing and special effects, including rewinds of clips from the original movie that I found annoying and obtrusive.

As this video came to an end, two feelings were predominant. First, I liked and respected Craig Bodeker and pretty much all of his interviewees. I particularly liked a couple of the blacks. It is refreshing to see people who are not burdened by "white guilt" speaking frankly and unapologetically about their racial interests. All the subjects had, of course, been well-catechized in the conventional wisdom about racism. But most of them had the potential to see beyond it with a little prodding.

Which leads me to the second feeling this DVD evoked, namely *hope*. Our system is based on lies: the lie of human equality, the lie of unique white depravity, the lie that diversity is a strength. These lies are so preposterous, so utterly contrary to human experience, that the system has to create an unsleeping, all-pervasive regime of propaganda and brainwashing to prevent people from looking at reality and thinking for themselves.

But it did not stop Craig Bodeker from creating *A Conversation About Race*. It did not stop him from putting an ad on Craigslist, interviewing people with an inexpensive camera, creating a documentary using inexpensive equipment, and promoting it with the internet. It did not stop him from opening the minds of his interviewees and countless viewers around the world.

As I said in my initial review, Craig Bodeker is a talent to be encouraged and emulated. Encourage him by buying his videos. Encourage him to do a new documentary. (I vote for *A Conversation About Diversity*.) As for emulating him, if there are any aspiring White Nationalist documentary filmmakers out there, please contact me. Perhaps we can put together a workshop.

You can purchase *More of . . . A Conversation About Race* from Craig Bodeker's website.[1]

TOQ Online, February 24, 2010

---

[1] http://www.aconversationaboutrace.com/part_2.asp

SMELLS LIKE ... WHITE GUILT:
CHRISTIAN LANDER'S *WHITER SHADES OF PALE*

Christian Lander
Whiter Shades of Pale:
The Stuff White People Like, Coast to Coast, from Seattle's Sweaters
to Maine's Microbrews
New York: Random House, 2010

I saw Christian Lander in San Francisco on Tuesday, December 2nd, 2010 speaking to a tiny, sweater-clad audience at a small independent bookstore in the Marina District. Lander told the story of the amazing success of his blog Stuff White People Like (http://stuffwhitepeoplelike.com/), which in about six months grew from a private joke to a *New York Times* best-selling book (with a reported $300,000 advance). (See Christopher Donovan's review of the *Stuff White People Like* book.[1])

In his talk, Lander made it very clear that he is not talking about all white people, but just "the right kind of white people," as opposed to "the wrong kind of white people."

The right kind of white people are urban, college-educated, and from upper-middle and upper-class backgrounds. And, most importantly, they are liberal.

Lander also adds that the right kind of white people are "rich": they live in expensive cities, go to expensive colleges, travel widely, and can afford to take a year off from time to time. They know how to trade their hip, grungy attire for expensive suits and ties, and their ironic detachment for "attaboy" attitude, when opportunities for advancement in the system present themselves (courtesy of people from their parents' generation and social circles).

And they know how to hold onto what's theirs. They can be cheap and multicultural at the same time simply by replacing

---

[1] http://www.counter-currents.com/2010/12/explicit-whiteness-christian-landers-stuff-white-people-like/

white workers with Guatemalans.

The wrong kind of white people live in suburbs and rural areas. They are not college educated, or, if they went to college, they were in frats and sororities, did not attend first tier schools, and did not take liberal arts degrees. They are working or middle class, or horrible businessmen and industrialists. And they are not liberal. They are Tea Partiers and Republicans. They watch Fox News.

The right kind of white people define themselves by looking down on the wrong type of white people. This sort of intra-white status competition is a perennial feature of colonial societies like the United States and Lander's native Canada, where an absence of fixed class distinctions creates immense social anxiety and a strong desire to distinguish oneself from "those people" through an ever-shifting set of conventional status markers that Lander focuses on with often uncanny perspicacity. (It takes a special kind of brilliance to see things that are so close to who we are that we cannot help but overlook them.)

I asked Lander "What percentage of white people are white people?" and he answered "90 percent" But it was clear he was talking only about 90 percent of the people *he knew*. In fact, 90 percent of the people he knows belong to the 20 percent of Americans who describe themselves as liberals. Lander also mentioned growing up in Toronto, where the white working and middle classes have been pretty much replaced by non-whites, which is a vision of the world being engineered by Lander's type of white people for the rest of us.

Lander's work is softball satire, not serious sociology. But it is nevertheless significant, because white liberals tend to think that they are generic, universal humans that all other humans aspire to imitate. In this, white liberals are true white supremacists. White Nationalists, who actually believe that the races are different, would never expect the other races to yearn to be just like us. We would sooner just let them be themselves.

By getting white liberals to realize that no, the things they like are not universal but parochially and ethnically white, Christian Lander has stumbled into something very subversive.

White liberals wish to give all the things they like the force of law: women's rights, gay rights, animal rights, environmentalism, historical preservationism, natural foods, walkable communities, general social tolerance. But the wrong type of white people stand in their way.

The solution is simple: dissolve the people and elect a new one. Destroy the wrong kind of white people by shipping their jobs overseas and importing non-whites to displace them at home. Destroy their will to reproduce by ridiculing and penalizing large white families. Destroy their ability to reproduce by taxing them to support large non-white families. And do whatever you can to make a buck producing a culture that leads the wrong kind of white people to political powerlessness, poverty, degradation, and death.

The right kind of white people think this will work, because they believe (1) that the new non-white peasantry will be grateful to them, (2) that deep down the grateful peasants all want to be just like them, and (3) that the emerging non-white majority will continue to accept the leadership of "the right kind of white people" even when they have dwindled to a minority segment of just another minority group. Lander talks about the magical process by which expensive colleges and urban environments transform select non-whites, mostly Asians, into white people.

Of course White Nationalists know that the white liberal plan for hegemony leads only to oblivion. The non-white hordes are well-aware of the parochial whiteness of liberal values. But non-white groups tend to be highly ethnocentric, and given the power, they will promote their own values, not the values of white liberals. Why in the world would they adopt the values of a people who have destroyed their civilization and handed their lands over to aliens?

In an America ruled by blacks, Hispanics, Asians, Hindus, and Muslims of all races, the stuff white liberals like — tolerance, feminism, gay rights, support for "the arts" (for white arts), environmentalism, historical preservationism (of white history), animal rights, etc. — will have pretty much the same status they have in every Third World country.

And aren't there *already* enough corrupt, violent, impoverished, misogynistic, filthy, environmentally devastated Third World countries?

Lander's work interests me for another reason. White Nationalism will not triumph if it is merely a phenomenon of the far Right. We need to work to make white racial consciousness hegemonic up and down the political spectrum. In a White Nationalist society, we will still be arguing about drug legalization, gay rights, environmentalism, abortion, etc. It is just that the Reds and the Blues will all be Whites, and whites will not have the opportunity to bring in non-whites to gain economic or political advantages in their battles with fellow whites.

So, how close are Christian Lander's "right kind of white people" to white racial consciousness? Sitting in that audience and listening to the smug, self-satisfied sniggering at Lander's gentle satire, I realized: they are already there.

The "right" kind of white people are supremely confident in their own superiority. Their self-esteem and sense of entitlement are rock solid. The right kind of white people believe that (1) all other human beings aspire to be just like them, and (2) they will always remain in power and able to secure and perpetuate their values. Those white people down at the Marina believe that the rising tide of color will float their boats.

One fellow asked Lander about what sort of criticism he gets. Apparently, a lot of Stormfront types take him to task for double standards: "How come it is OK to make fun of white people but not black or Hispanic or Asian people?" he asked in a mock-macho, working-class accent. Lander's answer stunned me: "It is always OK to make fun of white people, because no unhappy ending is possible." Translation: white people will always be on top and in control.

But the double standard is not limited to mockery. In the present social climate, whites and whites alone are not allowed to think of ourselves as white *unless we are mocking ourselves*. Whites are not allowed to take pride in our race and its achievements. But other races are encouraged to. We are not allowed to weigh policy questions in terms of our racial interests. But other races are encouraged to, and even helped by whites. Increasing racial and ethnic diversity is leading to increasing polarization and conflict, in which all groups *except whites* are encouraged to take their own side and get their share.

In this context, such a double standard can only have an unhappy ending: white dispossession. As Mike Polignano puts it in the title essay of his *Taking Our Own Side:*

> In the midst of a race war, there can be no greater folly than impartiality, than the pious rot that "there is only one race, the human race." Robert Frost once brilliantly described a liberal as a man who will not take his own side in a fight. In a fight to the death, such a policy is suicide.
>
> In every transaction between a partial man and an impartial man, the impartial man is at a disadvantage. When the impartial man has a benefit to confer, the partial man appeals to the other's impartiality and often walks off with the prize. But when the impartial man needs something from the partial man, his appeals to impartiality fall on deaf ears. As social interactions multiply, so do the partial man's advantages at the expense of the impartial man. (The essence of the Jewish strategy of dominance is to practice ruthless partiality while urging their victims to be free of prejudice and partiality.)
>
> Once the impartial man has nothing left to bargain with, once he has been reduced to powerlessness and penury, to what will he appeal to preserve his life and freedom? Impartiality? Universal notions of freedom and justice and rights? These are just pleading words unless one has the power to force others to respect them. But the impartial man has bargained all his power away. Pleading alone will not prevent him from being reduced to a slave or a corpse, and that is what we Whites will become unless we start taking our own side, and quickly.[2]

---

[2] Michael J. Polignano, *Taking Our Own Side*, ed. Greg Johnson (San Francisco: Counter-Currents Publishing, 2010), p. 4. Online version: http://www.counter-currents.com/2010/09/taking-our-own-side-2/

THE JEWISH QUESTION

Is Christian Lander Jewish? His humor definitely has a self-conscious, neurotic Jewish feel. On his website, there is a picture of him wearing a T-shirt with a Star of David and Hebrew lettering.[3] So is Christian Lander "white" in the same way that Tim Wise is "white": namely a Jew who pretends to be one of us so he can better mock us or sell us ethnocidal poison? Lander claims in his interview in *Heeb Magazine* that he is not Jewish. He just got the T-shirt at a thrift store.[4] He was wearing it "ironically." (In his talk, Lander gave examples of clothes that cannot be worn ironically by white people: Nazi uniforms and KKK robes.)

I believe Lander. The kind of white vs. white status competition he explores existed long before the rise of Jewish hegemony. It has been deftly exploited by Jews, but it was not created by them.

What is Jewish about Lander is his penchant for irony and self-mockery. By "irony," I do not mean the literary trope where one means something other than what one literally says. Instead, I mean a cynical pretense to have seen through the emptiness of something: an ideal, a practice, a religion, a whole culture, or a simple gesture like a handshake. Irony, of course, is incompatible with sincere commitment. Irony requires detachment, a step back, a look down. An ironist may still shake one's hand. He may even shake it vigorously. But inside, he is only acting. He sees the gesture as meaningless, but goes through with it anyway, feeling superior to those who are "fooled."

Diaspora Jews, of course, are natural ironists, because they are hostile aliens in every culture they inhabit. Jewish relations to non-Jews therefore are shot through with irony and mockery. Jewish cultural hegemony ensures that ironism is now the reigning attitude of high and middlebrow non-Jews as well. Jewish hostility to white society means that the only acceptable

---

[3] http://stuffwhitepeoplelike.com/2008/02/14/66-recycling/
[4] http://www.heebmagazine.com/stuff-white-people-likes-christian-lander-the-heeb-interview/

form of white self-consciousness is ironic self-mockery. Sincere ethnic pride, of course, is "hate" when practiced by white people (and only white people). Thus Christian Lander is simply a non-Jew who has mastered how to write as a self-conscious white man within Jewish-imposed boundaries of discourse.

THE BOTTOM LINE

So, is Christian Lander funny? Yes, but I think he is a lot funnier in person than in print. There is a great deal of smugness and self-satisfaction in Lander's brand of soothing satire. The right sort of white people look down on everybody else. When they read Lander, they also look down on themselves for just a second — but only at their most lovable little foibles — and in the end, their sense of superiority is merely reinforced. After all, they are not like those Stormfront rednecks who can't laugh at themselves.

Lander's big giveaway is #50: Christopher Guest Movies, the most smugly unfunny movies around.

Lander's white self-mockery smells like white guilt: self-congratulation disguised as self-abasement. Pity always involves invidious comparisons: one feels superior to those one pities. Moral self-deprecation has the same quality: one revels in one's superior self-consciousness. Every stroke of the flagellum is, in the end, just a pat on the back.

But in pointing this out, I don't want white people to engage in genuine guilt and self-abasement. I want us to take honest and straightforward pride in our virtues, not praise them under the guise of self-mockery. But I also want white elites to wake up and recognize that their hubris and snobbery endangers us all. I hope Lander's writings might contribute to this awakening, but honestly I think it will take an altogether more savage brand of mockery. God knows they open themselves up to it.

Lander lists 92 things that the "right sort" of white people like. The fun of this book is seeing how well one is reflected in it. (The Dutch translation of *Stuff White People Like* has a mirror on the cover.) I divided Lander's 92 "likes" into five categories. Here are my scores:

❖ Yes, I Like: **41**
❖ No me gusto: **37**
❖ Don't Know: **1** (Thailand)
❖ Above My Pay Grade: **2** (Ivy League, nannies)
❖ WTF?: **11** (These are probably things I would know about if I watched TV or went to malls. They include: #26 Adult Swim, #30 Ugly Sweater Parties [I regift all my ugly sweaters], #31 Anthropologie, #44 Roller Derby, #58 Hating People Who Wear Ed Hardy, and #87 Banksy)

My likes include #6 Foreign Accents (as long as they are European), #11 Moleskine Notebooks (wherein the first draft of this was written), #12 Messenger Bags (wherein the former was stashed), #15 Promising to Learn a New Language (Italian is next), #16 Political Prisoners (yes, like Ernst Zündel, Germar Rudolf, and Horst Mahler), #17 Disinfectant (hand sanitizer is a must for travel in Calcutta or New York City), #19 Bumper Stickers (I don't have a car, but I have bumper stickers, like "Bush: The Only Dope Worth Shooting" and "Annoy a Liberal: Kill, Hate, and Steal"), #35 Vespas, #36 Short Stories (as long as they are by H. P. Lovecraft or Flannery O'Connor), #37 Alternative Newspapers (actually I don't like any newspapers, but I wrote something for *The Aryan Alternative* once), #41 Halloween, #45 Appearing to Enjoy Classical Music (and really enjoying it, in my case), #49 Sweaters, #59 Swimming, #83 Taking a Year Off, #85 The Winter Olympics, #89 Old Maps (one of his uncanniest calls), and #90 IKEA.

Food-related likes include: #14 Raw Milk (right down to the glass bottles), #20 Berry Picking, #22 Community Supported Agriculture, #27 Whole Wheat, #28 Sea Salt, #42 Trader Joe's, #52 Small Batch Soda, #66 Hummus, #68 Heirloom Tomatoes, #70 Olives, and #84 Growing Their Own Food.

The most dead-on funny entries are on things that racially-aware white people don't like: #24 Self-Aware Hip-Hop References, #53 Black Music That Black People Don't Listen to Anymore, and #54 Bob Marley. Other standouts are #60 Google, #71 Facebook, #73 Cult Movies, and #88 Being Offended.

So what lessons does Christian Lander teach us about our white liberal brothers and sisters? Their white racial consciousness is alive and well. Their white pride is flourishing behind the masks of white guilt and irony.

But while Lander's "right kind of white people" are extremely secure of their status *vis-à-vis* non-whites, they are very insecure of their status *vis-à-vis* other white people, "the wrong kind," *our kind*. Thus white racial consciousness will not become hegemonic until the "right" whites start fearing non-whites more and hating other whites less.

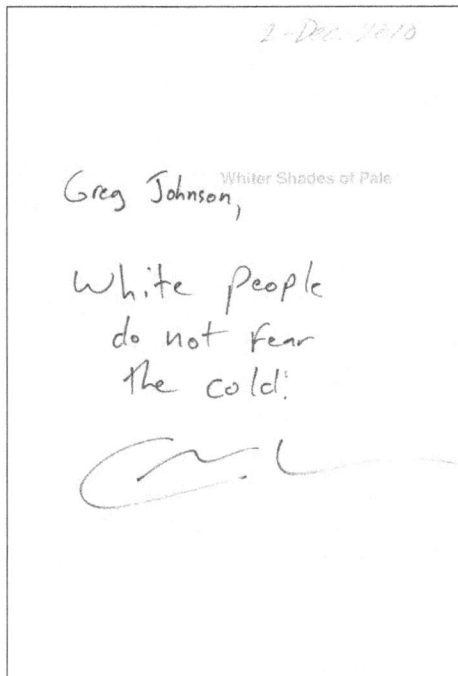

The Occidental Observer, December 7, 2010

TEA PARTY:
THE DOCUMENTARY FILM

Tea Party is a very informative, beautifully crafted, and often inspirational and funny documentary about a growing Right-wing political movement that now enjoys more public approval than Barack Obama and the Democratic Party.

Tea Party tells the overall story of the Tea Party movement, but it is not just a bloodless recitation of facts. It also seeks to build personal relationships between its audience and the Tea Party movement by focusing on particular activists, most of whom seem to be from the Atlanta area, where the director and producers are also located.

According to the film, the first stirrings of the Tea Party movement were near the end of the Bush administration in the waves of Right-wing discontent with the massive bailouts of banks and other large, powerful, well-connected companies that were deemed "too big to fail."

All of these companies were fierce advocates of private enterprise when they were making profits. But when they were losing money, they were only too eager adopt a kind of negative socialism in which the public only shares the losses, never the profits.

The bailouts just kept getting bigger after the election of Barack Obama, and with the signing of the profligate and corrupt "stimulus" bill on February 17, 2009, protests broke out around the nation.

The first specifically "Tea Party" protests took place on February 27, 2009. Almost 30,000 people participated in 50 events all over the country. These numbers are particularly impressive, given that the events were organized in only five days.

On April 15, 500,000 people participated in 850 Tea Party events around the country.

After that, sporadic Tea Parties took place all over the country to protest various big government initiatives, from taxes to bailouts, Cap and Trade, and health care reform.

More large-scale Tea Parties took place on July 4 and July 17.

The July 17 protests were focused on Obama's health care reform initiative. My favorite segment of the documentary follows a group of doctors who went to Washington to lobby Congress against Obamacare.

At one point, they entered a hearing on health care reform chaired by black Democrat John Conyers. We get a glimpse of the snake oil being peddled as reform. An unidentified speaker lauds a single payer system as the "magic solution" for the nation's health-care needs in the condescending tone of someone addressing schoolchildren.

Conyers, in a truly classy gesture, invited the Tea Party doctors to participate, even giving one of them—a very impressive Armenian named Vahan Kasabian—the lectern. It almost made me think that our system can still work.

But then Conyers scotched the whole discussion by asserting that the only reason for opposing Obamacare is the racist desire to defeat the first black president. Yes, it is childish. But remember we are dealing with a black man here.

The culmination of the documentary is the September 12 march on Washington, in which some 75,000 people from all over the United States converged to demonstrate the Tea Party movement's steady resolve and growing numbers. After a montage of sound-bites from the speakers, the documentary ends with members piously visiting various monuments and memorials around Washington.

The activists profiled include Jack, a forty-something white suburban dad; William, an older white minister of a black church who is also a painter and military re-enactor; Dr. Fred Shessel, a Jewish doctor who gets a lot of screen time because Jews are discomfited with the overwhelming non-Jewishness of the Tea Party movement; Dave, a white guy with a grin and big biceps; Jenny Beth Martin, a white suburban mother of two who lost her business to the recession and her house to foreclosure because she was not "too big to fail"; and Nate, a black Tea Partier who gets quite a lot of screen time because liberals, observing the overwhelming whiteness of the Tea Partiers, predictably accused them of being racists.

All of these activists are likable, sincere, and articulate. But I was most impressed by Jack and Jenny Beth.

Jack's unassuming but forceful calls to activism and his Aryan insistence that he does not deserve thanks or praise for merely doing his duty were quite powerful. The guy has the power to motivate people.

Jenny Beth Martin impressed me with her organizational skills and commitment. No, she is not a great orator. Yes, she talks in earnest about "tweeting" things. But she comes across as real, and sincerity is a rare and shining quality in politics today.

Other people who get screen time are Matt Kibbe of FreedomWorks, a libertarian/conservative non-profit organization; Georgia Representative Tom Price; and Joel Aaron, a talk radio personality.

I highly recommend *Tea Party*. It is a very good introductory documentary for people who know nothing about the Tea Party movement. It presupposes no background knowledge, and it is very easy to understand and follow. *Tea Party* should also be seen by anyone interested in Right-wing politics, grassroots political organizing, and documentary filmmaking.

In many ways, *Tea Party* is a model political documentary. It does not just inform and entertain. It motivates. People who see it will try to change the world.

It is encouraging to see just how much technical competence, artistic talent, good taste, and hipness can be found a little to the Right of mainstream. As someone still further to the Right, I realized just how much we have to learn, but I also feel hopeful that we can eventually do work of this quality as well.

You can purchase *Tea Party: The Documentary Film* from its website.[1] But skip the trailer, which is laughable. It makes the film sound like a monster truck rally or the latest release by Michael Bay.

WEAK TEA

Patrick Buchanan thinks that the Tea Party movement may

---

[1] http://www.teapartymovie.com/

save the Republic.[2] But I have read *The Death of the West*, so I know better.

Sure, in the short run, the Tea Party might lead to the election of more Republicans and stall some of the worst excesses of Obama and the Democrats.

But the Republicans can produce no lasting change.

The Republicans are the natural party of America's disappearing white majority. The Democrats are the natural party of America's emerging non-white majority. Whatever power the Republicans can wrest from the Left in the next few elections will inevitably be taken back *unless the erosion of the white majority can be halted*.

And nobody in the Republican party—or the Tea Party movement, or the Ron Paul movement, much less the Libertarians—even *wants* to do that. If the idea has crossed any of their minds, none of them has had the guts to utter it.

Furthermore, the ideas of the Tea Partiers—like those of Ron Paul—appeal only to a vanishingly small minority of the disappearing white majority. For every person who showed up at a Barack Obama rally, there were 100 potential voters who did not. For every person who showed up at a Ron Paul rally . . . well, they were pretty much the whole Ron Paul electorate.

The Tea Party movement has somewhat broader appeal, but people intelligent enough to understand its message and self-reliant enough not to be threatened by it are a small and shrinking minority.

I found myself smiling whenever Jenny Beth Martin raised her shrill voice seeking to energize the Tea Partiers with the mantra of "fiscal responsibility, constitutionally limited government, and free market economics." It would be nice. But it will never compete with "Liberty, Equality, Fraternity," much less "Welfare, Food Stamps, and Affirmative Action."

The Tea Partiers constantly invoke the US Constitution, but they have a largely mistaken view of its nature and its relationship to the American people. The Constitution did not create the American people, the American people created the Constitution.

---

[2] http://takimag.com/article/party_time/

Who are the American people? White people who came from Europe, settled this continent, and eventually decided that they could better govern themselves. The US Constitution was just one white American experiment in self-government. Nothing like it has ever been created by other races. Nothing like it has ever been successfully adopted by other races.

The Constitution and everything else that is good about America was created by white people. When white people disappear, all those good things will disappear with them.

Nobody is going to save the Republic without explicitly working to save the white majority.

And the Tea Partiers are not doing that.

DESIGNED TO FAIL

But it gets worse. The Tea Partiers, like the Republicans, actually obfuscate the necessity of preserving the white majority by playing by the rules of political correctness.

I'll bet there were all of five blacks at the September 12 march. Why do I think that? Because all five of them were featured in the documentary.

I'll bet there was one Latina at the march. Why? Because she was on screen too.

I suspect that the Jew, Dr. Fred Shessel, was highlighted in the film for similar reasons of diversity.

I am sure that the producers and director simply wished to immunize themselves against the predictable charges of racism by highlighting non-whites. Since they sincerely believe that they are selling universal, race-neutral ideas, they saw no downside to it.

But they have to understand: the rules of political correctness are designed by the Left to make effective Right-wing resistance to their agenda impossible. The enemy knows that *the only way the Right can win is by preserving the white majority*.

Therefore, the Left have bullied the Right into adopting the politically correct premise that white racial consciousness and white racial advocacy are simply immoral. Once Rightists have accepted that premise, all of their efforts will be in vain. The mainstream Right in America has accepted parameters that are designed to make them lose.

The Tea Party movement is overwhelmingly white. It manifests a great deal of what Kevin MacDonald calls "implicit" white racial consciousness.[3] This is why its enemies have branded it racist. To combat this charge, the creators of this documentary go out of their way to showcase non-whites.

But by showcasing non-whites, the Tea Partiers are fostering the same folly that helps the Republicans evade facing up to their inevitable demographic Armageddon.

They hope that significant numbers of non-whites will somehow decide — perhaps by repeating the magic mantra of "fiscal responsibility, constitutionally limited government, and free market economics" till their lips go numb — to stop riding on the system and start pulling it instead.

You see, Republicans and Tea Partiers are so terrified of defending the white majority that they have pinned all their hopes on fiscally responsible, law-abiding, hard-working . . . blacks.

The trouble is: there just aren't that many of them, and they'll have an uphill battle convincing the other 99.7 percent of their people.

The same is true of other non-white groups: there just aren't enough sensible ones to support the policies favored by the Tea Partiers.

If the Tea Partiers are going to win, they are going to have to break the taboo on *explicit* white racial consciousness and start working to preserve the white majority.

When that happens, they will have arrived at White Nationalism, which is a whole new cup of tea.

TOQ Online, December 27, 2009

---

[3] Kevin MacDonald, "Psychology and White Ethnocentrism," in *Cultural Insurrections: Essays on Western Civilization, Jewish Influence, and Anti-Semitism* (Atlanta: The Occidental Press, 2007).

SEPARATISM VS. SUPREMACISM

I wrote the following essay in June 2005. Again, it was circulated around the internet under the pen name Michael Meehan. I wrote it in response to a proposal in Edgar Steele's Defensive Racism, *which I learned about through a review by Mike Polignano.*

The problem with this critique (and with Steele's original proposal) is that it treats the issue of partition as a kind of abstract strategy board game, in which the power to do certain things is just assumed, so the only question is of what is desirable.

In the real world, I think it is very likely that a number of different states will emerge after the collapse of the United States. But they will emerge through physical force, and their boundaries will be determined by physical force. There will be no partition conference where politicians, lawyers, and plutocrats sip cocktails and decide whether Aztlan should be moved a little to the east.

I am reprinting it here since such abstract discussions can still be morally clarifying. I also think there are some good lines. Besides, even if it is flawed, it is still one of the bastard children of my pen that I now wish to acknowledge.

Many White Nationalists make a point of describing themselves as white "separatists" as opposed to white "supremacists." A separatist believes that all races have the right to survive, flourish, and pursue their own destinies, and this requires that each race exercise political control over an exclusive living space, a racial ethnostate. The supremacist, however, believes that his race should rule over other races.

There is much to recommend separatism over supremacism. Separatism is a racial "live and let live" philosophy. Separatism seems more moral and more just because it is fair to all races. Under separatism, all races get an equal chance to create the forms of life that express their distinct biological and spiritual natures, free from the interference of other races. Separatism is classical liberalism applied to races rather than to individuals. Liberalism is, of course, the "common sense" of American culture, which goes a long way to explaining the appeal of racial separatism.

Separatism often appeals to egalitarian sentiments by adopting the pretense that the separatist does not hold that some races are better than others, only that they are different, and all equally entitled to control over their own destinies.

I think this pretense is ridiculous. Every healthy race thinks itself superior to others, and no matter what dimension of comparison one chooses, one of them will always be right.

Separatism appeals to the ecologically-minded, because it recognizes that conflict is inevitable when different subspecies are forced to occupy the same ecological niche, and the only way to terminate such conflict is separation for both parties or extinction for one of them — through miscegenation or outright extermination. Separatism is, therefore, the best way of preserving biological diversity.

Separatism is also the best way of preserving cultural diversity. When multiple cultures exist in the same society, cultural differences inevitably give rise to friction and conflict. This friction can lead to two possible results: the violent splitting of a multicultural society into several culturally homogeneous societies, or the gradual wearing away of cultural distinctions, leaving a debased and homogenized cultural precipitate, which is related to a genuine culture like a pidgin is related to a genuine language, i.e., it is good enough for economic activity and expressing the basic, or just plain base, desires we all have in common, but it lacks a vocabulary to express anything higher or more spiritual, anything that differentiates one individual or one culture from another.

Supremacism is, by contrast, deeply illiberal in spirit. The supremacist wants his own race to have its own homeland(s) where it is free to control its own destiny. But he would deny the same freedom to other races. He wants his own race to rule over others. This hegemony need not be exploitative. It can be benign, even paternalistic and benevolent. But whatever form it takes, racial supremacism denies that all races have equal rights to self-determination.

Considered in the abstract, separatism is more attractive to me than supremacism. It accords with my love of natural diversity and my sense of fair play. I am also, frankly, sickened by the suffering and cruelty that is inevitable when one race or nation seeks to conquer and dominate another.

But when I contemplate how racial separatists propose to deal with present multiracial mess in the United States, it gives me pause.

For instance, Edgar Steele, in his recent book *Defensive Racism*, envisions the partition of the US into "New America" for whites, "Aztlan" for mestizos, "New Africa" for Negroes, and "New Israel" for Jews. (Perhaps we can locate "New Palestine," for our millions of Arabs, next door to New Israel.) Others have contemplated giving the San Francisco Bay Area and Hawaii to Orientals and Pacific Islanders.

Bear in mind that these plans for partition do not envision mere ethnic "reservations," which are non-sovereign entities under the control of the US government, but completely sovereign states.

The main problem with such a scheme is that the new ethnostates would threaten the security of the white homeland they would encircle.

If the San Francisco Bay Area were turned into an Oriental enclave, I have no doubt that, after a brief and brutal spasm of ethnic cleansing, it would be controlled by the Chinese, and that in a matter of years it would become a huge Red Chinese colony and military base, complete with nuclear weapons, on the West Coast of the North American continent. The Chinese would then be in a position to seize new territories either through nuclear blackmail or outright aggression.

If there were a New Israel on the North American continent (no doubt on the East Coast), it would lessen direct Jewish power over whites, but it would not stop the Jews from broadcasting filth and promoting decadence among us. Furthermore, why provide the Jews with another sovereign territory from which they can plot their global swindles and to which they can flee when their victims rise up against them?

Finally, unless we located New Palestine right next door to New Israel, I would predict that the Jews of Israel would move *en masse* to New Israel, complete with their nuclear, biological, and chemical arsenals with which they could blackmail us. After all, New Israel would be far safer. The present Israel had to be wrested by force from its inhabitants, whereas under the New Israel scheme, the inhabitants of the US would take a portion of the continent conquered and civilized with the blood, brains, and brawn of their kinsmen—indeed one of the most valuable portions—and give it away to the Jews, who deserve anything but a reward for their parasitism and nation-wrecking.

A black ethnostate on the North American continent would quickly follow the course of every other black state. The civilization built by whites would fall into ruin in the hands of blacks, who lack the intelligence, initiative, foresight, and moral character needed to create or sustain it.

Once ceded to blacks, whole states of the defunct US would become a vast Detroit. Depending on where the borders would fall, we would see magnificent cities like Savannah, Charleston, and New Orleans turn into burnt-out wastelands. There would be chaos, slaughter, civil war.

Horrified and soft-hearted whites would open their wallets to feed starving children and open their borders to pitiful refugees, and we would be right back where we started.

Eventually a dictator would emerge, a cannibal statesman like Idi Amin or Emperor Bokassa, who would become a natural ally of New Israel or the Red Chinese, or both, in putting the squeeze on Whitey.

A similar course would be followed by Aztlan. Southern California and the Southwest would become just like the other filthy, impoverished, corrupt, violent, backwards, Spanish-speaking, mestizo nations in this hemisphere. Then its residents would sneak across the border into the white homeland looking for jobs and handouts.

Although in the long run, Aztlan's interests would conflict with those of the Red Chinese, blacks, and Jews, in the short run they would be natural allies in looting and dispossessing whites.

And why wouldn't they?

The advocates of partition propose the following. The most powerful nation on Earth, with the most formidable military arsenal in history—a nation which in past generations ruthlessly conquered and civilized a vast portion of this continent—is going to surrender, without a fight, some of its richest and most beautiful territories. And to whom? To an army of dish washers and leaf blowers.

Any people so craven would never be able to rest secure behind the newly-drawn borders of their ethnostate. "If whites were unwilling to defend their borders before," our enemies will reason, "why would they defend them now?" "If they were unwilling to expel invaders before, why would they expel them now?"

And if whites would be willing to guard their borders and expel non-whites from a future ethnostate, *then why not do so now?*

If a pro-white government emerged with the power to partition the US into separate ethnostates, it would, *ipso facto,* also have the power to expel all non-whites from the present US. This, as I see it, is the most realistic and responsible form of racial separatism. (Except for the American Indians and native Hawaiians, for whom segregated ethnic reservations seem the just solution.)

There are certainly no practical impediments to mass expulsions. If it was possible for millions of people to come here, it is possible for them to leave. Whether or not a pro-white government would have the political will to do this is another matter altogether.

Another option for the separatist is to abandon the idea of sovereign ethnostates in favor of a system of segregated reservations for non-whites, reservations that might be internally self-governing, but whose relations with the rest of the world would be controlled by a white government. This, however, would be the very racial supremacism that the separatists want to avoid.

Counter-Currents/*North American New Right,*
October 25, 2010

TO CLEANSE AMERICA:
SOME PRACTICAL PROPOSALS

*The following short piece from 2003 has the same major flaw as
"Separatism vs. Supremacism," namely, it deals with the issue
in the abstract. Racial separation is not likely to happen this
way. Nonetheless, it has the virtue of broadening the reader's
sense of what is morally and practically possible.*

I hear a lot of defeatist talk among White Nationalists. A re-
curring theme is that there are too many non-whites in America to even consider an all-white nation. The most optimistic
solution is to partition the country into ethnically pure nations.

The answer to this kind of talk is simple: If it was not too
much trouble for all these people to come here, then it will not
be too much trouble for them to go back. If whites could conquer and settle this country once, then we can do it again. The
only thing stopping us from doing it again is lack of nerve, not
lack of ability. But an awakened white nation could quickly set
things right.

Part of the problem may be that people are trying to envision
a government program that could remove tens of millions of
non-whites. It seems impossible, so they give up in dismay. But
as a matter of fact, there have already been such programs. From
1929 to 1939, more than one million Mexicans—more than half
of them US citizens—were forced to return to Mexico. In the
1950s, more than one million Mexicans were again repatriated
by Operation Wetback. Surely with modern computers and law
enforcement techniques, it would be relatively easy to scale such
programs up to deal with more than 20 million Mexicans plus
other non-whites.

But does one really need a massive government operation to
cleanse America? After all, most non-whites did not come here
through government programs, but through private initiative.
They came because there were economic incentives to come.
They will leave when there are economic incentives to leave.

And I am not talking about the use of government money to bribe non-whites to leave. That was the feeble proposal of the British National Party, before they abandoned the idea of repatriation altogether as unfeasible.

We need to make a distinction between government programs, in which the state takes the initiative, and government policies, which allow or encourage private initiative. The economic incentives that lead to non-white immigration work only by the government's permission. If immigration were banned and the ban rigorously enforced, these incentives would become impotent. By the same token, the government can pass laws creating economic incentives for non-whites to go home.

Of course before we talk of incentives, we need to deal with the hundreds of thousands of non-whites, citizens and aliens, who are already incarcerated at public expense for breaking the law. These people should be immediately deported. Then we should crack down on non-white crime and automatically deport all new offenders. That would rid us of millions in short order.

As for non-whites who are here illegally, but who are not already incarcerated, we should first levy fines of $10,000 per day per alien on any business that employs them and any landlord who rents to them. That should send most of them scurrying for the border. After six months or so, the police can scour out the ones who remain and deport them. After another six months, the government can offer a bounty for those who slipped through the cracks.

As for the ones here legally: they should be immediately stripped of their citizenship and all the benefits that come from it. They should be denied any government or government subsidized benefits, e.g., education, welfare, unemployment insurance, health care. We should allow them to sell their property and take the proceeds with them. But to make a quick departure even more appealing, that option would expire after a year. Those who cannot take a hint would then be deported, with a bounty for those who remain.

Such policies, after a couple of years, would rid us of millions of non-whites. Only diplomats, tourists, and traveling businessmen would remain within our borders. Yes, these would be government policies. But the beauty of them is that they would encourage most non-whites to leave on their own initiative. The government would not have to track down, incarcerate, and deport each one, which would be an enormously expensive burden on the taxpayer and economy.

Instead, the policies I propose would stimulate economic activity, especially in travel and real estate. One appealing result is that home prices would drop, making it easier for white couples to get a start. Another result would be higher wages for white workers.

Only after the non-white population had been significantly reduced would a more active government role be necessary, but by that time the problem would be much more manageable.

"But there would be violence! There would be race war!" the defeatists will bleat. Of course there would be.

I am all for minimizing violence. But let's be real: There already is violence. There already is race war. There already is ethnic cleansing.

Every time a white is robbed, raped, or murdered by a non-white predator, that is race war. The Cincinnati riots were race war. The Wichita massacre was race war. "Beat up a White Kid Day" was race war. "Polar Bear Hunting" is race war. When tens of thousands of whites fled American cities and lost tens of millions in property because of desegregation, that was ethnic cleansing.

The race war and the cleansing are already upon us. It is just that we are not fighting back. And if we don't start fighting back, we are going to be destroyed.

Yes, there would be thousands of white race traitors marching and holding candlelight vigils. That's why we have rubber bullets and fire hoses. Yes, blacks and Mexicans would riot and burn down their neighborhoods and Korean convenience stores. But that's why we have police and the National Guard. In the end, non-white lawlessness would simply allow us to accelerate their expulsion.

Yes, violence would have economic costs, but they would be

nothing compared to the costs in crime, chaos, ugliness, and inefficiency of keeping these people here. Yes, there would be white casualties. But the white death toll would be nothing compared to the white death toll that is inevitable if we do nothing: namely, extinction.

"T. C. Lynch," *Vanguard News Network*, April 24, 2003

THE AUTOCHTHONY
ARGUMENT

One of the perennial accusations against white colonial societies around the globe — in the Americas, Africa, and the Antipodes — is that they are morally illegitimate because other people were there first. This is what I call the "autochthony argument," from the Greek "αὐτόχθων," meaning "springing from the land," i.e., indigenous. According to this argument, the original inhabitants of a land are its rightful owners ("finders-keepers"), and it is a violation of these rights for other peoples to displace them. Thus all European colonial societies, which more or less involve the displacement of indigenous peoples, are illegitimate.

The first thing to note is that those who appeal to the autochthony argument to dispossess white colonists quietly ignore it when dealing with the colonization of Europe by non-whites. In this case, it is Europeans who are indigenous and non-whites who are depriving indigenous people of control over their homelands. I feel for indigenous peoples around the globe, because as a white man, I too know what it is like to be displaced from one's home by aliens.

Of course some argue that European populations aren't really indigenous, since Europeans have invaded and colonized one another's societies for thousands of years. The indigenous people of England, for example, were invaded and colonized by Romans, Anglo-Saxons, Vikings, and Normans before the present waves of Africans and South Asians. So why should the descendants of Anglo-Saxons or Normans be considered any more "indigenous" than Jamaicans and Pakistanis?

The problem with this argument, of course, is that it still admits that *some* Europeans are indigenous. Moreover, since *all* European peoples are descended from the same racial stock, which is indigenous to Europe, when Europeans move from one part of Europe to another, they are not "displacing indigenous populations." They *are* the indigenous population, which is merely reshuffling itself.

This is not to discount the sufferings that Europeans have inflicted upon each other. But as bad as it was, it was not the displacement of an indigenous race by an alien one. It is simply different branches of the indigenous population fighting with one another, much like African tribes or American Indian tribes fight among each other. If racial infighting deprives Europeans of the right to call themselves indigenous, why does this not apply to non-whites as well?

Some people claim that the non-white colonization of Europe is tit for tat, since Europeans colonized non-white countries. This argument might be plausible for England, France, and Spain, which had vast colonial empires, and for Holland, Belgium, and Portugal, which had smaller empires. It applies to a much lesser extent to Germany and Italy. Denmark and Sweden also had negligible overseas colonies.

But if European colonization was wrong, then so is non-white colonization of Europe. Two wrongs don't make a right. Moreover, a punishment is a bad thing, and the advocates of diversity will never admit that non-white colonization is making Europe worse, although it obviously is. Finally, even if the historical injustice argument were valid, it would apply *only* to those European countries that had colonies, and it would grant rights of reverse colonization *only* to peoples that were once colonized, and *only* in the nations that once colonized them.

But the majority of European societies had no overseas empires: Ireland, Norway, Finland, Estonia, Latvia, Lithuania, Poland, Switzerland, Austria, Hungary, the Czech Republic, Slovakia, Romania, Bulgaria, Slovenia, Croatia, Serbia, Montenegro, Bosnia, Albania, Macedonia, Greece, Luxembourg, Monaco, Lichtenstein, Andorra, San Marino, etc. Yet all are targets for non-white colonization. Furthermore, the colonial powers are targeted for colonization by peoples they never colonized. It makes no sense that countries like Germany, Sweden, and Denmark, which never had colonies in the Muslim world, are suffering primarily from Muslim colonization.

Since non-white colonization of Europe cannot be justified as punishment for historical injustices, it is sold as a good thing because it increases "diversity" and because Europeans have a moral obligation to open their borders to immigrants who are fleeing poverty and oppression. The trouble with these arguments, however, is that they also support bad old European colonization, which increased ethnic diversity and was driven by poor people seeking resources and oppressed people seeking freedom. And if Europeans have to sacrifice ethnic homogeneity, political sovereignty, wealth, and freedom to accommodate non-white colonists, then why, exactly, was it wrong for Europeans to impose these costs on non-whites around the globe?

As tempting as it is to use the autochthony argument to defend Europe from non-white colonization, it has several problems.

First, it presupposes that *mere presence* in a territory is morally meaningful. The autochthony argument states that the *first* inhabitants of a land have a clean title. They did not have to displace anyone else through violence and trickery. Later occupants are illegitimate if they displace the first occupants and usurp their territories.

But if mere first presence in a territory confers rights, then why is this confined to biologically modern humans? Other animals are merely present where they live as well. Didn't Cro-Magnon man displace the Neanderthal? Didn't mammals displace the dinosaurs? Aren't practically all living things illegitimate interlopers in previously occupied ecological niches, until we get back to the original denizens of the primordial soup? But does it make sense to regard the entire history of life on this planet as a ghastly moral offense? So much for evolution, I guess.

A Darwinist, of course, would argue that one organism can displace another only by being better adapted for survival. Thus evolution is a process of improvement, rather than a fall from an original state of innocence. Social Darwinists argue that the conquest of the dark races by whites is evolution in action. And, if the darker races are now turning the table and conquering whites, that too is evolution in action. For Darwinists, success in the struggle for power is by definition the best outcome, no matter who ends up on top.

The autochthony argument holds, in essence, that the *first* organism on the scene is in the right, and all who follow are illegitimate interlopers. The Darwinist would argue that the *last* organism on the scene is in the right, simply because it is successful, and that all that came before have no legitimate claims, simply because they failed. Both arguments are equally morally absurd, because there is more to *right* than just being present at the beginning or the end of a struggle for power.

Second, the autochthony argument does not distinguish between *occupying* and *appropriating* territory. Just being on a piece of land does not necessarily make it one's own. To appropriate land, one has to *do something*. One has to *make something* of it, and in doing so, one *takes responsibility* for it.

Third, the autochthony argument also ignores the distinction between *nomadism* and *settled occupancy*. Often times, the first people were merely passing through. Nomads don't *own* land, they merely *inhabit* it, as do the buffalo. They do little to it, and they take little or no responsibility for it. Nomads are less tied to a piece of ground than settled people, and nomads can share the use of the same region, whereas settled ways of life require exclusive ownership. This is not to say that nomads have no interests and rights that more settled people need to respect. But to own land, is it sufficient merely to *be on it*, or does one have to *do something with it*—i.e., to improve it and take responsibility for it?

Fourth, the autochthony argument overlooks the fact that if one owns land, one can therefore disown it. If indigenous peoples actually own their homelands, then they can alienate them to newcomers. For instance, not all North American natives were dispossessed through wars of aggression. Many natives began by selling some of their lands to newcomers, and only later did conflicts arise. Moreover, American Indians were sometimes dispossessed after losing wars *they had started*. There is a huge moral difference between stealing land outright and securing one's own people by dispossessing and banishing aggressive and implacable enemies. Sometimes indigenous peoples lose their lands fair and square.

Fifth, the autochthony argument presupposes that legitimate ownership derives solely from the past (first occupancy) rather than from the future (what one is likely to do with it). For instance, even if the American Indians were the first people on this continent, *they weren't doing much with it*. It strikes me as a moralistic absurdity to declare that the farms, factories, highways, power plants, towns and cities of America, plus all of the cultural and technological achievements of Americans, from bluegrass music to the space program, are somehow illegitimate because there was a thin population of Stone Age people on the continent when our ancestors first arrived.

Even if we grant that *first occupancy* confers rights, doesn't *later use* also confer rights? And what is more important: how our people acquired our homelands or what we made of them? Given that the first occupants of all lands are primitives, whereas later occupants are usually more socially and technologically advanced, doesn't the autochthony argument contain a built-in bias against civilization, progress, and the races that can produce and sustain them? Why should whites, of all peoples, accept such a stacked moral deck? Encounters between radically different peoples almost always end up badly. But at least if one creates something great, the suffering and strife need not be in vain.

Sixth, the autochthony argument is usually offered in bad faith, as part of a swindle. In the United States, for instance, American Indians who did not suffer from the acts of white colonists in centuries past, demand apologies and favors from whites (including recent immigrants), who never did anything to harm an Indian.

The last thing these Indians want is for whites to take their guilt trip so seriously that they erase the wealth they created and leave the continent as their ancestors found it. Instead, Indians wish to increase their share in the bounty of white civilization through moral blackmail, which just happens to impeach the legitimacy of that civilization's very foundations. The Indians are untroubled by the moral contradictions of their position, but their aim is not justice but unearned wealth.

In truth, indigenous peoples who present themselves as

"historical" victims aren't victims at all. They are actually swindlers. And the whites they accuse of "historical" crimes are not criminals at all but victims of a moral swindle. Giving in to such moral blackmail does not right old ethnic wrongs (the victims and perpetrators of which are long dead). Instead creates fresh ethnic wrongs: new victims and new perpetrators and new resentments to fester down through the centuries. This can only impede amicable and just relations from emerging in the future.

What should the New Right's position be on colonialism and indigenous peoples? We are universal nationalists. We hold that the best way to secure peace and amicable relations between different peoples is to give every people a sovereign homeland. Where this is not possible — for instance with tribal relict populations in the Americas, Siberia, and elsewhere — the just solution is give these peoples ethnic reservations with maximum local autonomy.

But notice that our aim is to secure *a homeland* for every people, not to secure *the indigenous homeland* of every people. That would be nice, but sometimes it is just not possible, and sometimes autochthony should be overridden by the greater good of creating homelands for otherwise homeless peoples.

For instance, there is every reason to reverse the recent colonization of Europe and European diaspora societies by non-whites. There is every reason to reverse Chinese colonization of Tibet. In every case, the colonists have homelands to which they can return. In every case, there are living injustices that can be solved by repatriating invaders. There is, moreover, every reason to create an independent Kurdistan or white South Africa, for in both cases a people is suffering right now because it lacks a sovereign homeland.

But one cannot make an ethnonationalist case to restore the Byzantine Empire, for the Byzantines no longer need a homeland, but the Turks do. Nor can one make an ethnonationalist case for returning Israel to the Palestinians, because the world would be better off if Jews confined themselves to a Jewish homeland. So in the case of Israel and Palestine, the solution is to have two states. A similar solution would be desirable for

Europe's gypsy problem. (Perhaps next door to Birobidzhan.)

The focus of politics should always be the future. We cannot right all the wrongs of the past, but we can create an ethnonationalist world order that minimizes new wrongs in the future.

Counter-Currents/*North American New Right*
January 25, 2016

THREE QUESTIONS ON IDENTITARIANISM

The following answers are to a questionnaire from an academic researcher who is writing a book on the Identitarian movement.

1. DO YOU SEE COUNTER-CURRENTS AS AN IDENTITARIAN PUBLISHER?

Yes and no. I describe Counter-Currents as a New Right publisher, yet Identitarianism is related to the New Right as politics is related to metapolitics. I see Identitarianism as an essentially political movement, yet its metapolitical foundations have in part been laid down by the European New Right. I see the project of the New Right—both in Europe and North America—as the creation of a post-totalitarian Right, adapted to combating the post-war cultural hegemony of Leftist ideas. The ultimate aim of the New Right is to establish the biological and cultural survival and flourishing of European peoples as the highest political priority, because these values are being actively eroded by the homogenizing forces of globalization.

Racially, we are threatened with extinction through below-replacement birthrates, miscegenation, and the swamping of our homelands with non-white immigrants and their descendants.[1] Politically, we cannot resist these trends due to the loss of sovereignty to international and global institutions and elites. Culturally, we are being assimilated by a global consumerist monoculture which is hostile to European identity and self-assertion.

But cultural issues are trivial compared to our biological extinction. In any case, the artifacts of European high culture would be appreciated by Asians and Jews, even if the race that created them became extinct. If forced to choose, I would sacrifice the whole patrimony of European civilization to preserve

---

[1] See my essays "White Extinction" and "White Genocide" in Greg Johnson, *Truth, Justice, & a Nice White Country* (San Francisco: Counter-Currents, 2015).

the people that gave birth to it, and can give birth to the next Golden Age.

Even though the groundwork of Identitarianism was laid through decades of deep metapolitical thinking, writing, and teaching, the movement itself is ideologically minimalist, blunt, and plain-spoken. Europe belongs entirely to Europeans. The goal is to make that a reality once more. Non-whites must simply be repatriated. I think that most Identitarians would agree with a statement made by Jared Taylor, to the effect that "We have a right to be who we are, and only we can be who we are," i.e., only Frenchmen can be French; only whites can be Europeans; there will be no Europe without Europeans; a world without our kind is not something that any healthy person can contemplate with equanimity. Just as guerrilla fighters arm light to maximize mobility, Identitarian ideological minimalism allows them to nimbly step over the clichés of the mainstream's defenders and stay on the attack.

Counter-Currents, particularly in our webzine, has given a great deal of coverage to Identitarianism in Europe because we wish to encourage an Identitarian movement adapted to North American conditions, in which our population is largely of mixed European ancestry, and our national identities are abstract, propositional, and raceless. In such an environment, we can't be simply German or English or Italian, and being American or Canadian is racially non-specific. So what we have to fall back on in North America are deeper sources of identity than Old World nationalisms, namely our common racial identity and our common European cultural roots all the way back to the Paleolithic cave painters.

2. DO YOU THINK THAT IDENTITARIANISM IS REVOLUTIONARY?

Potentially, yes. Identitarianism is a youth movement. Its rank and file are in their teens and twenties. Its leaders are in their thirties and forties, max. This means that Identitarians are entirely products of multicultural Europe. Of course some have had more exposure than others to multiculturalism. And although they have more or less knowledge of European history, none of them have any experience of, or nostalgia for, Europe just before the plunge. This, I think, makes them constitutionally less inclined to bourgeois conservative compromise and half-measures. That is good, because half a solution is not a solution. This is the key to their revolutionary potential. But it is a conservative form of revolution, because even though they reject today's fallen Europe, they do so in the name of the rebirth of deeper and more authentic European identities.

3. WHAT DO YOU THINK OF THE "CLASH OF CIVILIZATIONS" THEORY?

I think that Samuel Huntington is basically correct, and my only disagreement with him is that he does not take his analysis far enough.

Huntington's clash of civilizations thesis is a reply to Francis Fukuyama's restatement of Alexandre Kojève's account of Hegel on the end of history. Hegel claimed that history would end when we discover and politically institutionalize the truth that all men are free. Kojève claimed that this required a "universal homogeneous state." And Fukuyama suggested that the triumph of liberal democratic capitalism after the end of the Cold War might fulfill the Hegelian-Kojèvian framework. Although Fukuyama was also acutely aware that a global bourgeois civilization might be vetoed by people who wish to start history over again, or by Muslims who wish to create a very different universal homogeneous *ummah*.

Huntington simply offers an account of distinct civilizational blocs. (I would add Jewish civilization to the list.) Even if one takes into account borrowings and influences between civilizations, and blended and liminal cultures, the fact remains that civilizations are plural. And since civilizations have different interests and ideals, tensions and conflicts will always exist. Thus the clash of civilizations. This means that history in the Hegelian sense,[2] and politics in Carl Schmitt's sense,[3] are ongoing.

---

[2] See my essay "Why Read Hegel? Notes on the 'End of History," http://www.counter-currents.com/2015/02/why-read-hegel/

[3] See my essay "Reflections on Carl Schmitt's *The Concept of the Political*," in Greg Johnson, *New Right vs. Old Right* (San Francisco: Counter-Currents, 2013).

In my view, there are real differences and thus real conflicts not just between civilizational blocs but also within them, and within different nation states. This is why I am an ethnonationalist. When different racial and ethnic groups are forced to coexist within the same political system, diversity gives rise to tensions, which both erode differences and cause differences to become flashpoints for hatred and violence. Thus the ethnonationalist vision—which is also the Identitarian vision—is of a world of homogeneous, sovereign homelands for all peoples.

A universal state would have to be homogeneous to work, which would require the destruction of every unique culture. Identitarians beg to differ. In fact, we will fight to differ. Thus, we veto the end of history.

But the political unification of Huntington's civilizational blocs would also be a bad thing for the same reason: to create the homogeneity conducive to political functioning, it erodes differences; it erodes identity. Every state, large and small, functions best when it has a homogeneous culture and population. Ethnonationalists think that the best way to achieve such homogeneity is to break states up along existing ethnic lines rather than to blend different peoples into a single mono-race and monoculture.

Now this does not mean that every tribe in the Amazon or Siberia needs a seat at the United Nations. Nor need it apply to every minority group that does not aspire to nationhood. But even in these cases, the goal should be maximum autonomy under the principle of subsidiarity.

As I argue in my article "Grandiose Nationalism,"[4] I think that European nations need to have some sort of loose federation that stops well short of political unification in order to mediate disputes among them and coordinate their policies toward other civilizational blocs. In my view, however, such a federation should encompass both the Western and Orthodox civilizations as described by Huntington.

Counter-Currents/*North American New Right*
March 10, 2015

---

[4] In *Truth, Justice, & a Nice White Country*.

CHRISTIANITY &
EUROPEAN IDENTITY

The following text is my opening statement for a debate with Jonas De Geer on Christianity and European revival held in Stockholm, Sweden, on Saturday, April 18, 2015. The debate was recorded and can be heard on YouTube; a full transcript is available at Counter-Currents.[1]

What is the relationship of Christianity and European identity? I do not say "Western Civilization," because I wish to speak of the whole of Europe, East and West, and the whole of European history and prehistory, not just the civilized bits.

There are two perspectives we can take on this question. One looks back at history. The other looks forward to the future.

Looking back at history, we see that Christianity played an important role in Europe for more than 1700 years. It might have been otherwise. Many wish it were otherwise. It might be different in the future. But even if there comes a day in which Europe is no longer Christian, there will never come a day when Europe has *never been* Christian. In that sense, Christianity will always be part of European identity. Just as pre-Christian religions and cultures stretching all the way back to the last Ice Age will also always be part of European identity.

But although there was a time when Europe was Christian, Christianity was never European. I am not referring to the Jewish origins of Christianity, although that should never be forgotten. From the start, though, Christianity was as Hellenic as it was Jewish. Moreover, it defined itself in contradistinction to Judaism, just as Judaism has defined itself in opposition to Christianity.

---

[1]Jonas De Geer and Greg Johnson, Debate on Christianity, transcript: http://www.counter-currents.com/2015/04/debate-on-christianity/; audio: https://www.youtube.com/watch?v=dMwrMl0tinQ&feature=youtu.be

What makes Christianity essentially non-European are the doctrines it shares with the ancient Greeks and Romans, and not with the Jews, namely the idea that *a universal truth is the foundation of a universal community*; if Christianity is true for all men, then it is a universal religion, not an ethnic religion. Because of its nature as a universal religion, Christianity is not tied to any particular race or people. Christendom is not and never has been co-extensive with Europe. European folk believed in Christianity, but Christianity was never a European folk religion. Many Europeans believe in the cause of Christianity, but Christianity has never believed in the cause of Europe. For the Christian cause is the salvation of all mankind.

Defenders of both Europe and Christianity point to the fact that, in the past, the Church supported the defense of Europe from Islam. But the Church was defending Europe only incidentally. What she was really defending was Christendom, which at the time was centered in Europe, but even then extended into Ethiopia, the Middle East, and as far away as China. And the Church has always been willing to shed European blood to defend and extend Christendom, from the Crusades to liberate the Holy Land on to centuries of global missionary work that continues to this day. Far from being an example of the harmony of Christianity and the ethnic-genetic interests of Europeans, the Crusades are an example of how the Church led Europeans to shed their blood to recoup lost Christian territories in the Middle East.

Let us now look to the future. If present trends are not reversed, European man will cease to exist. I do not fear for the artifacts of European civilization, since Bach and Rembrandt would continue to be prized by Jews and Orientals. I fear for the race that created these glories, and can create new glories. Our race is facing simple biological extinction due to below-replacement fertility, miscegenation, and the loss of our homelands to non-white invaders. If European man is to survive, we must exclude all non-whites from our homelands and adopt policies that cause our birthrates to rise, particularly the birthrates of the genetically best-endowed. In short, we need White Nationalism with pro-natal policies, preferably eugenic ones.

Is Christianity likely to help or to hinder White Nationalists in preventing the biological extinction of our race? To answer this question, we must first look at the actual behavior of the existing churches. All of the mainstream Christian denominations are opposed to White Nationalist policies. Instead, they provide intellectual and institutional support for ongoing white dispossession that is at least on a par with the support of the organized Jewish community, their senior partner in crime. Regardless of the views we may hold about "true" Christian teaching, if the white race is to be saved, we will have to fight the *existing* churches every step of the way.

Naturally, this battle will be aided if we have sympathizers inside the churches. All too often, White Nationalists who are also Christians spend their time battling against non-Christians in our ranks rather than against anti-whites in their churches. To prove that their White Nationalism is in good faith, they must instead take the battle to the churches. I wish them the best, but I also caution them. Political entryism within the churches will be no easy matter, since the churches were long ago subverted in just this manner, and the existing clergy are Old Masters in that particular black art. They will see you coming.

The battle within the churches will be aided if White Nationalists can find resources from the Bible and the traditions of the Church that support rather than oppose ethnonationalist politics. I have no doubt that such resources exist. Mobilizing them is an important metapolitical project, and it will be credible only if carried out by believers.

However, the battle within the Church is not likely to be successful unless our movement makes progress in the larger social realm, for the simple reason that the Church follows secular opinion rather than leads it. The church has a long history of supple accommodation to secular power, simply because its kingdom is not of this world. Its ultimate goal is the salvation of the soul. Thus, if White Nationalism achieves political power, the churches will hunt for Biblical precedents for our policies and reinterpret, downplay, or ignore contrary tendencies. The Church knows how to render unto Caesar what is Caesar's. Our job is to become Caesar.

Many defenders of Christianity argue that societies and individuals need religion, and they recommend Christianity simply because of its illustrious past and the fact that it is still here. Of course, this argument is somewhat premature, because the white race first has to survive before we can worry about how we might best organize a future white society.

Furthermore, in the last century, Christianity has been dramatically declining in Europe. Indeed, I have argued in *New Right vs. Old Right* that for three centuries now, liberalism, not Christianity, has been the *de facto* civil religion of Europe.[2] I see no reason to believe that Christianity will be more significant in the future than it is at present. It may revive; it may continue to decline; it may persist in diminished form; or it may cease to exist altogether.

Thus the mere fact that Christianity is here does not recommend it, if we are choosing a religion based merely on social utility. Indeed, if that is our primary concern, I have argued that we would be better served by trying to reform liberalism in a race-realist, non-individualist direction, since liberalism dominates everything today, even Christianity itself.

European Christianity will have a future only if European man has a future. But the Church is at best indifferent to white survival, and today it is actively working against it. Thus my recommendation to White Nationalists, Christian and non-Christian, is to focus primarily on white survival, which requires that we be more concerned with battling the churches than preserving them. The Christians among us must be White Nationalists among them. They must be our fifth column, doing whatever is possible to weaken the Church's opposition to us. They need not fear for the Church, which will survive even if whites do not. God will take care of His Church, but whites must take care of ourselves.

Counter-Currents/*North American New Right*
April 20, 2015

---

[2] See "Racial Civil Religion" and "That Old-Time Liberalism."

WHITE CIVILIZATION
IN THE DUMPSTER

Recently, I had an experience that made the ongoing destruction of our race and civilization very concrete and real. The woman who lived next door died a few months ago. Maybe she had no family. Maybe they just didn't care. But in any case, a large amount of her possessions were left in her house when it was sold to an Asian family, who are in the process of emptying it out.

A couple weeks ago, I noticed a stack of books bundled together with twine set out on the curb for the recycling pickup the next morning. The top volume was *The Black Book of Communism*. I asked a woman on the porch if I could have it, and she said sure. I took the bundle in and found that it contained a couple of P. J. O'Rourke books. (Was this the home of another childless Right-winger, I wondered?) Next were some *Calvin and Hobbes* and *Far Side* books, and at the bottom was a very large, very old hardcover book which turned out to be a Bible—a copy of the Latin *Biblia Sacra* with Andreas Osiander's commentaries printed in Nuremberg in 1618.

Judging from the inscriptions inside, this Bible had been in the same family since the 17th century. It had traveled to the New World, perhaps before the United States was even founded. It was passed down from generation to generation, until the family that owned it became extinct—or simply no longer knew or cared about its significance.

Then it fell into the hands of recent immigrants to whom it meant absolutely nothing. They weren't even curious if it had a merely monetary value. (It is worth $400 to $600.) Yes, I know Asia has ancient and very refined civilizations which also appreciate Western high culture. But to paraphrase Jared Taylor, Asia is not exporting connoisseurs of Ming ceramics to run convenience stores and laundromats in Brooklyn.

This is the story of our whole race in a nutshell. More whites are dying than being born, and whites are being replaced by non-whites in our own homelands. And what will happen to our history, our culture, and all our precious stuff when there are no white people around to care about it? Most of it will go in the dumpster.

None of what we do today *matters* if there is nobody around to carry it forward tomorrow. If your life is spent accumulating things and experiences that nobody would even want to remember or carry on, then I suggest that you are leading a meaningless, shallow, and selfish existence. And if you are doing things of genuine importance but you give no thought to making sure that they will persist and be appreciated by people after you die, then again, your life is empty and vain. So if you hunger for a meaningful life today, work to create a future of our people.

Counter-Currents/*North American New Right*
August 21, 2015

THE POLITICS OF
NOSTALGIA

Nostalgia is sentimentality about happier places and times. Leftists routinely bash conservatives for dressing up mere nostalgia as politics. Republicans, we are told, merely want to "turn back the clock" to the 1950s, or the 1980s, which is treated as a self-evidently stupid and laughable proposition.

Of course everyone has moments of nostalgia, which is why nostalgia is a multi-billion dollar industry. When we are teenagers, they sell us pop music. And when we hit middle age, they sell the same pop music back to us as nostalgia.

But the accusation of nostalgia is just another smug, lazy-minded Leftist canard — a canard that pops up all too often on the radical, anti-conservative Right as well.

First of all, the charge of nostalgia cuts both ways. How many Leftists wax boring with nostalgia for the 1960s? Ernest Callenbach's ludicrous novel *Ecotopia*, for instance, reeks with nostalgia for his college days.

How many Revolutionary Rightists pine with pseudo-nostalgia for interwar fascism, the Middle Ages, the Ancient World, or mythical Golden and Silver Ages? (It is pseudo-nostalgia, because it is not based on actual experiences.)

Second, to criticize an ideology, one must look at its strongest, most serious statements, not just attack straw men. And no serious thinker, Left or Right, bases a political theory on a snapshot from his childhood. Political philosophy deals with principles that are true of every time and place.

Third, since political philosophy is not an entirely *a priori* science, it is completely legitimate to look at historical examples of good and bad regimes, and this cannot be dismissed merely as a subjective attachment to one's own limited range of experience.

Fourth, although it is impossible to go back to the past, it is not impossible for the past to *come back* to us, meaning that we can and should restore past institutions if they worked better than present ones. If the Left accuses us of having a bias in favor of the past, we can accuse them of having a bias in favor of the present. But not every change is progress, and if we have good reason to reject modern innovations, we have good reason to restore what worked better in the past. And this has nothing to do with personal biases or even personal experience. Sometimes, we look longingly upon things because they are valuable in and of themselves.

Finally, there is an existential sense of nostalgia which is a legitimate part of political philosophy, particularly political nationalism. "Nostalgia" was coined in 1688 by the Swiss physician Johannes Hofer. Its roots are the Greek *nóstos* (homecoming) and *álgos* (pain). It basically means "homesickness," and it was classified as a form of melancholia. Apparently, the term was coined to describe the sufferings of Swiss mercenaries serving far from home.

Homesickness is possible only because there are places where we do *not* feel at home. If we belonged everywhere, we would not feel homesickness. But humans are not "citizens of the world." Different peoples originated in different places, where they feel most comfortable. Different peoples create different cultures that suit them like well-fitted clothes and properly sized shoes: they are comfortable and becoming. When forced into unsuitable environments and unintelligible cultures, we feel ill at ease. We don't feel like ourselves.

Homesickness is simply a desire to feel at home, to be comfortable, to be where we can be ourselves. Homesickness has nothing to do with fond memories of past experiences, for the simple reason that some of us have *never* really felt at home. Multiculturalism means that more and more of us grow up surrounded by peoples and cultures that are not related to us, not intelligible to us, and that make us feel uncomfortable and out of place. But that is no way to live. This, in part, explains the popularity of such television series as *Downton Abbey* and *Mad Men*. For the worlds the portray look far more comfortable for white people than the present.

The solution to this problem is not individualism. The problem is the loss of community. Individualism is both a cause and a consequence of this loss. It dissolves common cultures, opens us to outsiders, and exalts the private realm as a refuge from the alienating multicultural world it creates. The loss of community is a collective problem that requires collective solutions.

That is why the North American New Right stands for ethnonationalism. We are nationalists for all nations. We reject the one-size-fits-all totalitarian Mao suit of globalization and multiculturalism. We stand for the creation of sovereign homelands tailored to fit the different peoples of the world. Ultimately, the cure for homesickness is a homeland.

Counter-Currents/ *North American New Right*
September 17, 2015

THE "W" WORD

So there is a dirtier word than "nigger," and that word is "white."

How else to explain the political establishment's consternation over Hillary Clinton's statement in a *USA Today* interview that she is more electable than Barack Obama because she has more support from working-class white people?

This, according to a Democratic Party leader quoted by Peggy Noonan, is "unleashing the gates of hell." According to an Obama supporter quoted by Noonan, "Even Richard Nixon didn't say white, even with the Southern strategy."

Noonan herself adds:

> To play the race card as Mrs. Clinton has, to highlight and encourage a sense that we are crudely divided as a nation, to make your argument a brute and cynical "the black guy can't win but the white girl can" is—well, so vulgar, so cynical, so cold, that once again a Clinton is making us turn off the television in case the children walk by.

How dare you, Hillary? How dare you speak the dirty W-word?

Of course there is a glaring double standard here. Blacks, Jews, mestizos, and other ethnic minorities are strongly conscious of themselves as distinct groups with distinct interests—interests that often conflict with those of the white majority. None of these groups have any compunction about pursuing their interests, even at the expense of the white majority. Moreover, they select their leaders based on the strength of their ethnic consciousness and their willingness to pursue their collective interests.

But, according to Noonan, "If John McCain said, 'I got the white vote, baby!' his candidacy would be over." We whites, you see, are the only group that is not allowed to think of ourselves as a distinct group with distinct interests. We are the only group that is not allowed to select leaders based on their membership in our group and their commitment to our interests.

We whites are the race that dare not speak its name.

Instead, we whites are supposed to pretend that we do not exist as a people, but only as adherents of the abstract "color-blind" ideology of human equality. In the name of that ideology, we have to give away our wealth and power, debase our standards, corrupt our culture and institutions, and reduce ourselves to a minority. We have to do this any time members of selfish, race-conscious groups like Jews, blacks, mestizos, etc. demand something from us, as long as they cloak their demands in the language of equality.

What kind of people has to surrender everything to others, upon demand? A conquered people. We whites have to behave as a conquered people in our own country. If we persist in this long enough, of course, we will physically cease to exist as a people. We will succumb to miscegenation, demographic collapse, or outright mass murder, as conquered and enslaved peoples often do.

Obama's white supporters want to believe that his candidacy transcends race. They hope that by electing a black man president, they will absolve themselves of the burden of spurious "white guilt" that they have accepted. They hope that electing a black president will cause blacks to stop hating them and America. They hope that an articulate, intelligent black president will finally induce blacks to set aside their sullenness, resentment, and excuse-making and actually participate in American society. And, since deep-down most liberal whites are quite uncomfortable with the majority of blacks, they hope that President Obama will be the role model who will finally get the gang-bangers, crack heads, and welfare queens to abandon the bad manners, foul language, cornrows, gold teeth, doo-rags, silly names, and criminal mayhem and become like the blacks they see in television and movie fantasies, usually played by Bill Cosby, Denzel Washington, or Morgan Freeman.

Obama and his black supporters have no such illusions. Although Obama is half-black and half-white, he makes it clear in his books and speeches that he is obsessed with blackness and black authenticity. And the arbiters of black authenticity are not the "Oreos" white liberals celebrate, but the "inner city youths" that haunt their nightmares. An Obama administration would not be about transcending race, but about black authenticity and black empowerment. It would be the corruption, chaos, and buffoonery of the black city governments in Atlanta, New Orleans, Washington D.C., and Detroit writ large. With nukes. And "color-blind" whites will hand them the button.

As long as whites, and only whites, are not allowed to think of ourselves as a distinct group with distinct interests, the ultimate result will be white dispossession. Imagine a card game where the whole country is the stake. Each ethnic group has a hand and a stack of chips, but only non-whites get a trump: the "race card." No matter how huge the white pile of chips is at the beginning, as long as we play under those rules, we will eventually be left with nothing in the end.

Hillary Clinton is resisting white dispossession (well, just her own dispossession, but it is a start) in the only way possible: appealing to latent but real white racial consciousness and solidarity. And the establishment — and Republican lickspittles will trample and claw to take the lead on this matter — is in a frenzy to quash this insurrection.

The greatest threat to the establishment, after all, is frank discussion of white racial identity and interests along with the identities and interests of non-white groups.

The rule today is: if a black man wants something, Whitey has to defer. Liberals were all for this, when the blacks only wanted *those people's* wealth, power, and prerogatives. You know who *those people* are: white males, particularly Southern, rural, working or middle class white males; putative Republicans; the ungrateful, narrow-minded, backward peasants and cannon-fodder in "flyover country"; the "rednecks" who claim that they are losing their jobs and futures to "illegal aliens" and "less qualified Affirmative Action candidates." Extra points off for having more than two children or being serious about Christianity.

But now that a black man wants to ascend to the pinnacle of power, to which Hillary Clinton feels entitled (and, let's be honest, she is certainly much more qualified than Obama), Hillary will not quietly defer to the "less-qualified Affirmative Action candidate." Hillary Clinton has revealed that she is one Honky who is not going to back down. You go, girl!

It only takes a change of consciousness to halt white dispossession. Once whites awaken to the fact that we are a distinct group with distinct interests in competition with other groups, with incompatible interests, everything changes. We will refuse to play a game that we can only lose.

As liberals are constantly lecturing us, disadvantaged groups need "role models" to change their way of thinking. Could Hillary Clinton actually become a role model for feisty, active white racial consciousness? There have been greater ironies in history.

Thank goodness Hillary Clinton is selfish, ambitious, and doesn't really believe her professed liberal egalitarian multiculturalism. Thank goodness she has a self-righteous sense of entitlement that cannot be dissolved in the acid of "white guilt." This white woman will actually fight a black man for something valuable.

I wish more white people were like Hillary Clinton.

Western Voices World News, May 11, 2008

THE 2008 US
PRESIDENTIAL ELECTION

The election of Barack Obama as president of the United States is a good thing for White Nationalism.

Whites will regain control over our nation and our destiny only when we have a change of consciousness. First, we must again think of ourselves as a distinct ethnic group with distinct interests — interests that often conflict with those of other ethnic groups. Second, we must again believe that we are entitled — nay, obligated — to take our own side when our interests conflict with those of other groups.

Currently white identity and interests have been suppressed by the ideologies of universalism, multiculturalism, and white guilt. White consciousness and pride still exist, of course, but have been driven into the subconscious mind. Our race is a sleeping giant. The task of White Nationalism is to awaken it. And Barack Obama can only help us.

The recent presidential campaign has been racially divisive and polarizing, and that is a good thing. Countless whites have become newly conscious of their distinct racial identity and interests. Of course the Republican candidate, John McCain, did nothing to encourage this process. Nothing, that is, until he added Sarah Palin to the Republican ticket, which brought about a vicious and polarizing reaction from the Left, particularly Jews. Millions of whites, most of them from the productive minority that carries the rest of the country, spontaneously identified with Palin. Thus the establishment's hatred for her — and, by extension, them — was very instructive. Many became not just aware, but fighting mad.

But a McCain victory would only have dissipated this tendency to greater white racial consciousness. If McCain won, it would have been blamed on Republican racism, even though Obama would presumably have been defeated by racist Democrats who would have refused to vote for him. Republicans never would have considered voting for a Democrat in the first place, black or not. Nevertheless, a McCain administration would do everything in its power not to further white racial consciousness.

An Obama presidency, however, will only intensify racial polarization and stimulate greater white racial consciousness and self-assertiveness. More of the sleepers will awaken.

Whites, furthermore, will retake our nation only when we realize, finally, that it has been taken away from us. For the better part of a century, the United States has been ruled by a coalition of rootless white plutocrats and ethnocentric Jews, with the power of the Jews steadily growing at the expense of the whites. This ruling elite uses non-whites to gain advantage over the white majority.

For the white elites, it is more a status game than anything else. These people feel superior to lower class whites by advancing the interests of non-whites at the expense of *those people*: integrating those people's schools and neighborhoods, sacrificing those people's jobs, families, and futures with Affirmative Action, etc.

For Jews it is a much more serious game. They are after power. They use racial integration and non-white immigration to destroy the white working and middle classes (the kind of people who would vote for a racial nationalism other than Zionism), and they use Affirmative Action to crowd out the white elites (since there are not enough Jews to replace the entire white elite).

It is very difficult, however, to convince most whites that our country is ruled by race-traitors and aliens who govern on our backs and against our interests. It is hard, because most people will not listen to an argument, much less read the 624 pages of Wilmot Robertson's *The Dispossessed Majority*. Most people believe their eyes, and nothing else. And when they looked at their televisions, they saw white men in the White House.

Now they will see Barack Obama. That represents progress. It is truth in advertising. The symbolism now reveals rather than conceals the substance. This has not been our country for a long time. And now it no longer *looks* like our country.

There is no telling how Barack Obama will govern their country. There is no point in examining his platform or promises. He is a politician, after all. It is easy to tell when he is lying: his lips move. It is likely, however, that Obama will turn out rather like Bill Clinton. Both men may be Leftists by conviction. But, for them, there is something far more important than their convictions, namely, themselves. They are posturing, narcissistic empty suits.

Obama, like Clinton, will probably begin his administration with an orgy of high-minded oratory and high-priced social uplift programs, rapidly wear out his welcome, suffer a series of humiliating defeats, and end his administration as a centrist: exhausted, cynical, morally-compromised, an object of near-universal scorn. Despite this, Obama might gain re-election, if the Republicans nominate another old, feeble moderate like Bob Dole or John McCain—someone fit only to lose gracefully. In fact, I would bank on it.

This is a good thing for White Nationalists for two reasons. First, it is probably best that Obama not be able to enact far Left programs. Second, the threat of such programs will energize the Right.

During the Clinton years, there was a great deal of energy on the Right. Remember the conservative writers and commentators who offered principled, passionate, and inspiring critiques of liberalism—only to metamorphose into unprincipled Republican shills when George W. Bush was elected? Remember the conservative idealism and activism—exploited by phonies like Newt Gingrich? There was also, frankly, a lot of nasty personal hatred of Bill Clinton and his wife. But hatred, like all forms of energy, can be channeled into good things.

Obama (and his wife) will create similar energy on the Right. And this time White Nationalists are positioned to channel this energy into advancing our agenda. To give just one example: Now that a non-white has been elected president, it is possible to mobilize new energies and funds to abolish Affirmative Action as unnecessary.

Finally, in addition to Obama, the unfolding economic crisis—which looks more and more like a Greater Depression—

will provide immense opportunities for White Nationalists. For decades, movement people have been saying that the white masses will not be receptive to our message until there is a major economic downturn. There is a lot of truth in this view, although it has also functioned as an excuse for inactivity. Well, the downturn is here, and it is imperative that nationalists invest in the infrastructure necessary to get our message out to an increasingly receptive white majority. Please consider a donation to Counter-Currents today.

Now, some might think it odd to ask for funds in an economic downturn. But, first, it is possible to profit from an economic downturn, and, moreover, every white person with the capital and knowledge has a duty to profit from the system's decline. If the Right people profit, it will help us create a better world. Second, what kind of opposition only functions when the system flourishes and decides to pinch its pennies and pull its punches when the system is on the ropes? After the crash of 1929, the Communists piled on and made the 1930s the Red Decade. With your support, we'll make the next decade our own.

Western Voices World News, November 5, 2008

A TARIFF IN TIME . . .
SAVES BILLIONS:
THE PROPOSED AUTOMOTIVE
INDUSTRY BAILOUT

Free markets mean competition. Competition means winners and losers. Some losers even lose their shirts and go out of business. When a business fails, this should be regarded as a success for the capitalist system as a whole. That goes for really big businesses as well as small ones. In a capitalist system, nobody is "too big to fail."

Why, then, is nobody applauding the prospect of America's Big Three automakers—Ford, GM, and Chrysler—going out of business? Shouldn't this be counted as a sign that capitalism, free trade, and competition are working splendidly?

"Yes, but what about the suffering that will be borne by American workers?" But, again, one can't have a free market without the freedom to fail, and when businesses fail, workers lose their jobs. So job losses, which are a sign of local failures, are actually a sign of overall health for the system, just as sloughing off dead skin is the sign of a healthy snake.

So let's hear a big round of applause for free trade and free choice.

But aside from a few kooks, I'll wager the silence out there is deafening. I suspect that even most libertarians are not thrilled at the prospects of three million Americans losing their livelihoods. But if we are not willing to allow the Big Three to fail, then we really do not believe in free trade. When confronted with the ultimate consequences, we flinch.

But before we commit $25 billion to bailing out the Big Three, shouldn't we ask ourselves if there are *other* non-free market strategies that would be better at staving off the collapse of the US automotive industry? Is loaning out or giving away billions of dollars the best strategy conceivable? (Any loans would amount to massive giveaways, since inflation favors borrowers, and the US government has vastly increased the amount of dollars in circulation since the beginning of October. When the global financial markets regain their senses, the increased supply of dollars will lead to a massive devaluation, i.e., inflation.)

The main problem with giving or loaning money to the Big Three is that it does not address the underlying problem: US manufacturers are not able to compete with foreigners. And if the underlying problem is not dealt with, another bailout will just be required in the future. (Remember the Chrysler bailout of 1979?) In fact, a new bailout will probably increase the likelihood of a future bailout, since once the car industry receives huge loans, it will create pressure to bail them out again lest they default.

But how do we address the underlying cause: the inability of the Big Three to compete with foreigners? The solution I propose has two prongs: (1) tariffs on imported cars and car parts, and (2) regulations directed at increasing the quality of US manufactured cars.

Throughout most of US history, the federal government was largely funded by tariffs on foreign manufactured goods. Imagine if we had left those tariffs in place. The Big Three would be flourishing, not queuing up for billions of tax dollars, and the government would be collecting billions of tax dollars from people who insist on buying imported cars. The best way to ensure the long-term competitiveness of the US automotive industry is a return to protectionism.

But protectionism alone is not enough. Protectionism would remove foreign competition, but it would not make American cars genuinely competitive. That is to say, it would do nothing to improve the quality of American cars. In fact, it would remove incentives to improvement, insofar as competition with foreign manufacturers spurs the Big Three to make better cars. (American manufacturers would, of course, continue to compete with one another.)

Look at it another way: US citizens might gain by stabilizing the US car industry, but what's in it for US consumers? A good consumer is not necessarily a good citizen, and when the two conflict, the interests of the citizen should trump those of the

consumer. But shouldn't we do all we can to decrease the conflict? Wouldn't it be nice to have the best auto industry in the
world, so that one would not have to sacrifice being a good
consumer to being a good citizen?

To achieve that, the government cannot allow US auto manufacturers to get lazy behind the wall of tariffs. We need to use
carrots and sticks to encourage them to constantly improve
themselves. How could that be accomplished? People are justly
skeptical of the government's power to improve anything. But
that is because of the envious, leveling egalitarian agenda behind so many government programs, not because of a flaw in
government intervention *per se*. Government can also raise
standards rather than lower them. It can reward excellence rather than penalize it.

Consider seatbelts, for instance. It would be cheaper for car
manufacturers to leave them out, and in a highly competitive
market, they would have an incentive to leave them out of
some low end models. Seatbelts would become an option, an
extra, not standard for all cars. The government mandating that
seatbelts be included in all cars means that no manufacturer
has a competitive disadvantage in including them.

The same is true of all safety innovations. Imagine that GM
invents a better airbag. In a free market system, they might pa-
tent it, to gain a competitive advantage at the expense of overall public safety. What if, however, the government were to
mandate that new safety innovations be used across the whole
industry? The whole public would benefit, and other manufacturers could be compelled to pay GM a small royalty: not so
large as to constitute a real competitive disadvantage, but large
enough to recoup the research and development costs and off-
set the loss of a monopoly on a new safety invention. Presumably, as each manufacturer came up with new innovations that
were mandated to be adopted across the industry, these royal-
ties would balance each other out, and the rising standards
would lift the companies and consumers alike.

Tax laws could also be structured to encourage research and
development to improve safety, performance, and energy effi-
ciency, and to reduce pollution.

Is this approach Democratic or Republican, capitalist or socialist, conservative or liberal? None of the above, really. I do
not look at economic problems from the point of view of a capitalist, a laborer, or a consumer. These are partial viewpoints,
from which one cannot see the common good. Instead, I look at
economic issues from the point of view of what is required for
a healthy republic. Protectionism and regulation to progres-
sively raise standards are necessary to create and preserve a
strong middle-class society, a society with private property that
is broadly distributed. They are necessary to ensure a society
that is economically self-sufficient and technologically advanced enough to be competitive politically in a world of scarcity and Darwinian competition for planetary dominion.

To the extent that the interests of capital, labor, and consumers contradict the health of the community, they must be
trimmed back. The common good must come before every individual or factional interest.

My specific form of communitarianism is racial nationalism.
I look forward to the replacement of multicultural, multiracial
America with a homogeneous white ethnostate. But whatever
patriotism you hold, even an attachment to the present regime,
the proposals outlined above would be preferable to constantly
bailing out a sinking ship rather than just plugging the hull.

Western Voices World News, November 20, 2008

THE GATES CONTROVERSY

On July 16, 2009, Harvard Professor Henry Louis Gates, Jr. was arrested by Officer James Crowley of the Cambridge, Massachusetts Police department. A woman saw two men breaking into Gates' house and asked another woman to call 911. Apparently Gates had come home and found the front door of his house jammed, so he and his driver forced it open. When Officer Crowley arrived, Gates was in his house. But as far as the officer knew, Gates could have been a burglar.

Gates should have been grateful that his neighbors and the police were looking out for his property. He should have cooperated readily with the police to clear up the misunderstanding. But instead, he was uncooperative and verbally abusive, accusing the officer of racism. Officer Crowley arrested Gates for disorderly conduct and let his superiors sort it out. Once they did, they dropped the charges and released Gates. Gates then threatened to sue the Cambridge police for racism.

Racism is obviously not a factor. The police were not called because a black man was "just minding his own business," but because a man whose race was not identified by the caller was breaking into Gates' house. Gates was not arrested because he was a black man "just minding his own business," but because he was at the scene of a break-in and was uncooperative with the police. The same thing would have happened if he were white.

The fact is that a black gang-banger can be arrested standing over a corpse, machete in hand, blood up to his elbows, and he will still whine that he is being arrested "just because he is black." But this is just stupid. If the police wanted to arrest someone "just because he is black," there is no shortage of young black men loitering around "minding their own business" that they could nab. You don't exactly need a dragnet to find them.

In a country the size of America, it is inevitable that there will be some cases of mistaken arrest, arbitrary arrest, police prejudice, and police brutality.

But the fact remains, that the overwhelming reason why black males are so often arrested for crimes is that black males so often commit crimes. And law enforcement statistics show that black men are not arrested for crimes more often than they are reported by victims and witnesses to commit them.

Because of black criminality, it is rational for whites to fear and avoid blacks. Because of black criminality, it is right for police to be suspicious of blacks. And if blacks who really are "just minding their own business" are offended by this fact, they need to direct their complaints to their fellow blacks. How about trying to persuade blacks to stop committing crimes, rather than trying to bully the police into looking the other way?

But none of this even applies in the Gates case, because there is no question that the man was present at the scene of a break-in and refused to cooperate with the police.

It gives one pause that blacks from the dumbest street thug up to the Harvard faculty will latch onto the same transparently stupid ploy to evade responsibility and change the subject.

Did Gates think the "just because he is black" argument clever? If so, then he is clearly not smart enough to be a Harvard professor.

Or was Gates more calculating? Perhaps he knew he was talking nonsense but was hoping that Officer Crowley was a sufficiently "sensitive," guilty, and spineless to be intimidated. Gates might also have been laying the foundations for a lawsuit, grandstanding to the countless O. J. jurors out there in the black populace. If so, then he is clearly a cynic.

Another possibility is that Gates knew better but simply could not help himself. If so, perhaps we are dealing with a compulsive inability to take personal responsibility. Clearly this phenomenon is independent of IQ differences and seems to point to a deep psychological difference between blacks and whites.

There is also something morally obscene about Gates' behavior. After all, Gates is a tenured professor at insanely liberal Harvard, a resident of suicidally liberal Cambridge, a darling of the eastern liberal-Jewish establishment, and a friend of

President Obama. In short, Gates is a member of the power elite who could count on its backing. That makes him a powerful man.

James Crowley, by contrast, is an ordinary cop. As a white man, he is automatically classified by the establishment as an oppressor who shares the blame for all of society's ills. As a white cop, he is blamed for arresting America's plentiful black criminals, as if arresting them were somehow the greater crime.

Since Gates is the more powerful of the two, did he treat officer Crowley magnanimously, as powerful men are supposed to do with weaker men? Of course not. Magnanimity is an Aryan virtue. Instead, Gates played the victim, counting on being able to cast Crowley as another Mark Fuhrman. Gates has been lavishly rewarded for a lifetime of simpering about racism, so why would one expect anything else?

Gates is a bully playing the victim. The moral obscenity of his behavior is perfectly captured by an old Polish proverb: "The Jew cries out as he strikes you."

Chapter two of the Gates controversy began when President Barack Obama departed from his script at a press briefing on health care reform, siding with Gates and condemning the Cambridge police for acting "stupidly." Obama too was counting on lockstep agreement of the whole liberal-Jewish establishment and spinelessness from whites in general and the Cambridge police in particular.

Like Gates, however, Obama overestimated his hand. The Cambridge police stood solidly behind Officer Crowley. So too did a broad swath of the white public. The brains at the White House apparently looked at some polling data and decreed that Obama eat his words. Evidently they also judged the matter urgent enough that it could not wait until the next official appearance, so Obama popped into the White House Press Room for an unscheduled statement.

Unfortunately, Obama merely confounded the problem by issuing a studied non-apology, praising Officer Crowley in tepid words, and offering a condescending invitation to Crowley to "have a beer" with Obama and Gates at the White House. (What, no donuts?) I wish that Crowley had told Obama to take his beer and stick it, but eventually he accepted the invitation.

The end of the story remains to be seen, but already this much is apparent.

First, like Gates and countless other blacks, Obama apparently finds the "just because he's black" fallacy irresistible. Indeed, he claims in his autobiography that he had been stopped by the police "just because he is black." (Yeah. Prove it.)

Second, never has Obama seemed more of an empty suit. The man seems slick and sophisticated when sticking to a script, but as soon as he departs from it, it is just the same tired old black mischief.

Being a black man in a suit who can read from a teleprompter might qualify Obama to be a television news reader, but not the president of a serious country. It has never been clearer: Barack Obama is nothing but the mulatto press spokesman for the Rahm Emmanuel/Goldman-Sachs administration.

Obama had the face to insist that we use the Gates incident as "a teachable moment" (what a pompous, ugly phrase). Presumably this means yet another opportunity to lecture white Americans on how their wicked racism, rather than black criminality, is why police keep arresting black men.

The real lesson, of course, is that no matter how high we elevate blacks in white society—to the Harvard faculty, even to the White House—they still have chips on their shoulders. A chip on one's shoulder is a deep-seated, pre-existing grievance that shows up in inappropriate circumstances.

What sustains this black chip? The clash between ideology and reality. The ideology is racial equality. The reality is genetic racial inequality. White liberals keep telling blacks that they are equal to whites. To create the *appearance* of racial equality, white liberals have debased our standards and debauched our culture. They promote blacks to jobs they can't handle and give blacks money they can't earn. And they take the opportunities, and the money, from white men like James Crowley.

But in spite of it all, blacks still find that they are "over-represented" at the bottom of white society and "underrepresented" at the top. If blacks really are equal, then the only explanation for lingering inequality is white ill-will. This is the source of the simmering rage that sustains the "just because he is black" myth. It is also, no doubt, a major motive of the countless rapes, murders, and robberies perpetrated by blacks on white victims.

It is time to knock the chip off black America's shoulder by telling the truth: that racial inequality is based on genetic differences, that blacks will never flourish in a society created by white people and governed by white standards, and that it is time for Americans of all races to go our separate ways.

TOQ Online, July 29, 2009

THE PERSECUTION
OF KEVIN MACDONALD

On January 26, 2010, a new campaign of intellectual and political persecution was launched against Kevin MacDonald, Professor of Psychology at California State University, Long Beach. The express goal of this campaign is to get Professor MacDonald fired from his job because of his research and political convictions.

Professor MacDonald's research threatens the cultural and political hegemony of the organized Jewish community by exposing their ongoing subversion of Western civilization. This research has made Professor MacDonald a target of persecution by Jewish individuals, organizations, front groups, and their dupes for nearly a decade.

This persecution has intensified of late because of Professor MacDonald's affiliation with the newly-formed American Third Position political party, which threatens Jewish hegemony by explicitly representing the interests of white Americans, who are being culturally and politically dispossessed by Jews and their non-white allies.

Student agitators affiliated with Jewish front groups called "Students Fight Back" and the "Party for Socialism and Liberation" entered Professor MacDonald's classrooms on the first day of the Spring semester and passed out propaganda to induce students to drop his classes. The agitators also threatened to circulate a petition calling for Professor MacDonald's dismissal.

See Douglas Kauffman, "Long Beach students boycott fascist professor Kevin MacDonald,"[1] on the website of the Party for Socialism and Liberation and Sonia Scherr's "Student Activists Confront Anti-Semitic California Prof"[2] on the website of

---

[1] http://www.pslweb.org/site/News2?page=NewsArticle&id=13591&news_iv_ctrl=1030

[2] http://www.splcenter.org/blog/2010/01/29/student-activists-

Professor MacDonald's long-time persecutors the Southern Poverty Law Center.

Professor MacDonald has commented on the latest round of harassment on *The Occidental Observer Blog*: "The multicultural Left's broad definitions of 'racism' — and aggressive tactics"[3] and "The academic Left's involvement in politics."[4]

Professor MacDonald's enemies try to cloak their radical agenda in standard liberal pieties, but whether from cynicism or mere stupidity, their attempts are so clumsy that any child can see through them.

For instance, one of the agitators, Marylou Cabral, is concerned that Professor MacDonald's research and political commitments might color his teaching. The fact that she does not apply the same standards to politically engaged Leftist professors, indeed to entire politically engaged disciplines — women's studies, black studies, gay and lesbian studies, etc. — shows that her objection is not to academic political engagement *per se*, but merely to Professor MacDonald's views.

Another agitator, Douglas Kauffman, said: "Our campus is one of the most diverse in the country, and that really flies in the face of having a Nazi as a professor."[5] Student Shavanda Williams echoed these sentiments, asking: "Why is he here if he has these white supremacist ideas?"[6]

Genuine liberals should find such statements dismaying. After all, "liberal education" is not supposed to mean education by a bunch of dogmatic liberals who all think alike. Liberal education is an education that expands the horizons of students by exposing them to a variety of different viewpoints.

Thus, although it really is not fair to characterize Professor MacDonald as a Nazi or a white supremacist, even if he were, the presence of a faculty member with such unusual view-

confront-anti-semitic-california-prof/

[3] http://theoccidentalobserver.net/tooblog/?p=641

[4] http://theoccidentalobserver.net/tooblog/?p=662

[5] http://www.splcenter.org/blog/2010/01/29/student-activists-confront-anti-semitic-california-prof/

[6] http://www.pslweb.org/site/News2?page=NewsArticle&id=13591&news_iv_ctrl=1030

points would make CSLB more intellectually diverse

Of course Kauffman, Cabral, & Co. are not liberals. They are Left-wing totalitarians. For them, "diversity" is merely a euphemism for the stigmatization and dispossession of whites by Jews and non-whites.

"Diversity" does not mean diversity of opinion. It means black Leftists, lesbian Leftists, Asian Leftists, mestizo Leftists, feminist Leftists, etc. all working under the tutelage of Jewish Leftists to root out every possible form of white racial consciousness.

"Diversity" does not mean that all races and ethnic groups should take pride in themselves and watch out for their interests. No, when whites do that, it is not "diversity," it is "hate." And the fanatical persecution of "hate" is what Leftists call "tolerance" — and, presumably, "love" (they are all just snarling and sputtering with love).

Before Kevin MacDonald is nailed to the cross of tolerance, I hope we will hear some voices of protest from the genuine liberals — faculty, administrators, and students — at his university and in academia at large. Academia being what it is, we can't expect anything much better than sincere liberals. But genuine liberalism should be enough to protect Kevin MacDonald's freedom to think, write, teach, and exercise his political rights as he sees fit.

We will be watching.

TOQ Online, February 2, 2010

THE PERSECUTION OF
AMERICAN RENAISSANCE

The Ninth *American Renaissance* Conference, on "Defending the West," was canceled on February 15, 2010 after terroristic threats from egalitarian, multiculturalist love-mongers caused a third hotel to back out of their contract. (Let us hope that AmRen wrote hefty cancellation penalties into their contracts. If so, this non-conference may prove their most profitable ever.)

People from across the United States and a number of foreign countries were set to converge on Dulles Airport on February 19–21 to listen to a stellar lineup of speakers, including Nick Griffin of the British National Party, filmmaker Craig Bodeker, writer David Yeagley, Professor Raymond Wolters, speaker Sam Dickson, *American Renaissance* editor Jared Taylor, and others. In addition to providing a feast for the intellect, every AmRen conference is also a valuable opportunity for fellowship and networking.

But the cancellation also provides lessons and opportunities.

Whenever some Third World dictator cancels elections, shreds a constitution, or persecutes his political opponents, we all know what is happening. Given the choice between preserving the legitimacy of the system or preserving personal advantage, he chooses personal advantage and discards the props of legitimacy as just that: meaningless props.

America's ruling establishment now faces a similar choice.

The *American Renaissance* Conference was an entirely legal gathering. AmRen, its speakers, and its guests were exercising their constitutionally guaranteed rights to freedom of speech and freedom of association.

The conference was canceled because the hotel management feared that the system could not protect its staff and guests from death threats. The hotel may be a private organization, but freedom of speech means nothing if private organizations do not feel that they can safely host gatherings of controversial groups.

Thus the ruling establishment—the government, law-enforcement agencies, and the press—have to take a firm, public stand against terrorism and for freedom of speech and association. The hotels have to know that the full weight of the law will fall on those who seek to disrupt such gatherings.

Also, the hotels have to know that the establishment—as represented in the mainstream media—cares about freedom of speech and assembly as a matter of sacred principle.

The terrorists have to be publicly shamed. And so do the hotels for giving into them.

But shaming the hotels will not work unless they are reasonably sure that the moral stand is also the most practical one. And this means that the government must give plausible assurance that the terrorists will be punished.

I spoke to Jared Taylor on February 15, 2010. He emphasized that the AmRen Conference was an entirely legal gathering, protected by the Constitution itself. He also went on to stress that anyone who thinks in terms of principles can see that "If AmRen can be shut down this way, then anyone can be shut down. The meatpackers meeting can be shut down by PETA." This can be prevented only if the establishment takes a strong and decisive stand against terrorism and for freedom of speech and assembly.

Taylor fears, however, that the government and media will greet the cancellation of AmRen with silent gloating rather than howls of righteous indignation. After all, Jared Taylor and his readers are heretics, dissenters from our secular religion of racial egalitarianism and multiculturalism. By shutting down AmRen, the terrorists remove a challenge to the establishment's power. The only problem is that by remaining silent, the current establishment preserves its power while undermining the system's legitimacy.

We will be watching the response of politicians, law enforcement, and the media.

The terrorists, and potential terrorists, will be watching as well.

If AmRen is shut down with impunity, then Left-wing terrorists will repeat their winning strategy.

But Right-wing terrorists may also be encouraged.

Within the White Nationalist community, *American Renaissance* stands for gentlemanly debate and strict legality. The underlying assumption of this approach is that White Nationalists can work within the American system. America was a *de facto* White Nationalist society. America became a multiculturalist society *within the system*. And America can be reborn as an explicitly White Nationalist society *within the system as well*. The American system is not so broken that it cannot be fixed.

But there is another faction in the White Nationalist movement: those who feel that the American system cannot be reformed and must simply be replaced. And before it can be replaced, it must be destroyed. Some are banking on the system destroying itself. Others are hankering to lend a hand. Call this the revolutionary faction.

If *American Renaissance* can be shut down with impunity, the ranks and influence of the reformist faction will shrink as those of the revolutionary faction grow.

Furthermore, as with all revolutionary movements, Left and Right, White Nationalism's revolutionary faction has a largely sociopathic fringe just itching for opportunities and excuses for violence. This fringe's influence will grow as well.

I asked Jared Taylor if he thought that a soft response or non-response by the establishment to the shutdown of the AmRen Conference might encourage violence from White Nationalist fringe elements. Taylor said that he hoped not, but feared this it might happen: "That is a danger. If people think that the game is rigged, they might be tempted to just kick over the table. I hope that doesn't happen."

White Nationalists need to do more than just wait for the establishment's response. We need to encourage it. There are three things we can all do:

❖ Contact the media and demand coverage.
❖ Contact political figures and law enforcement and demand justice.
❖ Contact your friends and acquaintances and spread

the word about this outrage.

Finally, I have a personal recommendation for Jared Taylor, and I am sure I speak for many others as well: *fight.*

Keep my registration fee. But I would feel better about it if you used it to actively fight. Don't wait for the press to call you. Hire a press agent and get this publicized. Take out full-page advertisements in the *New York Times* and the *Washington Post.* Don't wait for law enforcement to track down the perpetrators of this crime. Offer a reward for information that leads to the arrest of the terrorists. Hire a private investigator to conduct a perfectly legal search. And when you find the perpetrators, don't wait for a criminal prosecution. Look into a civil suit too.

There is no better proof that multiculturalism is bringing on a new Dark Age of scientific obscurantism, moralistic fanaticism, and political repression than these low and frantic attempts to abort an American Renaissance.

TOQ Online, February 15, 2010

9/11 TEN YEARS LATER

I wish I had an arresting "what I was doing when the twin towers were hit" story. But the truth is that I had slept through the whole thing. The night before, I had stayed up into the wee hours reading Savitri Devi's *The Lightning and the Sun* (I had just found a copy of the unabridged version). I first heard around 3 pm when an Aryan barbarian from Alabama (nobody you would have heard of) called me to ask me what I thought.

"About what?"

"Terrorists hijacked two jetliners and crashed them into the World Trade Center towers, then the towers collapsed."

"Yeah, sure . . ." I said, as I flipped on the TV (I still had TV then) and saw the second tower collapsing in slow motion. My first thought, I am ashamed to say, was of the huge Miró tapestry I had once seen in one of the lobbies. Then, with horror, I realized I had *been* there. This could have happened to me! I thought of the terror of the people in the airplanes and the buildings. For the rest of the afternoon, I was glued to the TV.

That evening, I went to the regular Tuesday evening "hate dinner" in Atlanta. Instead of the usual eight or ten people, there were more than twenty. Quite frankly, there was a good deal of gallows humor and *Schadenfreude* around the table. One person quipped that at least this would get Chandra Levy off the news.

We had all pretty much concluded that the hijackers were Muslims who had targeted us because of the US government's slavish subservience to Israel and our domestic Jewish community. There was also a consensus that 9/11 was a superb opportunity to awaken our people on the Jewish domination of American foreign policy and the Jewish question in general.

But the public was pretty much already there. Later in the week, Tom Brokaw reported that NBC and Reuters announced that two-thirds of Americans polled believed that we had been attacked because of America's close ties with Israel. I wondered how (not if, just how) the establishment would spin this.

The answer was soon to come when the *New York Times* found a "face" to put on a position held by two-thirds of the American public. They went to West Virginia to the "compound" of "neo-Nazi" Dr. William Pierce, leader of the National Alliance, who was of the opinion that 9/11 took place because of Jewish domination of American foreign policy. The *Times*, in short, sought to marginalize a mainstream position by linking it to a marginal figure.

Don't get me wrong. I am not blaming Dr. Pierce for anything, certainly not for representing the opinions of two-thirds of the American people. I blame the whole political mainstream for failing to represent us. Apparently every politician and political commentator knows that pandering to the Jewish minority is always more important than pandering to the American majority.

Still, 9/11 was the occasion for my first attempts at open white advocacy under my own name. And I know that I was not alone. I also know many people whose first racial awakening came from 9/11.

We all had high hopes. I was very encouraged when I learned of the arrest of Israeli spies who were filming the attack on the World Trade Center and celebrating. Clearly they had advance knowledge of the attacks and believed them to be "good for the Jews." Then I heard that a large Israeli spy network had been arrested, including people who had been shadowing the 9/11 hijackers. There was also the story of a text message sent by Odigo, a text-messaging company in Israel, warning of the attack. Carl Cameron began piecing the Israel connection together for Fox.

But then Jewish power intervened. The spies were released and sent home. Cameron's investigation was quashed and his stories pulled. And the United States went to war. First in Afghanistan, which was at least connected with Al Qaeda, then with Iraq, which was targeted because of Israeli interests, not American interests. It was child's play, really, for the Jews to lie and manipulate Americans to spill their blood and treasure for the benefit of Israel. Organized Jewry had already brought the United States into World War I and World War II.

I think that the most reasonable account of 9/11 is the following.

Nineteen Muslims armed with box cutters hijacked four airplanes, crashing two of them into the World Trade Center and one into the Pentagon. The fourth crashed in Pennsylvania for reasons unknown.

The government of Israel had been shadowing the hijackers and clearly had advance knowledge of the attacks. Reliable Israeli agents in the US government may also have had advance knowledge. But no attempt was made to warn the American government to stop the attacks. 9/11 was allowed to happen because the Jews needed a new Lusitania, a new Pearl Harbor, as a pretext to bring America into a new war, or wars, in the Middle East on Israel's behalf. Iraq, Syria, and Iran were at the top of Israel's hit list. So far, they have had to settle for Iraq. The war in Afghanistan, from a Jewish perspective, was a mere distraction, although it certainly eases the road to war with Iran.

The conclusion and practical implications could not be clearer: Israel is not our friend. American Jews, who if forced to choose between serving US interests or Israeli interests, would overwhelmingly choose Israel, are not our friends either. America's Jewish community is the reason why US foreign policy is conducted for Israeli not American interests. If America is to prevent another 9/11, we must break the power of American Jewry over our political system. But that will not be possible without addressing Jewish power in the media, the economy, academia, and all realms of culture. Jews need to be excluded from all channels of power and influence in our society. And the only practical way to accomplish that is to expel them as a community from the US. And naturally we should send back our Muslims while we are at it.

On 9/12, some two-thirds of the American public already agreed with part of that message, and they certainly would have been willing to hear more. But White Nationalists did not have the money, the talent, the infrastructure, or the organizational maturity necessary to make our message competitive with the Jewish angle. Our people had the ears to hear, but we could not get our message out.

Ten years later, we are in essentially the same position. Yes, there are new webzines, new publishers, and new podcasts. But there have also been considerable losses. William Pierce died and the National Alliance is a shadow of its former self. National Vanguard has collapsed; its excellent webzine is gone; Kevin Strom has been essentially silenced. American Renaissance has been pretty much driven out of the conference business. And so forth.

It has been worse than two steps forward, one step back, because that presupposes marching in one direction. The course of our movement, however, more resembles a jitterbug contest or a mosh pit. With a trajectory like that, it is impossible to calculate progress. But overall I am optimistic, because in my experience, the average age of people in our movement is far lower and the average quality is far higher than ten years ago.

As for the 9/11 "conspiracy" theories, I have three thoughts.

First, from a purely pragmatic point of view, the 9/11 account I have outlined above is far superior to any of the more complex theories, because it supports every practical consequence that we want, and it has the added advantages of being based on easily verified facts and being easy to explain.

Second, from a rational point of view, most of the conspiracy theories violate basic principles like Occam's Razor, namely that the simplest explanation of a given fact is to be preferred. Generally, people lead with their strongest arguments, but nothing I have seen makes me want to inquire more deeply. It is laughable, for instance, that people who claim that no planes hit the Pentagon or crashed in Pennsylvania don't feel a need to explain what really did happen to the airplanes. And as for the claims that the twin towers were brought down by explosives, well doesn't that seem like overkill? Sure, it looks spectacular on TV. But crashing jetliners into the buildings would have been sufficient to achieve any of the posited motives, from starting a war to totaling the buildings for insurance purposes.

Third, because 9/11 right on its surface is so damaging to Jewish power, and because the official American story (they attacked us because they hate our freedoms) is so absurd, and two out of three Americans knew it, I believe that the enemy felt the need to create a disinformation campaign that would taint even the most cautious and rational critiques of the "official story" with the stench of lunacy. Because the net effect of all the excited talk about disappearing airplanes, controlled demolitions, and false flags manufactured at the highest levels of the US government is that even reasonable alternatives to the official story are dismissed as just more internet conspiracy crankery. Well, maybe that's what we are supposed to think. Maybe the 9/11 "truth" movement is the real "false flag."

Counter-Currents/*North American New Right*
September 11, 2011

THE "GROUND ZERO"
MOSQUE CONTROVERSY

People on the real Right are correct to be skeptical of the phony Right. The leaders of the phony Right are suffered or promoted by the establishment because they do not threaten it. The phony Right are obsessed with maintaining their status as a "respectable" opposition, a status awarded by their enemies. But the only respectable opposition is an ineffectual opposition. The phony Right send mixed and misleading messages. They get people asking the wrong questions and fighting the wrong enemies. They channel genuine discontent into fake causes. They take idealism, activism, and resources that could threaten the system . . . and waste them.

The current controversy about building a mosque near "Ground Zero" — the site of the World Trade Center buildings destroyed on September 11, 2001 — has all the marks of a phony Right campaign: orchestrated by Jews and propagated by Fox News to stir up hatred against Muslims and grease the way for more war in the Middle East.

Even using the term "Ground Zero" is grotesque. It was originally coined to describe the centers of the atomic blasts that destroyed Hiroshima and Nagasaki. At these "Grounds Zero," more than 150,000 people were immediately killed, and as many as 250,000 additional victims died in the following years: more people in two cities than the entire US military lost in the Second World War.

Yet in the baffling arithmetic of moral imbecility, when 3,000-odd Americans die in Manhattan, that is "Ground Zero" too. I remember the stampede to cash in on America's newfound collective victimhood, which is the coin of entitlement in our morally inverted realm. No doubt "Ground Zero" would have been called America's "Holocaust" if Jews were not so zealous in maintaining their trademark and their status as the world's supreme victims, which entitles them to be the world's supreme bullies.

The events of 9/11 have been used to justify nearly a decade of US-led wars in Afghanistan and Iraq. These wars have killed, wounded, displaced, and aggrieved millions of Muslims. Thus playing the 9/11 victim card to stop the construction of a mosque can only be seen a moral obscenity, and not just in the eyes of the Muslim world.

But it is worse than an obscenity, it is a mistake. It is evil to be a dealer of death and destruction the world over. Yet such a bully is at least feared, and from fear comes a grudging respect. But a global bully who wallows in self-pity over a comparative hangnail is contemptible. And it is not wise to make oneself contemptible as well as hated.

That said, the "Ground Zero" mosque controversy has some unintended good consequences for White America.

1. The "Ground Zero" mosque controversy exposes the moral imbecility of liberalism.

On August 13, 2010, Barack Obama endorsed the mosque in front of a Muslim audience at "the annual White House Iftar dinner" (!) celebrating the Muslim holy month of Ramadan. The next day, Obama retreated from his endorsement by claiming that he was merely commenting on the *rights* of Muslims to religious freedom and to build the mosque on private property. Obama expressly denied that he had commented on the *wisdom* — i.e., the *rightness* — of building the mosque and claimed that he *would not* comment on it.

From that point on, the liberal tactic was to dodge the issue with pious harrumphing about rights, while conservatives consistently held that the issue was not "rights" but "right or wrong." (To show that moral imbecility is not a monopoly of the Left, Ron Paul also tried to reduce the whole issue to a matter of rights.)

The hardest thing to teach in today's relativistic culture is that there is more to morality than just rights. "Rights talk" makes Americans morally stupid. But suddenly the momentous distinction between "rights" and "right or wrong" was being made loud and clear by conservative politicians and pundits. That's a good thing for white people, because when we stop talking about the "rights" of non-whites and immigrants and start talking about whether multiculturalism, racial integration, and non-white immigration are "right or wrong" for this country, the political landscape will look very different, and new things will suddenly become politically possible.

2. WHITE AMERICANS ARE NOW DEMANDING RECIPROCAL "SENSITIVITY" FROM OUTSIDERS.

Multiculturalism is just a euphemism for white dispossession, because only whites are asked to tolerate other cultures, accommodate other cultures, efface and adulterate our own cultures in the name of "enrichment." Thus the first stirrings of protest against the mosque were predictably met with a scolding about "sensitivity." Amazingly, though, white Americans did not retreat. Instead, they demanded that *Muslims be sensitive to us for a change.*

Once white Americans start "taking our own side" in cultural clashes, white dispossession will be halted and reversed. Once we start demanding that other cultures tolerate us, accommodate us, enrich themselves by becoming more like us, we will see that multiculturalism is not a two way street, but a one way street leading to the dead end of racial and cultural extinction.

Will white historians 200 years from now look back and say that here, with the resistance to the "Ground Zero" mosque, the tide began to turn?

Counter-Currents/*North American New Right*,
September 2, 2010

JEWS TO MORMONS:
WE'LL TELL YOU WHAT TO THINK

Mormons believe that the spirits of the dead can be baptized, allowing them to accept Jesus as their savior and thus enter heaven. Mormons think this is an improvement over mainstream Christianity, which teaches that those who do not accept Jesus as their savior are condemned to hell even if they merely lived in the wrong place at the wrong time and thus never even heard of Christianity. Furthermore, Mormons believe that people living today can baptize the spirits of the dead, or accept baptism for them. The primary recipients of posthumous baptism are the ancestors of living Mormons, hence the Mormon genealogical database. Finally, Mormons believe that the spirits of the dead have the power to reject Jesus. So posthumous baptism does not conscript people into heaven. It merely offers them a chance to receive salvation, which they can reject if they wish.

Personally, I am not too concerned what happens to me after I die. I would like my body to be cremated. I would like there to be a memorial service, and I don't want it to be a "celebration of life" either. I want it to be somber, because I rather hope that I will be missed. Eventually, my name will be forgotten, just like Marcus Aurelius says it will. But it would be nice to delay oblivion as long as the Sage Emperor has. On matters spiritual, I confess that I am very interested in the possible survival of the spirit after death. But I remain an agnostic on the matter. All told, I don't worry too much about what will happen to me after death, *because I suspect that I really will be dead.*

The last thing I am worried about is being posthumously baptized in a Mormon temple somewhere. I have been dodging Mormon missionaries my whole life. But I can't really get mad at them for trying one last time. After all, I don't really think they can send me to heaven. If I believed that, I would be a Mormon today. So I really think that posthumous baptism is all in their heads. It is just one more quaint religious belief, like Buddhist prayer wheels and Egyptian gods with the heads of crocodiles and dogs. This this does not alter the fact that Mormons are among the finest people I know.

Although posthumous baptism cannot affect me in the next life, what do I think of it in this life? Frankly, I think the idea is rather sweet. It is an act of kindness. I don't care if people try to baptize me after I am dead or pray for my salvation while I am living. That's their opinion. It doesn't affect me. And they have every right to go on believing what they do.

After all, *it would be churlish to get angry at people who wish me well*, even if their happy thoughts make no difference one way or another. It is also *stupid* to get angry about such things when there are people who wish me ill, and who are very effective at putting their thoughts into action. There is far too much real evil in this world. Frankly, I would have to be hypersensitive, narcissistic, and aggressive—and have far too much time on my hands—to get excited about the menace of posthumous baptism. Only an asshole would make an issue of it.

But assholes are in plentiful supply. For instance, in a CBS News article from February 14, 2012, "Mormons Apologize for Baptizing Dead Jews," we learn that the Mormon Church has apologized to the family of Simon Wiesenthal for posthumously baptizing his parents. We also learn that this is not the first time that Jews have protested posthumous baptism. Apparently, in 1995 the Mormon Church actually reached an agreement with Jewry promising not to baptize the spirits of dead Jews.

But this did not prevent Asher and Rosa Rapp Wiesenthal from being baptized by proxy in Mormon temples in Arizona and Utah in late January. "We are outraged that such insensitive actions continue in the Mormon temples," said Rabbi Abraham Cooper, associate dean at the Simon Wiesenthal Center, which operates a Museum of Tolerance.

In its apology, the Mormon Church blamed the posthumous baptism on overzealous individuals who have been barred from future use of the Mormon genealogical database. Being entered into the database is the first step toward posthumous baptism. In 2010, the Mormon Church made changes to its genealogical database to prevent Holocaust victims from being put on the queue for eternal salvation. But that is not enough.

The database is carefully monitored by a renegade ex-Mormon, Helen Radkey, who tattles to Jewish organizations when Jews are threatened with salvation. It was she who discovered the Wiesenthal outrage. And she also discovered that Elie Wiesel and several of his relatives have been placed in the database. (Wiesel, of course, is still alive, so perhaps he is at risk of being cast alive into the bliss of heaven.) Jewish genealogist Gary Mokotoff thinks there need to be "consequences" for renegade Mormons who try to save Jews from hell: "If the word gets out that there are consequences, they'll stop." (When Jews start talking about consequences, I start thinking of the Gulag.)

Of course, no Jew believes that his departed relatives are actually being saved by Mormon posthumous baptism. Jews think that the whole thing is merely a silly belief that Mormons cooked up. So for Jews, the issue is not preventing fellow Jews from going to heaven. The issue is controlling what Mormons *think* about Jews. (In fairness to Jews, the Catholic Church has also protested posthumous baptism, but apparently Catholics have not gone nearly as far as Jews.)

Unfortunately, the Mormon Church is all too willing to let Jews control their thoughts. If the leaders of the Mormon Church actually believe their theology, then their ban on posthumous baptism of Jews means that these individuals are being condemned to hell. By banning Mormons who try to save Jews from using the church's genealogical database, they are surely preventing the posthumous salvation of non-Jews as well. But apparently the Mormon Church thinks that this is a small price to pay to appease the lords of this world.

The only sincere people in this whole fiasco are the renegade Mormons who apparently believe their church's teachings about posthumous baptism and are also innocent enough to believe the teachings of Elie Wiesel and Simon Wiesenthal that Jews, especially Holocaust victims and survivors, are such select and holy people that they deserve special treatment to get them into heaven.

Counter-Currents/*North American New Right*
February 21, 2012

THE 2010 US
MIDTERM ELECTIONS

As I write, it looks like the Democratic party will retain control of the US Senate by a narrowed margin and the Republican party will gain control of the US House of Representatives by a narrow margin. The likely result: gridlock, centrism, pervasive dissatisfaction, and ever-increasing polarization. In short: This has been a good election viewed in terms of the long-term interests of white Americans.

(1) This election is a repudiation of the presidency of Barack Obama, specifically Obama as a "post-racial" and Leftist president. In my essay on the 2008 election reprinted above, I predicted the following:

> Obama, like Clinton, will probably begin his administration with an orgy of high-minded oratory and high-priced social uplift programs, rapidly wear out his welcome, suffer a series of humiliating defeats, and end his administration as a centrist: exhausted, cynical, morally-compromised, an object of near-universal scorn.

I never dreamed, however, that Obama's presidency would collapse so fast, a function of the man's essential emptiness. He is the weakest president since Carter, the most despised since Nixon. Furthermore, unlike Carter and Nixon, Obama's stature will not rise when he leaves office. In their own ways, Nixon and Carter were too big for the office, thus they blossomed when they were not being "handled" and "fed" things to say. But we all know what happens when Obama does not have a teleprompter or Rahm Emanuel around. I am betting that Obama will be a one term president. The real question is whether he runs again in 2012. The 2012 presidential election is the Republicans' to lose.

(2) The best thing for white Americans is continued racial and political polarization until the system cracks. In my 2008 election

article, I wrote:

> The recent presidential campaign has been racially divisive and polarizing, and that is a good thing. Countless whites have become newly conscious of their distinct racial identity and interests. Of course the Republican candidate, John McCain, did nothing to encourage this process. Nothing, that is, until he added Sarah Palin to the Republican ticket, which brought about a vicious and polarizing reaction from the Left, particularly Jews. Millions of whites, most of them from the productive minority that carries the rest of the country, spontaneously identified with Palin. Thus the establishment's hatred for her—and, by extension, them—was very instructive. Many became not just aware, but fighting mad.

Sarah Palin, of course, is still a polarizing figure. I hope she stays out there attracting liberal lightning bolts, but the Republicans would have to be the Stupid Party to run her for president in 2012. A much greater cause for hope is the phenomenal growth of the Tea Party movement. Like Palin, the Tea Partiers profess anti-racist, universalist Americanism of the classical liberal variety. But to the Left they still just look like a bunch of rednecks and crackers, and as Matt Parrott has pointed out, if you call a white man a white man long enough he might just take your ugly insult to heart.[1]

In short, the racial polarization of 2008 has continued and intensified.

Gridlock, however, will do far more to further racial polarization than a Republican sweep of both the House and the Senate. As I wrote in 2008:

> . . . a McCain victory would only have dissipated this tendency to greater white racial consciousness. If McCain won, it would have been blamed on Republican racism,

---

[1] http://www.counter-currents.com/2010/11/americas-first-third-world-election/

even though Obama would presumably have been defeated by racist Democrats who would have refused to vote
for him. Republicans never would have considered voting
for a Democrat in the first place, black or not. Nevertheless, a McCain administration would do everything in its
power not to further white racial consciousness.

An Obama presidency, however, will only intensify racial polarization and stimulate greater white racial consciousness and self-assertiveness. More of the sleepers will
awaken.

(3) The only thing I hoped for from the present election is a
strong showing for anti-immigration candidates. Immigration is
really the only political issue that White Nationalists should
bother with today, since we desperately need to close the borders, and we can make real progress in that direction.

An immigration cut-off would not decrease racial tension and
polarization, since differential birthrates would still doom
whites to eventual demographic eclipse even if the borders were
sealed today.

What an immigration freeze would give us is time, and given
the sorry state of the White Nationalist movement today, we
need all the time we can get. We need time to organize ourselves, so that changing circumstances will give us more than
mere opportunities to congratulate ourselves on our prescience.
When events break our way, we need to be able to convert them
into real political power.

In terms of immigration, this election has been a mixed bag.
Symbolically, the best victories would have been Tom Tancredo
as governor of Colorado and Sharon Angle as senator from Nevada. Both were long-shots, but both were defeated. In terms of
substance, however, the House and Senate both will be seating a
solid group of immigration restrictionists.

(4) Gridlock in Washington means that nothing will be done
to alleviate the current economic depression, and this provides
another important opportunity for White Nationalists. Already,
at the end of 2009, the US Census Bureau pushed back the date
when whites become a minority from 2042 to 2050, citing the

depression as the main reason for the slowed demographic changes.

If only two years of depression bought us eight years of breathing space, I say let the bad times roll!

The Great Depression of the 1930s was also the Red Decade, because the Communists took it as an opportunity to organize, not as an excuse to close their purses and pull their punches. White Nationalists need to be just as smart. Let future historians call this the "White Century," the first of many to come.

This election, in short, is good news for White Nationalists.

Even though our cause is just, truth is on our side, and eventually we will win, we can't lose sight of the fact that, at present, we are a small, despised, poorly-organized, and powerless minority. The political system is stacked against us. The predominant moral climate holds racism to be the ultimate evil. Aside from the internet, we have no way to get our arguments to the masses.

Thus the best we can hope for from an election are events that argue in our favor and opportunities for action and growth. This election guarantees continued racial polarization and offers real opportunities for a respite on immigration. So let's get to work.

Counter-Currents/*North American New Right*,
November 3, 2010

IMPLICIT WHITENESS
& THE REPUBLICANS

Kevin MacDonald's work on the concept of "implicit white-ness" in his essay "Psychology and White Ethnocentrism"[1] is a major breakthrough for White Nationalism. Ethnocentrism — usually stigmatized as "xenophobia" and "racism" — is a pref-erence to be around genetically similar people. Anti-ethnocentrism — a preference for people unlike ourselves — is sold today as "diversity," the secret ingredient that adds "strength" wherever it is found.

According to MacDonald, ethnocentrism is a natural phe-nomenon, hard-wired into the oldest and deepest levels of the brain. Anti-ethnocentrism, however, exists as a conscious mor-al conviction. From a psychological point of view, therefore, anti-ethnocentrism is relatively superficial, even though it cur-rently dominates our culture and politics.

Anti-ethnocentrism is dominant because its advocates con-trol the forces that shape our explicit consciousness: education, the arts, the news and entertainment media. But unconscious ethnocentrism persists and can never be extirpated because it is hard-wired into the brain.

Thus when Leftists accuse whites of "unconscious" racism, they are correct. Unconscious white ethnocentrism manifests itself in affiliation patterns. In particular, MacDonald cites country music, NASCAR, and the Republican Party as foci of implicitly white affiliation.

But because ethnocentrism is hard-wired, anti-racists can't really do anything about it. At best, anti-racist "consciousness raising" can only institute a permanent state of inner psycho-logical conflict.

The Leftists thought that by controlling the explicit culture,

---

[1] Kevin MacDonald, "Psychology and White Ethnocentrism," in *Cultural Insurrections: Essays on Western Civilization, Jewish Influence, and Anti-Semitism* (Atlanta: The Occidental Press, 2007).

they could eliminate ethnocentrism once and for all. But they can't. They can only create a psychologically draining conflict between our conscious convictions and our conscious instincts. And they can never rest, because if they let up on the conditioning for just a minute, they may see all their gains — and all their power — swept away.

Contrary to enemy propaganda, ethnocentrism is a perfectly normal and healthy psychological trait. A racially aware individual, who consciously believes that his ethnocentric instincts are morally *right*, enjoys inner psychological harmony, the peace of mind that is denied to anti-racists, who exist in a constant state of inner conflict between their natural instincts and their unnatural moral convictions.

Anti-racists are, in a real sense, mentally ill, whereas those of us who are self-consciously and proudly ethnocentric are mentally healthy (at least in that respect). And, because so much of the mental energy of anti-racists is drained away in internal conflict, other things being equal, we "racists" are stronger, happier, and more capable of transforming the world.

Thus MacDonald's research is cause for hope:

❖ The Left cannot win, because they can only control our conscious convictions but not our unconscious instincts.
❖ Nature is on our side, because in their hearts, people want what we want.
❖ Time is on our side, because anti-racism introduces internal psychological conflicts that are bound to be debilitating over the long run.

What is the path to racial salvation? Ultimately, it is a metapolitical struggle to gain control of the forces that shape people's conscious convictions about what is right. Once we can bring people's conscious convictions in line with their deepest instincts, the resistance to the political changes we seek will fall as a matter of course.

Unfortunately, the import of MacDonald's research is often misunderstood when applied to party politics. The euphoric reaction of some White Nationalists to the Republican gains in

the recent midterm elections is a case in point. White Nationalists are claiming that "we" have taken control of the House,
that "we" have made significant progress toward immigration
restriction, that "whites" are taking our country back.

White Nationalists were, of course, mostly spectators in the
last election. "We" White Nationalists did not take control of
the House, the Republicans did. So this talk about what "we"
won is based on the power of make-believe, in exactly the same
way that a Giants fan says that "we" won the World Series.
Fans form an imaginative identification with "their" team and
vicariously experience their triumphs and tragedies as their
own.

I have seen obese couch potatoes pantomiming touchdowns
and toddling around beer-sodden rec rooms in victory laps,
pumping their fists in the air as if they were star athletes. I have
seen rock concerts where countless teenage boys, bombed out
of their minds, play air guitar and feel like the crowd is cheering for them. In men, testosterone production actually rises and
falls based on the performance of their sports teams. It may be
good, clean fun. But it is not the foundation of sober political
analysis.

The misuse of the idea of "implicit whiteness" is another
factor contributing to giddiness about the Republicans and the
Tea Party. Yes, the Republicans may be benefitting from implicit ethnocentrism on the part of whites, but that is a far cry
from explicit White Nationalists enjoying any sort of political
power or influence.

First of all, the fact that Republican voters may be motivated
by unconscious ethnocentrism does not imply that they are receptive to explicit White Nationalism. Most Republicans would
vehemently reject the "accusation" that they have any racial
fellow-feeling at all. Yes, this resistance to white racial consciousness is waning, partly because it is just tiring to fight
against one's natural instincts, and partly because White Nationalists are slowly getting our message out through the internet and through personal interactions. But we have a long metapolitical educational process ahead of us before we can turn
implicit whiteness into widespread explicit whiteness.

Second, the fact that Republican *voters* may be motivated by implicit racial consciousness does not mean that Republican *politicians* will serve white interests. Quite the contrary, they would be the first to deny any hint of racism. They would deny it *strenuously*.

Republicans have a long history of taking the money, efforts, and votes of explicitly conservative and pro-life voters . . . and then betraying them. Why, then, would one expect them to be responsive to the merely *implicit* racial consciousness of white voters—many of whom would deny they are racially conscious altogether?

The sad truth is that Republicans will not cater to the interests of whites even out of the "base" motive of self-preservation. In their hearts, Republicans know that their party is doomed by the rising tide of color. But they will do *anything* rather than admit this fact and work to preserve the white majority.

Just as their corporate masters are committed to the racial replacement of white workers, Republicans are committed to the racial replacement of white voters by winning the votes of responsible, hard-working blacks and browns. Sure, most of them know it is a pipe-dream. But they are more afraid of being called racists today than of their party disappearing in a generation.

Other Republicans are committed to staving off political death through racial gerrymandering and ever more intense exploitation of the shrinking white voter base. They are praying for the Left to rile up Republican voters by promoting further "progress" toward insanity: socialized medicine for pets, tax-funded sex change operations, the right to marry one's pet, and the like. Republicans will do just about anything but speak the dreaded "W" word.

The barriers to moving the Republicans toward explicit whiteness can be appreciated with an analogy. Imagine an organization consisting largely of unmarried men that has an explicitly anti-homosexual culture yet a pattern of recruiting and promoting young men based largely on sex appeal. Such an organization could accurately be described as "implicitly" or "latently" homosexual. Would such an organization, therefore, be a likely ally for the homosexual lobby?

Of course not. Its members would frantically rebuff any proffered alliance. Individually, many of the members might be sympathetic. But any sympathies would be cancelled by fear of the disapproval of their peers, because status in the organization depends on conformity to the explicit culture, and those who dissent from the party line will be replaced by those who toe it.

The same is true of explicitly white Nationalists trying to reach out to latently white Republicans. Status in Republican circles depends on adherence to anti-racism (except, of course, in the case of Zionism, which must be subsidized with tax dollars). Even if every leading Republican felt, in the privacy of his or her own mind, that anti-racism is nonsense, what are the chances that they would all level with one another at the same time? Because if a courageous individual stuck his neck out on his own, he might find his honesty turned against him by somebody who believes the exact same thing but is more concerned with gaining advantage over him in a struggle for personal advancement.

In fact, I believe that White Nationalists are more likely to find allies on some issues among black and Hispanic nationalist groups, since members of these organizations don't need to constantly prove their anti-white credentials like Republicans do. And that is the full measure of Republican depravity.

As I argued in the previous chapter, the 2010 midterm elections turned out about as well as could be expected for White Nationalists, given that racially conscious whites are a tiny, despised, and almost voiceless minority. Let's not forget that of the hundreds of candidates who ran, only Jim Russell in New York's 18th district is an explicit advocate for white interests, and he lost by a landslide.

Kevin MacDonald's work on implicit whiteness is a conceptual breakthrough for White Nationalism, a source of hope for the long run viability of our cause. But let's not get carried away by elections. But there is still a vast gulf between implicit and explicit whiteness, a gulf that politics alone cannot bridge.

The Occidental Observer, November 11, 2010

THE 2012 US PRESIDENTIAL ELECTION

On November 5, 2008, I wrote an article arguing that the election of Barack Obama as president of the United States was a good thing for White Nationalism. And I was right. Thus I am going to copy and quote liberally from that article to argue that four more years of Obama will be good for White Nationalism as well.

Whites will regain control over our nations and our destiny only when we have a change of consciousness. First, we must again think of ourselves as a distinct ethnic group with distinct interests — interests that often conflict with those of other ethnic groups. Second, we must again believe that we are entitled — nay, obligated — to take our own side when our interests conflict with those of other groups.

Currently white identity and interests have been suppressed by the ideologies of universalism, multiculturalism, and white guilt. White consciousness and pride still exist, of course, but have been driven into the subconscious mind. Our race is a sleeping giant. The task of White Nationalism is to awaken it. And four more years of Barack Obama in the White House can only help us.

As in 2008, the present presidential campaign has been racially divisive and polarizing, and that is a good thing. Countless whites have become newly conscious of their distinct racial identity and interests. Of course the Republican candidate, Mitt Romney, is doing nothing to encourage this process, making every effort to woo the zero point zero something percent of the Black vote that he will receive in November — which will be pretty much the number he can expect due to voter error. As for white voters, well he can take those for granted.

A Romney victory would only dissipate this tendency to greater white racial consciousness. If Romney wins, it will predictably be blamed on Republican racism, even though Obama would presumably be defeated by racist Democrats refusing to vote for him, since most Republicans never would vote for a Democrat, black or white, anyway. Nevertheless, a Romney administration inaugurated under a cloud of whining about white racism would do everything in its power not to further white racial consciousness.

Four more years of an Obama presidency, however, will only intensify racial polarization and stimulate greater white racial consciousness and self-assertiveness. More of our sleeping people will awaken.

Whites, furthermore, will retake our nation only when we realize, finally, that it has been taken away from us. For the better part of a century, the United States has been ruled by a coalition of rootless white plutocrats and ethnocentric Jews, with the power of the Jews steadily growing at the expense of the whites. This ruling elite uses non-whites to gain advantage over the white majority, depressing our wages and diluting our political power.

For the white elites, it is more a status game than anything else. These people feel superior to lower class whites by advancing the interests of non-whites at the expense of *those people*: integrating *those people's* schools and neighborhoods, sacrificing *those people's* jobs, families, and futures with Affirmative Action, etc.

For Jews it is a much more serious game. They are after power. They use racial integration and non-white immigration to destroy the white working and middle classes (the kind of people who would vote for a racial nationalism other than Zionism), and they use affirmative action to crowd out the white elites (since there are not enough Jews to replace the entire white elite).

It is very difficult, however, to convince most whites that our country is ruled by race-traitors and aliens who govern on our backs and against our interests. It is hard, because most people will not listen to an argument, much less read the 624 pages of Wilmot Robertson's *The Dispossessed Majority*. Most people believe their eyes, and nothing else. And when they looked at their televisions, they saw white men in the White House.

Now they see Barack Obama. That represents real progress. It is truth in advertising. The symbolism now reveals rather than conceals the substance. This has not been our country for a long time. And now it no longer *looks* like our country. The last thing we need is another white face on a system that is promoting nothing less than the genocide of the white race.

In 2008, I wrote:

> There is no telling how Barack Obama will govern their country. There is no point in examining his platform or promises. He is a politician, after all. It is easy to tell when he is lying: his lips move. It is likely, however, that Obama will turn out rather like Bill Clinton. Both men may be Leftists by conviction. But, for them, there is something far more important than their convictions, namely, themselves. They are posturing, narcissistic empty suits.
>
> Obama, like Clinton, will probably begin his administration with an orgy of high-minded oratory and high-priced social uplift programs, rapidly wear out his welcome, suffer a series of humiliating defeats, and end his administration as a centrist: exhausted, cynical, morally-compromised, an object of near-universal scorn. Despite this, Obama might gain re-election, if the Republicans nominate another old, feeble moderate like Bob Dole or John McCain — someone fit only to lose gracefully. In fact, I would bank on it.

I think I pretty much nailed it.

I also argued that a failed Obama presidency would be a good thing for White Nationalists for two reasons. First, it is probably best that Obama not be able to enact far Left programs. Second, the threat of such programs will energize the Right. As I wrote then:

> During the Clinton years, there was a great deal of energy on the Right. Remember the conservative writers and commentators who offered principled, passionate, and

inspiring critiques of liberalism—only to metamorphose
into unprincipled Republican shills when George W.
Bush was elected? Remember the conservative idealism
and activism—exploited by phonies like Newt Gingrich?
There was also, frankly, a lot of nasty personal hatred of
Bill Clinton and his wife. But hatred, like all forms of energy, can be channeled into good things. . . . Obama (and
his wife) will create similar energy on the Right.

I wrote this just a few months before the birth of the Tea Party.

But I also said something that turned out to be almost completely wrong:

And this time White Nationalists are positioned to channel this energy into advancing our agenda. To give just
one example: Now that a non-white has been elected
president, it is possible to mobilize new energies and
funds to abolish Affirmative Action as unnecessary.

Obama gave White Nationalists a golden opportunity, and
for the most part we blew it. Why? Because instead of channel-
ing racial discontent in our direction, too many of us allowed
system politicians to channel our energies and funds into dead
ends. Because instead of investing in our own movement, too
many of us fell for the folly of "mainstreaming." The same
people who had been giddy over the Ron Paul movement in
2008 became giddy over the Tea Party and then over Ron Paul
all over again.

Yes, of course Ron Paul and the Tea Party advocate forms of
race-blind classical liberalism, which is philosophically opposed to White Nationalism. Yes, of course Ron Paul and the
Tea Party went out of their way not to be branded racist. Yes,
of course Ron Paul and the Tea Party were all too glad to take
the money and labor of White Nationalists, so long as they
gave us nothing in return.

Libertarians understand the power of ideas and the necessity of metapolitics. Libertarians spent decades laying the intellectual and organizational groundwork that made Ron Paul

and Tea Party possible. Only a fundamental lack of appreciation for ideas and principles, *a fundamental lack of seriousness*,
can explain why some White Nationalists thought they could
somehow ride on the coattails of Ron Paul and the Tea Party . . .
and arrive at anything like White Nationalism, which libertarians reject as immoral *in principle*.

Part of the trouble, of course, is that, aside from the issue of
race, a lot of White Nationalists are nothing but classical liberals or conservative Republicans anyway.

Another part of the problem is sheer giddiness. After decades of White Nationalism going nowhere, it was nice to be
part of a movement that was going *somewhere*. Just look at the
crowds! And too many of our people were willing to overlook
the fact that Ron Paul and the Tea Party were *going in the wrong
direction*.

So we were counseled to shut up, blend in, and work to
spread non-racialist ideas, advance non-racialist agendas, and
elect non-racialist politicians. Unsurprisingly, none of this advanced *our* cause. What is surprising is that anybody thought it
would.

How do we advance White Nationalism? By articulating
and spreading *our own* message, not the message of our enemies. By working and donating our money to build up *our own*
institutions, not those of our enemies. There are legions of libertarians and paleocons and Republicans. They can take care of
themselves. But fully awakened White Nationalists are a rare
and precious breed. If we don't put our time and money into
spreading our own message, building our own institutions,
and developing our own community *nobody else will*.

I concluded my original article by arguing that the economic
crisis would also provide immense opportunities for White Nationalists. That is still true, no matter who wins the upcoming
election. For decades, movement people have been saying that
the white masses will not be receptive to our message until
there is a major economic downturn. There is a lot of truth in
this view, although it has also functioned as an excuse for inactivity.

Well, we are almost four years into downturn, and White

Nationalists have done precious little to invest in the ideas and infrastructure necessary to get our message out to an increasingly receptive white majority. That's why you should give a donation to Counter-Currents today.

Now somebody might object to asking for money during an economic downturn. They certainly objected four years ago, but my answer was simple: What kind of opposition only functions when the system flourishes and decides to pinch its pennies and pull its punches when the system is on the ropes? After the crash of 1929, the Communists piled on and made the 1930s the Red Decade. With your support, we'll make the next decade our own.

Counter-Currents/*North American New Right*
September 10, 2012

Being "Nice" Will Not Save Us

I try not to follow news of black crime in America, because there is too damn much of it, it is depressingly stupid and savage, and I made my mind up about blacks long ago. But on August 26, 2015 I could not tune out the live on-air murder of two white journalists in Roanoke, Virgina—reporter Alison Parker (24) and cameraman Adam Ward (27)—by a paranoid, hateful black man named Vester Lee Flanagan II (41), professionally known as Bryce Williams, a failed news reporter who showed clear signs of personality disorders and had a history of filing bogus complaints for racism and sexual harassment (he was homosexual).

Flanagan's crime was meticulously premeditated. He filmed the murders and uploaded the video to his Twitter and Facebook accounts. No, I did not watch it. The screen capture was horrifying enough, prompting me to make another fledgling foray into the meme wars, by adapting Harold Covington's mantra: "If white people had a country of our own, this would not be happening."

Two hours after the crime, Flanagan faxed ABC News a 23-page suicide note and manifesto explaining his actions. ABC has quoted from the document, but at this writing it has not been released to the public. Flanagan also called ABC and confessed.

Police used Flanagan's cell phone signal to locate him. After a brief chase, Flanagan's car went off the road, and he committed suicide. Police found several license plates and disguises in the car, further evidence of planning.

By all accounts, Alison Parker and Adam Ward were nice, liberal, anti-racist white people. And Vester Flanagan, far from being a victim of racism and homophobia, was actually a privileged beneficiary of affirmative action and the willingness of whites to repeatedly give him jobs and the benefit of the doubt. So why did he decide that his former colleagues were racist crackers deserving of death?

To say that Flanagan was "crazy" is an evasion. He clearly had some sort of personality disorder. But what stoked his paranoia and resentment into a murderous rage is the false ideology of political correctness about race. Political correctness is just a form of *lying* and *injustice*. The basic lie is that blacks are equal to whites in every way, such that one would expect that both races would be equally represented among society's winners and losers.

When this lie conflicts with reality, the politically correct lie again to exculpate blacks from responsibility and blame all their failures on whites. Black underrepresentation in the professions and overrepresentation in prisons are attributed to white malevolence, i.e., "racism." And since overt white racism is in short supply, blacks are encouraged to use magnifying glasses and tweezers to find "microagressions" to complain about.

For instance, Vester Flanagan believed that his coworkers were racist for eating watermelon at work. Other racist provocations were phrases like "swing by" a location, which perhaps connoted apes or lynching victims swinging from trees, and getting "out in the field," which apparently triggered ancestral memories of picking cotton. Alison Parker was even accused of racism for having a friend who lived on Cotton Hill Road in Roanoke.

The lesson here is that, try as we might, white people are never going to be able to placate blacks by being "nice." On average, blacks are inferior to whites in intelligence, impulse control, planning for the future, and a host of other traits relevant to success in white civilization. Thus they are always going to be underrepresented among winners and overrepresented among losers. I won't say "even if they were treated fairly," because in truth blacks are given a whole host of unfair privileges, and for all that, they are still the sorriest race in America.

The only real solution is what White Nationalism stands for: *truth* about racial differences, *justice* in assigning rewards and responsibility, and a *nice white country*, for if white people had a country of our own, this would not have happened. The North American New Right advocates nationalism for all nations, i.e., the creation of racially and ethnically homogeneous homelands for all peoples.

Counter-Currents/*North American New Right*
September 2, 2015

THE NIGGER WORD

At Counter-Currents/*North American New Right*, our aim is to raise the social status, intellectual rigor, and stylistic tone of racialist discourse. Thus we do not use the nigger word and other crude racial slurs. However, although the distinction between "using" a word and merely "mentioning" it is lost on the low-IQ and the high-PC alike, it is possible to strictly avoid *using* a given word but still *mention* and even *discuss* it, e.g., by putting the word in quotes or referring to it as the such-and-such word. For instance, it is possible to *mention* that Trayvon Martin used the word "nigger" to refer to himself without actually *using* the nigger word. Similarly, it is possible to mention that Paula Deen used the nigger word to describe a black armed robber without actually using the word "nigger."

The reluctance to use the nigger word is far older than today's modern political correctness, racial integration, rampant egalitarianism, and Negro worship. Indeed, many whites who believed that blacks were inferior to whites in everything important to the creation and perpetuation of European civilization would still feel dirty calling them "niggers." Whites who believed that it was a great misfortune that blacks were bought to the Western hemisphere and wanted them strictly segregated from white society or even shipped back to Africa, still regarded the nigger word as an expletive that should not be uttered.

Class snobbery is definitely part of the longstanding disdain for the nigger word. I remember in Junior High School when a notorious dullard, bully, and slob pronounced the African nation of Niger—which David Irving sensitively refers to as "the n-country"—as if it had two g's. Apparently he didn't know any better. The class roared with mockery, and I smugly reveled in the fact that I was not one of "those people." (The fact that blacks use the nigger word constantly merely declasses it further.)

But there's more to it than just snobbery. "Nigger" is an expletive, like "fuck," "shit," "asshole," "cunt," "kike," "gook," or "Jeezus Fuckin' Christ." It is a word that names an ugly thing, or names a beautiful thing in an ugly way. Such words are usually uttered in anger, often with the intention to wound. Using expletives is a sign of poor self-control, as well as lack of imagination, taste, or intellect. These are not good traits.

But in my book, priggishness, cant, and hypocrisy are far worse. People who genuinely disapprove of expletives still use them in anger and extremity. Furthermore, there are also circumstances in which expletives really are the only appropriate word. For instance, Paula Deen is probably a sincere anti-racist and a genteel Southern woman who thinks the nigger word is low class. But when she described a black robber who stuck a gun in her face, it was completely understandable that her inhibitions about the nigger word would be overcome by righteous indignation and the undeniable fact that she was dealing with the genuine article. To pretend otherwise is simply dishonest. It is to maintain the absurdity that it is worse to be called a "nigger" than to act like one.

When faced with a genuinely ugly reality, the person of true class — i.e., nobility, courage, honor, honesty — does not resort to euphemisms. He does not speak of a "rest room" when he wants to use the toilet. He does not say "guuul-durn it!" when he mean "God damn it!" He disapproves of using expletives loosely, but he disapproves even more of using euphemisms when only good honest expletives will do. Euphemisms are for timid, prudish, conformist, mealy-mouthed, small-minded, middle-class, Low-Church philistines, which pretty much describes the default moral programming of mainstream white Americans, which keeps us a docile herd of cattle moving toward the kosher butcher at the end of the trail.

The most ridiculous euphemism of our times is "the n-word." Apparently, in the past, legislators banned sodomy but could not bring themselves to actually describe what they were banning. Today, the nation can be convulsed with a scandal about a simple word, but nobody can bring himself to say what the word actually is. Thus whenever I hear people use "the n-word," I play dumb.

"What word is that?"

"You know, the 'n-word.'"

"Nevada?"

"No!"

"Come on! Out with it then."

"Surely you know?"

"Sorry, I don't. You know me. Head in the clouds."

After squirming a bit, people will look to the left, then look to the right, then, *sotto voce*, come out with the nigger word. One woman mouthed it silently, hoping I could read her lips. Naturally I squinted and leaned in and finally wrung it out of her.

These people are not, mind you, actually *using* the nigger word. They fear to even *mention* it. This is, of course, an absurd act of appeasement of blacks, who are typically too dumb to distinguish between use and mention, and of the Politically Correct who are too hateful and unjust to care.

It also contributes to the ridiculous cult of the "numinous Negro," which has led Morgan Freeman to be typecast as God. Just as you can't criticize those who hold true power, you can't name those who are truly holy. Thus whites are conditioned to speak of blacks as a wise, innocent, and holy race when, in reality, all of us—liberal and conservative alike—both patronize them as "half-child" and fear them as "half-devil," to use the words of Nobel Laureate Rudyard Kipling.

Thus I completely understand Jim Goad's desire for massive resistance to this absurd taboo by *using* the nigger word as much as possible, although I cannot endorse it. After all, Counter-Currents does not use the nigger word. But I can at least show SWPL solidarity with the author of *The Redneck Manifesto* by *mentioning* the nigger word in this article, from time to time.

I believe that White Nationalism will win for many reasons, but they all boil down to the fact that we are the only people telling the truth about race, and the lies, evasions, excuses, and euphemisms have become so massive and absurd that people with even a shred of intelligence and honor are finding it increasingly difficult to believe in the diversity cult. So we need to keep speaking out and standing up for the truth. We don't have to be hateful. We don't have to be strident. We don't have to be crude. All we have to be is real.

Counter-Currents/*North American New Right*
July 29, 2013

ANDERS BEHRING BREIVIK:
THE NEO-CONSERVATIVE RAMBO

White Nationalists, European nationalists, counter-jihadists, immigration restrictionists, even the Tea Party are being smeared by being "linked" and "associated" with accused Norwegian spree-killer Anders Behring Breivik.

Most of these links exist only in the minds of dishonest Leftists (and Kosher conservatives) seeking to squeeze political advantage from the corpses of teenagers.

But some linkages are real—as real as anything on the internet can be. For instance, I immediately recognized Breivik's photo because I have seen it on Facebook a couple of times. (At the time of the attack, he had more than 7,000 Facebook friends.)

I remember him distinctly because of his photos, which look like professional modeling shots, not the typical candid snaps people use for their Facebook avatars.

I recall looking at his profile and deciding that he was not really in sync with the Counter-Currents agenda. He described himself as conservative and Christian (which are not necessarily red flags), but he aligned himself with Europe's philo-Semitic anti-Islamic movement (which is a very big red flag, and often a Jewish false one at that).

Also, the second time I encountered Breivik's picture on Facebook, I noticed that his name had been changed. After his picture appeared in news stories, I found it on Facebook under yet a third name (a name other than Anders Behring Breivik), but when I searched again a few minutes later, I could not find that profile.

This gave me an uneasy feeling: There are far too many ideological shape- and name-shifters in our milieu, and these behaviors are usually correlated with a high degree of narcissism as well as deeper psychological disorders. (I get the same creepy vibe from people who change their Facebook avatars a lot.) I have learned from bitter experience that nothing good for our race and cause comes out of association with the insane, so I prefer to err on the side of caution and avoid people who show signs of flakiness.

Initially, I held off writing about Breivik because his motives were not clear. Then Kevin Slaughter scooped the whole world of journalism by bringing Breivik's rationale to light: *2083: A European Declaration of Independence,* a 1,518 page manifesto outlining his worldview and the plans for his attacks. Breivik also created a very well-made video that summarizes his views and illustrates them with effective images. (These were published under the name Andrew Berwick. The book indicates London as the place of publication. The photos in the back, however, are of Anders Breivik.)

Although the crimes of which Breivik is accused bring to mind the Oklahoma City bombing, Breivik's carefully worked-out manifesto is more in the style of "Unabomber" Ted Kaczynski (although Breivik is not as deep a thinker; nor, unfortunately, is he as concise).

Breivik is a European nationalist whose primary concern is Islamic colonization. He is a conservative, an anti-Communist and opponent of "cultural Marxism," a Freemason, a Christian who sees Christianity as a cultural force for the unification of Europe against Islam (but obviously not a Christian fundamentalist as claimed by the mainstream media), a philo-Semite and pro-Zionist, an anti-racist, and an anti-National Socialist, who constantly uses Nazism as a paradigm for evil. (Breivik calls Adolf Hitler "the Great Satan" and blames him for our race's decline.)

Although the North American New Right belongs to the same genus, Euro-Nationalist, I can't imagine a more fundamentally different species than Breivik, for at the core of his thinking is an intellectual (or, more likely, moral) failing that makes it possible to embrace Jewry (and one of its tentacles, Freemasonry) while fighting its consequences ("cultural Marxism," the Islamization of Europe) and maligning National Socialism and other forms of Euro-Nationalism that get to the root of the problem.

Breivik's aim was, apparently, to spark a new crusade to

drive Islam out of Europe. His model is the Knights Templar, one of the spiritual-military orders that rolled back Islam during the Crusades. Breivik's photo of himself in Masonic garb is clearly based on the Masonic claim of descent from the Knights Templar.

Breivik devotes countless pages to outlining in detail the structure of his new Knights Templar, complete with ranks, oaths, rituals, and actual prototypes of uniforms and medals. Anyone familiar with role-playing games will immediately recognize this type of literature.

How, precisely, did Breivik think that he could resurrect the Knights Templar and spark a Europe-wide crusade against Islam by gunning down teenagers? Well, perhaps I speed-read right by it, but I did not see a connection.

Breivik has erected a skyscraper of words, but the elevators do not go all the way to the top. He spent 300,000 Euros (!) preparing for his operation, but left a gap between his means and ultimate ends that you could drive a truck bomb through.

Breivik's tome also includes tips for looking your best for photo shoots. Which makes me wonder: Was the disconnect between Breivik's political aims and his actions bridged by the sheer narcissism of this smug but deadly dork?

Was Breivik so captivated by his logic, his rhetoric, and his snazzy uniforms that he thought that millions of European men would rise up to follow him after he splattered the addled liberal brains of enough high-school students? When the crusade does not materialize, do you think that he will merely conclude that he needed to kill just a few more people, or maybe spend more time in a tanning bed? Did all these people die because a wealthy, alienated nerd was consumed by his own fantasy world?

If Breivik is indeed the perpetrator of the Norway killings, then I have a very simple message for him: You have done far more, and far worse, than killing 90-odd Norwegians, as terrible as that may be. You have set back the cause of saving the white race as a whole from extinction. For the predictable consequences of this sort of pointless terrorism do not include the revival of the Knights Templar. Rather, they include (1) politi-

cal crackdowns on dissenters, and (2) increased public resistance to our message by normal people, who are repulsed by
mass murder, especially of cute blonde teenagers.

Yes, of course this climate of opinion is being manipulated
by our enemies. Yes, our enemies get away with far worse
crimes all the time. Yes, it does not have to be this way. But
still, this is the reality of the situation. They have the power to
smear us, so of course they are going to use it. Terrorism is a
fight we cannot win, in the realm of politics or in the realm of
publicity. And only a fool picks a fight he cannot win.

And why, in the name of Odin, did the killer choose to target teenagers? (Who are being spun by the media into "children" and "kids" for extra horror.) Yes, there was a certain logic to targeting a youth camp for the ruling social democratic
Labor Party. Like all traitorous Western elites, the Norwegian
Labor Party condemns ordinary Norwegians to being preyed
upon by Third World thieves, rapists, and murderers, whom
they import and coddle. Yet they shelter themselves and their
families from the chaos they inflict on others. Breivik may have
decided to show these hypocrites that they are not invulnerable, that they cannot insulate themselves from the consequences of their own actions.

If that was his intended message, then it was perfectly futile.
The Oklahoma City bombing and the 9/11 terrorist attacks
proved that the United States government and its functionaries
are not invulnerable to the consequences of their actions either.
But if these attacks produced one second of moral reflection in
the citadels of power, a single moment of clarity about the evil
and hubris of American policy, I have yet to see any sign of it.
Instead, it produced just more domestic repression and foreign
adventurism: more lies, more wars, more victims.

Yes, 9/11 did manage to wake up a lot of Americans, but the
Oklahoma City bombing was a huge setback to the patriot and
militia movements. Again, only a fool picks a fight he cannot
win. If all you can do is wound a monster, then you are better
off leaving it alone.

In the aftermath of the attempt to smear *American Renaissance* by linking it to Arizona spree killer Jared Lee Loughner, I

argued that armed struggle against our enemies is futile, because they are stronger than us.[1] It is also unnecessary, because they are pursuing policies that will weaken and destroy themselves in the long run.

I also argued that merely *verbal* condemnations of violence by White Nationalists have no intellectual or moral credibility. The only credible step we can take to avoid senseless and counter-productive killing sprees like Breivik's is to stop coddling the insane among us. Elitism needs to begin at home.

Counter-Currents/*North American New Right*
July 24, 2011

---

[1] See my "On Violence" in *New Right vs. Old Right*.

THE COWARD CANARD

Patrick Buchanan's recent column on Anders Breivik is almost note perfect, until the very end, where he calls Breivik a "coward."[1] Buchanan is not the only one to use this canard when discussing Breivik. It is a stock accusation directed at all terrorists.

Remember when George W. Bush crept out of his secure location to accuse the 9/11 hijackers of cowardice? But this is just an abuse of language motivated by anger. Breivik may be a lot of things, but he is no coward.

What is cowardice? Cowardice the inability to master fear. Courage is the ability to master fear so that one can act, or not act, appropriately. The paradigm of fear is of death in battle. But there are many lesser fears that one needs to master as well: the fears of social disapproval, personal failure, and public embarrassment are often greater than the fear of death.

Courage, therefore, is not just one virtue. It is a virtue that makes other virtues possible. We need courage to be honest, just, moderate, wise, and so forth, for almost every decent act carries with it the risk of personal failure or public opposition.

There is a sense in which courage and cowardice are morally neutral. It takes courage to do bad things as well as good ones. Indeed, it takes *more* courage to do bad things than good ones, because more people will oppose you. So if someone is doing evil, decent people should pray that his courage fails; cowardice suddenly becomes praiseworthy.

I think that Breivik's killing spree was evil. It is not evil because violence *per se* is evil. Aside from complete pacifists, everyone recognizes situations in which violence is morally justified. It is not even evil because it is an act of terrorism. A single act by a single man might be terrorism. But a whole series of such acts by a group of men is a war or a revolution. And wars and revolutions can be morally justified.

---

[1] http://takimag.com/article/a_fire_bell_in_the_night_for_norway

No, Breivik's acts were evil simply because he targeted people who were largely innocent of the crimes he deplored: government clerks and passersby in Oslo, teenagers and young adults at a Labor Party youth camp. The full horror sinks in with a question: How many of you, dear readers, were politically liberal at age sixteen? How many of you simply believed what your parents believed?

Breivik's acts were also evil because they will hinder rather than help those trying to save Europe from declining white birthrates and rising non-white immigration. And from my point of view, saving the white race is the most important thing in the world, an end that can justify *any* means — provided they *really are* means.

But as evil as Breivik's acts may have been, they still took nerves of steel; they took courage. Breivik knew very well that he might be facing death. Or, if he survived, he would face a nightmare for the rest of his life: the hatred of healthy people and the adulation of the insane; the betrayal of friends and family; the indignities of interrogation, trial, and imprisonment.

It takes courage to face death. It takes even more courage to face a life of infamy. (A very high percentage of suicides are out of cowardice.)

As Breivik planned and carried out his mission, there were thousands moments of decision when his courage could have failed, but he continued. He did horrible things with his own hands, things that he saw before his very eyes, things that probably sickened him. But he steeled his nerves and kept on killing.

Personally speaking, I am too much of a coward to do what Breivik did, and too much of a coward to have faced the consequences. And I suspect the same is true of the bloggers hurling the word "coward" into cyberspace from the safety of their studies. But we can console ourselves that *our* form of cowardice — cowardice in the commission of evil — is, after all, a praiseworthy thing.

But Breivik killed people who were unarmed. Doesn't that make him cowardly? No. It still took courage to do what he did. Yes, it would have taken more courage to face down armed opponents. But as far as he knew, there could have been armed opponents on that island. And even if he knew that his opponents were unarmed, his task still entailed risks. He could have been rushed as he reloaded, for instance. (I would like to know if anything like that was even attempted.) Moreover, he surely had to struggle to master feelings of horror at what he had accomplished.

Granted, the most honorable battle is a duel in which both parties fight with the same weapons out in the open under conditions of strictest equality so that only valor and martial skill matter. It entails the maximum risk and therefore requires the maximum courage.

But it is just wishful thinking to demand that an opponent who enjoys a strategic advantage give that up merely out of a romantic notion of chivalry, particularly since one's real motive is hardly chivalrous either. It is simply to increase one's own chances of success.

"Come out here and face me like a man, you coward!" merely translates to "Come out here so I can get an easier shot at you." One merely phrases it in the language of a playground taunt in the unlikely event that one's enemy is insecure enough to risk his life proving something to a person he sees fit to kill.

Courage is one of the most important traits we can cultivate. With courage, we can face down the impediments to living a decent and honorable life. Without it, none of our other virtues really matter. Yes, courage in evil is a terrible possibility. But that is possible only because courage makes all things possible.

Because courage is so important, we have to know exactly what it means — and what its opposite means. Thus we cannot afford to abuse words like "coward," even when our anger is righteous. There is a long list of vices and expletives that can justly describe Anders Berhing Breivik. But coward is not among them.

Counter-Currents/*North American New Right*
July 28, 2011

BREIVIK:
A STRANGE NEW RESPECT

My initial reaction to Anders Breivik's killing spree on July 22, 2011 was largely anger, because I feared that his actions would harm not just Norwegian ethnonationalism but white nationalism around the world.

I was relieved to learn that Breivik was a product of the Jewish-controlled Counter-Jihadist movement, which eschews racial nationalism and builds a case against the Muslim colonization of Europe on "Judeo-Christian" religious and cultural grounds. I was quite content to let them take the heat. But of course both our enemies and our chosen audience are none too concerned about such fine distinctions.

I also, frankly, took a visceral dislike to Breivik, who struck me as a creepy, narcissistic dork.

However, since Breivik went on trial last month, I have found a strange new respect for him. He has comported himself in a dignified manner and made a forceful, intelligent, well-argued case for his views and actions. His only real gaffe has been to insist on the existence of his make-believe Knights Templar organization.

By the end of the first week, the trial was being pulled from front pages around the world, for the simple reason that Breivik was making too much sense to too many people.

Breivik admits to the killings. But he demands to be acquitted on the grounds of "necessity," but what it boils down to is *ethnic self-defense*. Based on news coverage, machine translations of trial transcripts posted on the internet, particularly at Tanstaafl's Age of Treason and Attack on the Labor Party, and our own Andrew Hamilton's translation of Breivik's Opening Statement on the second day of his trial, the rationale for Breivik's attack and his defense is the following.[1]

---

[1] http://www.counter-currents.com/2012/05/anders-breiviks-opening-statement/

The Norwegian Labor Party and its allies in the press are primarily responsible for imposing non-white immigration on Norway and for stigmatizing and silencing Norwegian opposition. The Labor Party has imposed multiculturalism without a popular referendum. Their policies have led to the rape, murder, brutalization, and ethnic displacement of Norwegians by non-white immigrants — crimes to which the Norwegian establishment, including the media, has responded with lies, cover-ups, and psychological warfare against Norwegians, labeling them "racist" and "xenophobic" and denigrating their culture and traditions.

Since, moreover, these non-white immigrants are far more prolific than Norwegians, who are taxed to subsidize the invaders, the long term consequence of the Labor Party's policies is the destruction of Norwegians as a distinct people.

Although Breivik does not, to my knowledge, use the term, this is actually *genocide* as defined by the United Nations, which holds that genocide is not merely the outright murder of a people, but the creation of conditions that make its long term survival as a people impossible.

Thus the Norwegian Labor Party and its allies have imposed a genocidal regime on Norway. And if there are any absolutes in the world today, the moral rectitude of resisting genocide is chief among them.

Under international law, the leaders of the Norwegian Labor Party, as well as their collaborators, should be removed from power and tried and punished for genocide. But dissenting voices about multiculturalism are silenced, so rational debate and peaceful political change are impossible. As Breivik says in his Opening Statement:

> More and more cultural conservatives realize that the democratic struggle is pointless. It is not possible to win when no real freedom of speech exists. As more realize this in the coming decades it is a short path to the weapon.
>
> When a peaceful revolution is impossible, a violent revolution is the only possibility.

Thus, Breivik planned and executed his attacks.

The purpose of the attacks appears to be fourfold.

First, Breivik wished to punish people in the Labor Party who were responsible for instituting anti-Norwegian genocide. He failed at this, because most of his victims were innocent by-standers, low-level functionaries, and youth activists.

Second, Breivik wished to publicize his 1518 page manifesto, *2083: A European Declaration of Independence*, a compendium of Counter-Jihadist writings. In this, he was wildly successful.

It is unfortunate, however, that his manifesto was such a vast and indigestible data-dump. If it had been a slender, concise work, like *The Communist Manifesto* or the Unabomber's *Industrial Society and Its Future*, it would have had a far greater impact, because it would actually have been *read* by far more people.

Furthermore, although Breivik did not expect to survive his attack, he has used his imprisonment and trial to refine his message and garner new publicity. At this, he has been extremely successful.

Third, Breivik hoped to inspire imitators, perhaps even someone who will actually bring into existence the fictional Knights Templar order outlined in his manifesto. To my knowledge, he has not yet succeeded in this aim. But it seems inevitable, given enough time, that others will follow Breivik's example.

Fourth, Breivik hoped to increase political tension and polarization, perhaps even provoking a crackdown on moderate nationalists, including the various democratic nationalist parties that are actually making some progress in Europe. This, of course, is what I fear the most, and I find it especially galling that Breivik *intended* this outcome. His rationale is that such a crackdown will radicalize nationalists to take up arms.

But if one is going to polarize the political field in order to empty the middle ground by forcing moderates to the extremes, *one needs to give them somewhere else to go* — somewhere *real*, not a fantasy order of Knights Templar elaborated with all the detail one would expect from someone who spent countless hours in online role-playing games. Otherwise, polarizing the field will only lead right-leaning moderates to give up entirely.

Furthermore, the existence of moderate shades of political opinion in nationalist circles actually provides channels of influence bridging the gap between the mainstream and the radical fringe. Radicals can actually utilize this moderate infrastructure to influence and radicalize people who might otherwise be unavailable to them.

Finally, although nationalists today labor under huge handicaps, we still enjoy some freedom of speech and association, and we benefit far more from them than we would from the possible radicalizing effects of a real crackdown.

Even though Breivik is stridently anti-Nazi and anti-Communist, his basic political model shares much with the Old Right and the Old Left. He hoped to create an armed, conspiratorial, revolutionary party (in the form of an initiatic knightly order) as a vehicle for violently halting and reversing the Islamic colonization of Europe.

From a New Right perspective, Breivik's overall strategy is counter-productive. Our race will not be saved by armed struggle, but by the transformation of consciousness and culture. The Norwegian Labor Party did not come to power by force of arms, but because the New Left laid the intellectual and cultural groundwork. For the New Right to do the same, we need to maintain freedom of speech and association and learn to use the infrastructure of the whole political spectrum to spread our message outward and draw people and resources inward, in a more radical direction.

It is necessary for the New Right to draw a bold, clear line between our approach and Old Right approaches like Breivik's, because his approach does not complement ours but fundamentally undermines it.

As for Breivik's rationale for violence, he claims that indigenous peoples have special rights to their homelands, which entitle them to resist invaders with violence. It is a principle of ethnic self-defense. It is true that indigenous peoples have the right to ethnic self-defense. But surely that right extends to all peoples. All peoples have the right to resist genocide by all necessary means, including violence.

Breivik also makes a utilitarian argument, claiming that his acts were justified because he killed today to save a much greater number of people in the future, who will die unless multiculturalism is stopped.

Morally speaking, there is simply no valid argument against political violence *per se*, particularly in resistance to genocide. The justification of a particular act of violence depends entirely upon whether or not it actually is necessary to serve a moral end.

The weakness of Breivik's case is not the moral premise, but the choice of his targets: If he had killed the actual leadership of Norway's Labor Party, or the leaders of the Norwegian press — as opposed to people as young as 14 — his defense might actually hold water. It is really shocking that Breivik put so much thought and planning into his acts, but didn't think *just a bit more* about his targets. He chose the wrong targets, both from the point of view of their culpability and from the point of view of publicity, of propaganda of the deed.

Breivik was not indifferent to innocent life. But some "collateral damage," i.e., killing of the innocent, is necessary and unavoidable even in just struggles. Breivik tried to minimize such deaths. His error was in ascribing culpability to young people whose only crime may have been to believe the multicultural propaganda they were steeped in from birth.

The leaders of the Norwegian Labor Party have taken one of Europe's most homogeneous, harmonious, and happy societies and colonized it with hostile, fast-breeding aliens. Since racially, culturally, and religiously diverse peoples inevitably end up hating and killing one another when forced to coexist within the same system, the Norwegian Labor Party has responded to these tensions by hushing up both crimes and criticism. They created a boiling cauldron of social and psychological turmoil. Then they clamped a lid down on it. Then they were shocked — shocked! — that the whole thing exploded in their faces. First and foremost, Breivik needs to be seen as the inevitable consequence of the Labor Party's policies.

The establishment obviously wished to use the Breivik trial to stigmatize ethnonationalist sentiments. But Breivik was making too much sense, so they are drawing a veil of censorship over the proceedings. In short, they are doing the very thing that made Breivik's rampage necessary in the first place.

Will they ever learn?

I grew up around a lot of Norwegian Americans in the Pacific Northwest. They are known for being taciturn and reserved about expressing their feelings. I still remember the only Norwegian joke I ever heard: "Did you hear the one about the Norwegian man who loved his wife so much that he *almost told her*?" Nordics don't just keep back positive emotions, either. They are notorious for bottling up their anger, suffering in silence until, eventually, there is an explosion and someone goes Viking.

There will be more Breiviks. Of course the multiculturalists will merely blame Breivik for that. But the truth is that Breivik himself was merely a product of the hatred and violence that multiculturalism predictably brings. The Norwegian Labor Party is responsible for all of the violence caused by their policies, including the inevitable violence by Norwegians who get fed up and finally fight back. That includes Breivik. Primarily he needs to be seen as a victim of an evil system. (Breivik, of course, bears some responsibility for his acts. These were not crimes of passion but the products of lengthy, meticulous premeditation.)

Yet in the end, for all of his crimes and mistakes, I cannot judge Breivik too harshly. He is an awakened white man, and those are all too rare. In spite of his errors, he was acting out of loyalty to our people, and that matters a great deal. Yes, he committed crimes. But he committed them out of love.

Granted, when Breivik awakened he fled one form of Jewish ideology for another, namely the Counter-Jihad movement. But the whole reason that such false opposition groups exist is to deceive, deflect, and delay awakened whites. Still, many whites eventually see through them. And, as Breivik's Opening Statement indicates, since his arrest, his thinking has evolved in the direction of explicit ethnonationalism. Given time, he might even evolve toward a consistent New Right outlook.

Breivik is going to spend many years in prison. If I could

whisper to the Norns, this is the wyrd I would have them spin. I hope he continues his intellectual evolution in a New Right trajectory, renouncing violence and emphasizing intellectual and cultural strategies of change (the only strategies that will be available to him, in any case). I hope that he comments on Norwegian and international affairs and develops a following. Surely events in the coming decades will only argue in his favor. More and more Norwegians — and Europeans around the world — would come to sympathize with his outlook.

Eventually, he could become a pundit, a prophet, a guru, a cult figure. Political prisoners definitely have a glamor. People may someday rifle through his garbage for relics. Women will want to bear his children. His face might end up on t-shirts, just like Che Guevara. And when he gets out of prison, who knows, perhaps Breivik will follow the path of rehabilitated ex-terrorists like Nelson Mandela and Menachem Begin. Perhaps he will end up a Prime Minister or a Nobel Peace Prize winner. He would not be the first to have used dynamite along the way.

Counter-Currents/*North American New Right*
May 18, 2012

On the Necessity
of a New Right

I have been asked for my opinion of long-time White Nationalist Frazier Glenn Miller's shooting spree in Overland Park, Kansas, on April 13, 2014, in which he murdered three white people, including a 14-year-old boy, outside a Jewish Community Center and a Jewish old folks home, apparently while shouting Adolf Hitler's name.

There's no point in lingering too long over the layer upon layer of idiocy and evil in this act. Miller wanted to strike at Jews, whom he blames with good reason for the ongoing destruction of our people, and he killed three of our people, hastening the day when whites become extinct, increasing public sympathy for Jews, and putting White Nationalism in an even worse light. If the white race still exists on this planet in 200 years, it will be no thanks to Glenn Miller.

Even if he had killed three Jews, did he really imagine that by randomly selecting three Jews in Kansas, he was striking at the leadership of the Jewish community? Or did he think that all Jews are equally responsible for what their leaders promote? And even if he had struck down three Jewish leaders, did he imagine that this would do anything but increase our people's sympathy for Jews and reinforce negative opinions of White Nationalists?

Didn't Miller believe that Jews control the media and thus have the power to paint his actions in a way that helps their cause and harms ours? Of course, that is easy, because only a fool could think that Miller's actions help our cause.

And why was he taking Hitler's name in vain? Did he really think that Hitler would have approved of such pointless terrorism? Even if Hitler were every bit as evil as his enemies make out, he wasn't stupid.

The reason I wrote my essay "New Right vs. Old Right"[1] in

---

[1] The title essay in my *New Right vs. Old Right*.

May of 2012 is because I wished to draw a bright clear line between the project of the North American New Right and what I call the Old Right, namely classical National Socialism and Fascism and their latter-day imitators, including people like William Pierce, Alex Linder, and, down at the bottom of the barrel, Glenn Miller, Wade Michael Page,[2] Anders Breivik, and other gun-toting, spree-killing retards.

The North American New Right rejects the totalitarianism, terrorism, imperialism, and genocide of the Old Right.

It was perfectly logical for the National Socialists and Fascists to form uniformed paramilitaries when they were battling Communists who wished to impose a totalitarian dictatorship by terrorism and force of arms. And, given the proven inability of liberal democracies and old aristocracies to resist Bolshevism, it made sense for them to set up one party dictatorships which suppressed dissent and unified their nations by dint of propaganda and force — although they were never so "totalitarian" as the Bolsheviks. The Old Right's methods were, in short, perfectly adapted to the methods of their enemies. They merely took a gun to a gun fight.

But Jewish political dominance in America was not imposed by Bolshevik methods. It was achieved within the framework of liberal democracy by first attaining *metapolitical* hegemony through propaganda and institutional subversion.[3] Thus the New Right proposes to fight them the same way: through changing minds, culture, and institutions. One fights bad ideas with better ideas, cultural subversion with cultural renewal, institutional subversion with institutional renewal.

These counter-measures are not just appropriate to the enemy's attack, but they play to our strengths. The moral, scientific, and historical case for White Nationalism has never been stronger, even though we lack money, organizational competence, and political power. The enemy, by contrast, has never been richer, better organized, or more politically powerful. But

---

[2] http://www.counter-currents.com/2012/08/understanding-the-sikh-temple-massacre/

[3] See my essay "Hegemony" in *New Right vs. Old Right*.

they have never been weaker on moral, scientific, and historical grounds. And as human beings, they have never been more corrupt, decadent, and repulsive to healthy people.

What is the Old Right response to this strategic situation? Based on Alex Linder's *Vanguard News Network Forum*, which Glenn Miller frequented, the Old Right approach is to drop our strongest weapons (particularly morality), to put together a cadre of people who are even more repulsive and crazy than the enemy leadership, and then to charge the enemy at his strongest point.

Old Right types typically accuse me of bringing a pen to a gunfight, but I accuse them of bringing a gun to a battle of ideas. Glenn Miller shows us how well that works out.

Counter-Currents/*North American New Right*
April 15, 2014

UNDERSTANDING THE CHARLESTON CHURCH MASSACRE

On Wednesday, June 17th, 2015, a 21-year-old white man, Dylann Storm Roof, entered the Emanuel African Methodist Episcopal Church in Charleston, South Carolina, and killed nine blacks gathered for Bible study with a 45. pistol, then fled the scene. He was arrested the next day in North Carolina and returned to Charleston less than a day after the killings.

As a white person, I look down upon the criminals among us. I do not reflexively defend and glorify them. This was a terrible act, an act that was illegal under slavery, illegal under Jim Crow, and illegal today. I hope Storm receives a fair trial and just punishment, but that seems unlikely given the racially charged atmosphere in America today.

We obviously don't know all the facts yet, but apparently the killings were racially motivated. Still, I can say three things with confidence.

First, this could not have happened in a homogeneously white society. I have no desire to absolve Dylann Roof, much less blame his victims. But he would not be a killer, and they would not be dead, if blacks and whites did not live in the same society. When different races are forced to live together in the same system, frictions are inevitable. These frictions give rise to misunderstandings, distrust, alienation, and long-simmering resentments, which flare up into hatred, violence, and social upheaval. Dylan Roof's actions are predictable consequences of multiculturalism — as are the far more numerous racially-motivated hate crimes committed by blacks against whites, crimes which the establishment and media prefer to ignore.

Blacks and whites have shared North America for almost 400 years, and race relations are getting worse rather than better. If this were a marriage, we would have filed for divorce long ago. Thus the New Right stands for the principle of racial divorce.[1] It is time for whites and blacks to go our separate ways and pursue their our own destinies. We stand for the creation of separate racially homogeneous societies, through the peaceful and humane process of redrawing borders and shifting populations.[2]

In the case of recent immigrant populations, the best solution is for them to return to their homelands. I also think that is the best solution for groups like Jews, Japanese, and Chinese who have been in America for a long time but still maintain strong ties to their homelands. In the case of indigenous peoples and some older immigrant populations (including the descendants of African slaves), territorial partition would seem to be in order.

Second, we should resist dismissing Dylann Roof with the all-too-easy claim that he was "crazy." Sure, he looks dweeby and autistic. Sure, there are reports of illegal drug use, which is often both an effect and a cause of mental illness. Sure, there are reports that he was prescribed mind-altering legal drugs as well.

But I am not going to simply disown Dylann Roof and label him "one of them": one of those evil, crazy white racists who are fundamentally different from the rest of us, the "good," "sane," "tolerant" white people. For the truth is, Dylann Storm Roof is "one of us."

By "one of us," I simply mean that he is a white man, and all white people have innate ethnocentric tendencies, wired deep in our brains. We love our own and we fear strangers. As diversity increases, all of us will bear increased psychic costs, even those who pursue wealth and status by selling out their own people in favor of foreigners.

Roof and people like him may be nothing more than canaries in a coal mine: the first to sense the presence of a threat to the survival of us all. Roof may have just been abnormally sensitive to the terrible psychic consequences of losing control of

---

[1] See my "Irreconcilable Differences: The Case for Racial Divorce," in *Truth, Justice, & a Nice White Country*.
[2] http://www.counter-currents.com/2014/06/the-slow-cleanse/

our society to aliens: stress, alienation, anger, hatred, rage, etc. This heightened sensitivity might also go along with a whole suite of other abnormal traits. But we dismiss people like Roof at our own risk. For in the end, all of us will feel the same effects — unless we heed the warning signs and turn back the rising tide of color.

Third, Roof's "solution" to his rage and alienation — killing innocent people — just makes the racial situation worse rather than better. There is no evidence so far that Roof was affiliated with or influenced by any white racialist group. But his actions certainly resemble those of racially-motivated spree killers like Anders Breivik, Wade Michael Page, and Glenn Miller, all of whom are products of what I call "Old Right" thinking.

By the "Old Right," I mean classical Fascism and National Socialism and their contemporary imitators who believe that White Nationalism can be advanced through such means as one party-politics, terrorism, totalitarianism, imperialism, and genocide. Today's Old Right scene is rife with fantasies of race war, lone wolf attacks on non-whites, and heroic last stands that end in a hail of police bullets. Intelligent and honorable people have emerged from this milieu. But there have been more than a few spree-killers as well.

This kind of violence is worse than a crime. It is a mistake. It does nothing to advance our cause and much to set us back.

Given that reason, science, and history are all on our side, and the greatest apparatus of coercion and brainwashing in human history is on the enemy's side, doesn't it make sense to attack the enemy at his weakest point rather than at his strongest? This is why the North American New Right pursues White Nationalism through intellectual and cultural means: we critique the hegemony of anti-white ideas and seek to establish a counter-hegemony of pro-white ideas.

Only a fool picks a battle he cannot win, and we cannot win with violence. Fortunately, we don't have to. The Left lost the Cold War but won the peace through the establishment of intellectual and cultural hegemony. We can beat them the same way, and we don't have to all be rocket scientists to do it, since anyone of even moderate intelligence can make real progress by simply repeating Bob Whitaker's talking points about white genocide.

Furthermore, the only form of violence that even has *a chance* to be productive in halting multiculturalism and non-white immigration would target the people *responsible* for these policies, not random innocents. Moreover, killing innocent people (at a place of worship!) has entirely predictable results. First, such violence creates sympathy for the victims. (*Even I feel sympathy for them, and I would deport them all tomorrow if I had the power.*) Second, it plays into the establishment narrative of evil, crazy, intolerant whites whose gun rights must be taken away.

So Roof's choice of targets was superficial and frankly stupid. (Yes, he killed a state senator. But what are the chances that he knew that?) Was he even thinking about the greater good of our people? Or was he merely indulging in blind, self-destructive spite? And how exactly does praising repugnant killers help White Nationalists establish ourselves as representatives of the long-term best interests of our people?

I wish I could erect a wall between myself and the kind of unstable, undisciplined people who go on killing sprees, but you can't change the world from a bunker. Thus responsible white advocates need to adopt the next best course of action: (1) we must be alert to the signs of mental instability and inclinations toward violence and rigorously screen out such people, and (2) we need draw clear, unambiguous intellectual lines between New Right and Old Right approaches.

I just hope I don't have to do this *often*. But apparently it will be often enough that I have been able to dust off one of my previous spree-killer essays and merely change a few particulars.[3]

Counter-Currents/*North American New Right*
June 19, 2015

---

[3] http://www.counter-currents.com/2012/08/understanding-the-sikh-temple-massacre/

WEST-COAST WHITE NATIONALISM

Years ago, when a young woman set out from Alabama to go to college in California, her uncle told her the story of how California was born. America, you see, was populated by people who just did not fit in back in Europe: religious fanatics, horse thieves, bail jumpers, fortune seekers, and other footloose folk. When they settled on the East Coast, the ones who didn't fit in there moved a little further West and settled. Those who didn't fit in there, moved still further West. And so on, and so forth, until they reached the West Coast and couldn't go any further. Then they started collecting. And that's what explains California, the great cultural granola of fruits, nuts, and flakes.

I laughed, of course, when she told this story, because as a native Westerner, I know that it is true. I grew up in the inland Northwest, but when I first visited the West Coast, I knew that I was at home. The West Coast of the United States, from San Diego to Seattle, is the closest thing I have experienced to an earthly paradise. We have the best climate in the country. The temperature is almost always mild, no matter where one's area falls on the spectrum from steady sunshine to perpetual twilight. Aside from the coastline itself, we have some of America's most beautiful landscapes, ranging from deserts to towering snow-capped volcanoes to rainforests. We have America's best food and wines, some of its most beautiful cities, and some pretty formidable cultural resources. No, we do not have the art museums of New York City, Washington, D.C., and Boston. No, we do not have the Metropolitan Opera. But we can always visit them during the two weeks of the year when those cities are neither freezing nor sweltering, then hasten back to where living is easy.

The West Coast also has a lot of white people. Seattle and Portland are the whitest large cities in the United States, and outside the cities, Washington and Oregon are even whiter. California, of course, is now majority non-white, although whites remain the largest ethnic group.

The racial quality of Western whites is also very high. Furthermore, white Westerners really are more "laid back" and fun-loving. Western friendliness is not just politeness. It is combined with genuine openness and civic-mindedness. City folk out West tend to be much less pretentious than city folk back East. Even in San Francisco.

Many White Nationalists hope that when the United States falls apart, a White Republic will emerge in the Pacific Northwest, encompassing Washington, Oregon, Idaho, and parts of Montana and even some parts of Northern California. Harold Covington is the chief promoter of this idea, but he is not its originator or sole proponent. There are White Nationalists moving to the Northwest who are not part of Covington's Northwest Front.

The chief objection to the idea of a Northwest Homeland is that the West Coast tends to be socially and politically liberal, even though the inland West tends to be socially and politically conservative. So, the argument goes, the Pacific Northwest is less hospitable to a White Republic than other, more uniformly conservative areas. (Of course the creation of a White Republic will be an uphill battle anywhere in America.)

White Nationalism is, of course, overwhelmingly associated with the political Right both in Europe and America. But White Nationalism will never triumph if it remains confined to the political Right. White consciousness must become hegemonic throughout the political spectrum. White liberals and Leftists will have to realize that their values are not universal aspirations of all mankind. They are, instead, expressions of a distinctly white consciousness and will not survive or flourish in a non-white society.

There is nothing absurd about the idea of a racially conscious Left, much less a racially conscious Left on the West Coast. Indeed, it has already existed, and its headquarters were right here in the San Francisco Bay Area. It was here that Denis Kearney, 1847–1907, an immigrant from Ireland, founded the California Workingman's Party to combat Chinese immigration. It was here that Jack London, 1876–1916, wrote passionately on behalf of both socialism and racialism (and experimented with ecologically sustainable agriculture). It was here that Michael O'Meara was born in 1946 and began his intellectual odyssey from Marxist and revolutionary syndicalist to White Nationalist and prophet of the White Republic.

Furthermore, I have noticed that today's West Coast White Nationalists tend to be socially and even politically more Leftwing than White Nationalists from other parts of the United States. I'll never forget the evening in 2003 when, at a David Irving lecture in San Francisco, I met a daughter of the '60s counter-culture who told me that her two favorite books are *The Lord of the Rings* and *Mein Kampf.*

- ❖ West Coast White Nationalists tend to have higher SWPLQs ("Stuff White People Like" Quotients) than White Nationalists in other parts of the US. (I liked 122/150 SWPL in the first *Stuff White People Like* book, but only 41/92 SWPL in *Whiter Shades of Pale.*)
- ❖ West Coast White Nationalists tend to be more strongly concerned with environmental preservation, healthy and sustainable lifestyles, and combating cruelty to animals than White Nationalists in other parts of the US. If Savitri Devi were alive today, she would be smuggling stray cats into an organic gardening commune in Berkeley.
- ❖ West Coast White Nationalists tend to be more critical of the workings of unrestrained global capitalism. We are pro-labor, protectionist, pro-zoning, and pro-small business.
- ❖ West Coast White Nationalists tend to be more non-Christian and to be more honest about it than other White Nationalists. I know atheists, agnostics, neo-pagans, New Agers, and even some who have made extensive study and practice of Eastern philosophies and religions. Religious pluralism and tolerance would definitely be features of a West Coast White Republic.
- ❖ West Coast White Nationalists tend to be more toler-

ant of homosexuals, bisexuals, "androphiles," and "none of the aboves" who put their racial identity first.

❖ West Coast White Nationalists tend to be more tolerant of drugs like marijuana and psychedelics.

❖ West Coast White Nationalists are far less hung up on sub-racial distinctions and Old World feuds than White Nationalists in the East and South. We tend to think of ourselves as whites first and foremost.

These are, of course, generalizations based on personal experience, not sociological surveys. They are, furthermore, tendencies, not general rules or universal generalizations. There are obviously many exceptions. But White Nationalism is the stuff of dreams anyway. So with that caveat, I think there is reason to believe that, if a racially conscious Left arises again, it will be on the West Coast.

Counter-Currents/*North American New Right*,
December 10, 2010

IS RACIAL PURISM DECADENT?

"Those who talk too much about
race no longer have it in them."
—Oswald Spengler

Recently I spent a good deal of time re-reading the great Oswald Spengler: for general enlightenment, but also with an eye to criticizing his teachings about race, which seemed at first reading confused, bizarre, and dangerous. Much to my surprise, however, I have come to see much sense and truth in Spengler's views.

BIOLOGICAL RACE

Although Spengler speaks dismissively of Darwinism, he does not deny that race is a biological phenomenon. For Spengler, races are extended families, people who share the same "blood" (i.e., genes). Spengler even speaks of a race as a vast collective body of individuals through which the same genes circulate.

But Spengler denies that biology is all there is to race. Race, it turns out, has both psychological and cultural aspects as well.

Like Darwinists, Spengler believes that biological races are mutable. They change over time. According to Spengler, the principal force that shapes races is "landscape," i.e., environment. This is consistent with the biological view that a distinct race emerges when a human population is isolated and subjected to unique environmental conditions. These conditions select for certain genetic variations. These variations then spread throughout the entire population through inbreeding. (If there are barriers to breeding between different parts of the population, then multiple new races or subraces will emerge.)

Where Spengler departs from sound biology is his belief that landscape can shape a population *independent of genetic change*, and that different races, when placed in the same landscape, will converge in their traits *without genetic blending*. Spengler even refers to Franz Boas's false and probably fraudulent claims that in America, the offspring of different European racial stocks had convergent biological traits that were products of environment alone. But none of Spengler's conclusions about race depend on these false assumptions, which can be excised without changing his overall viewpoint.

PSYCHOLOGICAL RACE

What is "psychological" race? Spengler often speaks of "having race" and being "of race." But having race is not merely having certain genes. It is a matter of having a certain *feeling*: a primitive, vital urge to propagate oneself. It is the drive to immortalize oneself through one's progeny. In *The Hour of Decision*, Spengler writes:

A woman of race does not desire to be a "companion" or a "lover," but a *mother*; and not the mother of *one* child, to serve as a toy and distraction, but of many: the instinct of a strong race speaks in the pride that large families inspire, in the feeling that barrenness is the hardest curse that can befall a woman and through her the race. Out of this instinct arises the primitive jealousy which leads one woman to take away from another the man whom she covets as the father of her children. The more intellectual jealousy of the great cities . . . betrays the waning of the race urge to permanence; and that instinct for permanence cannot be reawakened by speeches and writing. . . . A man wants stout sons who will perpetuate his name and his deeds beyond his death into the future and enhance them, just as he has done himself through feeling himself heir to the calling and works of his ancestors. That is the *Nordic* idea of immortality. These peoples have known no other and desired none. It is the source of that tremendous yearning for fame, the wish to live on among posterity through one's work, to see one's name perpetuated on monuments or at the least held in honourable memory.[1]

---

[1] Oswald Spengler, *The Hour of Decision, Part One: Germany and*

This feeling of race is not "racial consciousness," i.e., awareness of belonging to a certain race. The feeling of race is forward-looking. Racial consciousness is backwards-looking. The feeling of race impels us to create new life. Racial consciousness is merely awareness of life that has already been created, the life handed down to us. The feeling of race is the stirring of the same creative force in ourselves.

RACE & CULTURE

How, then, is race also "cultural"? If a race is a collective body that exists and propagates itself through individual bodies, a culture is a collective mind that exists in and through individual minds, propagating itself by means of language.

Race shapes and limits culture. But once culture arises, it turns back on and reshapes its racial substratum in the light of ideas that are not dictated by biology. These ideas include conceptions of beauty and fitness that guide mate selection, myths and religious beliefs that regulate sexual behavior, moral ideals that promote the propagation of certain types, etc.

Cultural selection may be eugenic, dysgenic, or both, but if exercised over a long enough period of time, it can produce human populations as varied as different breeds of dog.

RACE CHANGE

Spengler puts great stock in the mutability of races.

He denies what might be called "race Platonism," namely the idea that races are immutable kinds that are more or less well-instantiated by particular individuals. For Spengler, a race is just a collection of individuals with common blood. If a race can be likened to a collective organism, this organism does not exist over and above its individual members. Instead it exists only in and through them.

Spengler also denies what can be called "race Traditionalism," the idea that in the distant past, a godlike super-race existed, which has since declined because of miscegenation with infe-

World-Historical Evolution, trans. Charles Francis Atkinson (New York: Alfred A. Knopf, 1934), 220–21.

rior races or spiritual transgressions or both.

Race Platonism sees every concrete, living organism as an imperfect reflection of its ideal archetype. Race Traditionalism sees all change as degeneration. Both views see change as metaphysically inferior to timeless perfection, and the Traditionalists think that as time rolls on, things usually go from bad to worse.

But if race Platonism and race Traditionalism are false, then change is not *necessarily* a bad thing. Life is constant change, and stasis — even frozen perfection — is death.

In Spengler's view, a race *just is* a constantly changing group of individuals who share the same genetic traits at any given point in time. But these traits are not timeless and permanent either. (That would be just a sneaky, immanent form of Platonism, i.e., Aristotelianism.) Genetic traits also change over time. This means that if we go far enough back in our family trees, we will find people quite unlike ourselves.

The unity of a race, therefore, is ultimately not defined by the persistence of something that remains unchanged in time, but merely the continuity of an ever-changing process, one of the strands of the ever-changing process that is nature itself.

RACE PRESERVATION?

What is race preservation? Most race preservationists will answer that it consists of maintaining a certain set of genes. This is, for instance, the core of Frank Salter's concept of Ethnic Genetic Interests.

But if Spengler's view of race is correct, then this is tantamount to the demand that time stop. It is tantamount to taking a snapshot of a moving process and demanding that no further change take place.

Yet if a race is a constantly changing collective organism, then the demand to "preserve" it at a certain arbitrarily chosen moment is actually the demand to kill it. It is analogous to "preserving" a bird at the height of its beauty — by shooting it and taking it to the taxidermist.

Every generation of a race is shaped in part by the conscious and unconscious choices of its forebears. Each new generation will be slightly different, and when we compare our remote ancestors and our remote descendants, they will hardly resemble one another.

At one end of the family tree, there will be the ape-like primitives of *2001: A Space Odyssey*. At the other end, there might be something like the macrocephalic, telepathic "butt heads" of the original *Star Trek* series. But they will still be "one" race, one extended family.

Allowing that story to unfold is the only genuine form of race preservation that is possible.

The false race preservationist, however, decides that his generation—or some previous generation—is the "right" generation to preserve. Then he seeks to hold onto—or "get back" to—a particular genetic snapshot or cross-section of the race's life.

All generations before that point were not just shaped by previous generations, they also shaped subsequent generations. But the race preservationist decides that from a certain point on, every generation will be *made by* previous generations. But they will not be allowed to make future generations in their turn. They will no longer be agents of change, but merely agents of preservation.

Who are they to change anything?

RACIAL PURISM AS DECADENCE

Spengler regards such a mindset as decadent. Consider the following passage from *The Hour of Decision*:

> . . . in speaking of race, it is not intended in the sense in which it is the fashion among anti-Semites in Europe and America to use it today: Darwinistically, materially. Race purity is a grotesque word in view of the fact that for centuries all stocks and species have been mixed, and that warlike—that is, healthy—generations with a future before them have from time immemorial always welcomed a stranger into the family if he had "race," to whatever race it was he belonged. Those who talk too much about race no longer have it in them. What is needed is not a

pure race, but a *strong* one, which has a nation within it.

This manifests itself above all in self-evident elemental fecundity, in an abundance of children, which historical life can consume without ever exhausting the supply. God is, in the familiar words of Frederick the Great, always on the side of the big battalions, and now if ever this shows itself. The millions who fell in the World War were the pick of all the white world had in the way of race, but the test of race is the speed with which it can replace itself. A Russian once said to me: "The Russian woman will make good in ten years what we sacrificed in the Revolution." *That* is the right instinct. Such races are irresistible.[2]

Following Nietzsche, Spengler holds that positive values and a healthy culture are the products of "ascending life." Negative values and a decadent culture are products of declining life.

Ascending life is active, conscious of what it can do, of its power to change the future. Declining life is passive, conscious of what has been done to it and cannot be undone.

Ascending life is vital and life-giving. Declining life is devitalized and devitalizing.

Ascending life is forward-looking and hopeful; it creates and embraces change; it pursues gain rather than avoids loss; it is motivated by love and passion, not fear; it is warlike, willing to risk life for higher gains.

Declining life is backward-looking, fearful of the future, fearful of change, fearful of loss, fearful of risk and conflict, conservative, stinking of senility, hemmed by shrinking horizons, chilled by looming death.

Ascending life is aware of the past, but selectively so: it remembers what is empowering and forgets what is not. When the past becomes restrictive, it sloughs it off like a snake discards an old skin.

Declining life is less selective. It has a long memory, brood-

---

[2] *The Hour of Decision*, 219–20.

ing over old mistakes and picking at old wounds. Declining life is defined by the past, which it carries as an ever-growing burden, like a snail adding to its lifeless shell even as its living substance wanes, until finally it is crushed under the dead weight.

According to Spengler, when the healthy man thinks of race, he is less concerned with the race we have been than the race we will become. He may feel grateful to his ancestors for the positive gifts — the strengths — they have bequeathed him. He gives no thought to their mistakes and imperfections, even those that mark him. It is enough to be aware *that* they were not perfect, that there is room for improvement. And a healthy man thinks that he can make improvements. He thinks that he can bequeath more to his progeny than his ancestors bequeathed to him.

Thus the healthy man "of race" is not concerned with racial purity — defined as the preservation of a certain set of gene frequencies, whether his own or his ancestors'. He is pleased with the good traits he has received, and he would like to pass them on. But, as Spengler says, he is more concerned with *strong* sons than *pure* ones, and he would not hesitate to breed with an outsider if he thought this would improve his progeny.

For Spengler, a concern with racial purity is a sign of racial decadence, of a lack of racial vitality. The racial purist looks to the past, not the future, because *he does not have the vitality in him necessary to create a future.* He is defined by the past and feels that he does not have the power or the right to change it, only to repeat it (or talk about repeating it, and urge others to repeat it).

As Spengler writes, "Those who talk too much about race no longer have it in them." This means that the people who talk the most about reproduction do it the least. And, Spengler might add, that is a good thing. Let the sapless branches rattle in the wind all they want, as long as they spare us their shriveled fruit.

WHITE NATIONALISM: A DEGENERATE MOVEMENT?

Racial purists often claim that their intellectual opposition to miscegenation is merely a healthy "instinct." They also claim that there is something biologically sick about the instincts of miscegenators.

Spengler thinks that the exact opposite is true. He would predict that those who intellectually oppose miscegenation and advocate racial purity and preservation would be, on average, less virile, less fecund, and less mentally and physically healthy than the average person, including the average miscegenator.

Based on ten years of experience in the American White Nationalist movement, I have to say that Spengler's prediction is absolutely correct. White Nationalism in America is an overwhelmingly degenerate movement, and I do not exempt myself from this judgment.

But what does this mean, exactly? It means merely that, *from the point of view of biological vitality,* a white man who preaches racial purity but has no children is less healthy than a white man who chooses to have children with a non-white woman.

It does not mean that the White Nationalist is *wrong in his convictions* about biology and politics. It does not mean that, from a eugenic point of view, whites have anything to gain from mixing with other races. (As a matter of fact, I think we do not.)

Decadent people can be right, and healthy people can be wrong.

But there is a lot more to politics than simply being *right.*

And from the point of view of practical politics, we White Nationalists need to take a good hard look at ourselves. Can such a degenerate movement win?

Should it win? For the sake of all that is holy, shouldn't we want to keep nostalgia-addled kooks away from any power over the future of life, lest they murder and mummify the race in their quest to preserve its purity?

VITALIZING WHITE NATIONALISM?

What would a vital White Nationalism look like? This is where Spengler's views of how culture shapes race come in. I also take inspiration from Michael O'Meara's essays on myth and politics in his *Toward the White Republic*[3] and Alex Kurtagić's "Learning from the Right" and related essays.[4]

White Nationalists love sobering facts, so let's begin with one. The White Nationalist movement, which seeks the salvation of nature's fairest and most talented race, is less capable of motivating *real world* activity than *Star Trek*, a silly but entertaining set of movies and TV shows about multiracial and miscegenating liberals who live in Tupperware, dress in pajamas, and fly around the galaxy preaching high-minded, hypocritical twaddle about tolerance and pluralism and diversity.

Even if we correct for the differences in the size of audiences, Trekkies accomplish more in the real world than an equal number of White Nationalists.

Why is that? It has nothing to do with idealism. Both movements are highly idealistic. It has everything to do with animal vitality. For all its silliness, there is something about *Star Trek* that motivates human action and creativity — that taps into pure animal vitality — better than White Nationalism.

Present-day White Nationalism is *conservative*: backward-looking, devitalized, decadent, and gloomy. *Star Trek* is *progressive*: forward-looking, optimistic, and hopeful. (Nauseatingly so.)

With this in mind, ask yourself who is more likely to preserve the white race: (1) the present White Nationalist movement, or (2) a group of kooks who, taking Tolkien as their bible, decide that through eugenics, they are going to mold every successive generation of their progeny closer to the archetype of the elves, the fairest and wisest race?

The elves have it. Why? Because, kooky though it may be, creating a race of elves far better captures the imagination and mobilizes human vitality than dark predictions about the rising tide of color.

---

[3] See the first six essays of Michael O'Meara, *Toward the White Republic*, ed. Greg Johnson (San Francisco: Counter-Currents Publishing, 2010).

[4] http://www.theoccidentalobserver.net/2010/06/learning-from-the-right/

A vital White Nationalist movement would be a utopian, progressivist, eugenicist mythical-cultural phenomenon. It would not be founded on empirical studies of how race influences culture. It would not propagate itself through academic conferences and policy studies. It would be founded on a grand culture-creating, race-shaping myth, propagated through art and religion, that enthralls and mobilizes a whole people. (No, I don't have one handy.)

It would be less concerned about the race we were or the race we are than about the race we can become. It would not brood over whether the Finns or Armenians or Sicilians are white enough. It would not obsess over the odd Jew or Amerindian in someone's ancestry, as long as he or she makes a net contribution to the coming race. (No, this is not special pleading on my part.) Besides, eventually, we will be able to just edit out undesirable genetic code, although I hope we will be more concerned with the perfections we can write in.

Most importantly, a vital White Nationalist movement should require its leaders to lead by example, by marrying wisely and fruitfully. No, the movement should not and cannot turn away talented people who have the misfortune of being unwilling or unable to reproduce. But the movement should definitely have a hierarchy, and anyone who wants to rise to the top needs to do more than *talk* about a future for white children. He needs to contribute white children to the future.

The Occidental Observer, July 10, 2010

RACE-MIXING:
NOT JUST FOR LOSERS ANYMORE?

When most people see whites dating non-whites, the immediate assumption is that there is something wrong with the white. Usually the defects are obvious. We know why a homely or obese white woman is sleeping with blacks or Mexicans: They are willing to overlook her faults *because she is white*. We know why a geeky, acne-scarred white man gravitates toward Asians: They are willing to overlook his faults *because he is white* (and of course the aliens are angling for green cards and money as well).

And what about attractive whites who date non-whites? In recent years, more and more white men who are not obvious losers are dating Asians. But according to the conventional wisdom, they probably have hidden physical or psychological defects, such as a self-esteem problem. (Seems pretty reasonable to me.)

Race-mixing is sold as an expression of progress in racial equality. Fair Romeos will no longer be separated from their dusky Juliets by the antiquated prejudices of their parents' generation. But the ugly truth is that race-mixing usually *presupposes* racism and racial hierarchies. The whites feel that they are dating or marrying *down*, and the non-whites feel that they are dating or marrying *up*.

White losers are attracted to marrying down, because they feel that their grateful partners will overlook their flaws for the privilege of marrying into a superior race, and their non-white partners think the same thing: they could never get a normal white, but they are willing to take up with a subnormal one, because they want to marry into a superior race.

An allied attitude is that non-whites can't be blamed for wanting to date or marry whites. Their racial betrayal is seen as a completely healthy impulse. The attitude is: "Who could blame black men for pursuing white women? Have you *seen* black women?" "Who could blame Asian women for wanting to date white men? Just look at Asian men!" (Everybody also knows that Asian men and black women are the big losers in the interracial dating game.)

These are not, moreover, the attitudes of hardcore racists alone. Virtually *everyone* believes this, white and non-white, race-mixers included.

I hold these views, even though I know that there are obviously some cases in which they are not true. There is enough interaction between the races now that perfectly normal people can form friendships that turn into romances.

But the attitudes persist, because they are what Burke calls "wise prejudices" — based on past experience, repeatedly confirmed by new experiences, and therefore handy heuristic assumptions to maintain when visiting the Bay Area.

But even though everyone believes that white race-mixers are defective, nobody really *talks* about it. Even the diversity police who obsessively try to expose every other instance of hidden racism, real or imagined, remain silent. I suspect they are silent because they know that a widespread discussion of this attitude would inhibit race-mixing, and they don't want to do that.

White race-mixers may know they are defective, but they think that others do not divine this fact when they parade their non-white paramours in public. If they knew that others saw them as defective, they might not be so enthusiastic about race-mixing. This is especially true of otherwise attractive and normal-looking white race-mixers, who would not be suspected of having hidden flaws if they did not advertise them by pursuing non-white sexual partners.

There has been a certain normalization of white men dating Asians. Because feminism has made so many otherwise attractive white women into bitches, it is easy to understand why perfectly normal white men are tempted to settle for Asian women, as they seem to be more feminine, submissive, and oriented toward home and family.

But even those who defend whites dating Asians as a normal and healthy reaction to a sick society, will immediately assume that there must be something wrong with a white man who dates a *black* woman. Even the most delirious Yellow Fever victims balk at that. Hence the normalization of white male/black female pairings has emerged as an identifiable action item on the agenda for white genocide.

For a long time, such pairings were quite rare in television and the movies. It seemed easier to sell images of black men as wise mentors, crime fighters, scientific geniuses, US Presidents, and God, than black women as attractive sexual partners for normal, non-defective white men.

Yes, there was the famous kiss between Captain Kirk (William Shatner) and Lt. Uhuru (Nichelle Nichols) in the original *Star Trek* series, but Kirk was under alien influence. Yes, there was race-mixing in *Mandingo* (the Marquis de Sade meets *Uncle Tom's Cabin*), but the white race-mixers were explicitly shown to be physically and psychologically defective. The same is true in *Roots*. Yes, there was the neighbor across the hall in *The Jeffersons*. But he was a dweeb. James Bond, of course, is one of the earliest white miscegenators on the big screen, but we assume he is closing his eyes, holding his nose, and thinking about England. And when Bond marries, he marries a white woman.

But in recent years, there has been a trend toward pairing white Alpha males with black women. Not just normal white males, but superior white males. Heroic white males. Winners, not losers.

The first time this struck me was in Oliver Stone's 2004 film *Alexander*, in which Alexander the Great (you can't get more Alpha than Alexander the Great), played by Colin Farrell, is paired with the mulatto Rosario Dawson, who is cast as Roxane, Alexander's queen. (The historical Roxane was the daughter of a Persian aristocrat. She was reputed to be one of the most beautiful women in the Empire. She was probably as Aryan as Alexander himself.)

Then there is Joss Whedon's superb but short-lived 2002 science fiction series *Firefly*, in which starship pilot Hoban Washburne, played by the very Nordic Alan Tudyk, is married to Zoë, a black Amazon with grotesquely large lips played by Gina Torres. The character of "Wash" is something of a dork, and he is not the captain of the ship, so he is not the real Alpha. The captain, Malcolm Reynolds (played by Nathan Fillion) is a true Alpha male, and his romantic interest is a white woman, Inara (played by the beautiful Morena Baccarin). But in one episode he is shown lusting after Zoë as well.

In another science fiction series, the new *Battlestar Galactica*, Alpha male Lee Adama, played by the Nordic Jamie Bamber, marries green-eyed mulatto Dualla, played by Kandyse McClure. (Admittedly, the character is punishing himself and the white woman he really wants to marry. But he could have punished himself with another white woman.)

Finally, in the new *Star Trek* movie, the Alpha male, Captain Kirk, played by the Nordic Chris Pine, is shown lusting after a black woman and even a *green* woman—but never a white woman. (This essay originally began as a review of *Star Trek*, but I have nothing to add to Jonathan Pyle's superb *Occidental Observer* essay "Star Trek and the Multiracial Future."[1])

I am sure that many other examples can be provided.

Why is Hollywood portraying white Alpha males pursuing and even marrying black women? Because they want the Beta males, the Gamma males, and everybody else down to the Omega males, to follow them down the path to white racial extinction.

The people who create these movies—the directors, the writers, the producers, the casting directors—are not artists. They are abortionists. They are aborting the whole future of the white race. And they are not doing it by accident. We know this, because so many of them are Jews, who are constantly reminded from birth that marrying out leads to extinction for them, and they know that goes for us too. (The fact that many of these Jews marry out make them even worse. It means that they are committing genocide against their own people as well as ours.)

When the White Nationalist movement can mobilize the numbers, the idealism, and the physical courage evoked by the

---

[1] http://www.theoccidentalobserver.net/2009/05/star-trek-and-the-multi-racial-future/

anti-abortion movement, then I will stop fearing for the future of my race. And even then, it will take a full-blown revolution, not merely a constitutional amendment, to save us.

"Trevor Lynch," *TOQ Online*, June 5, 2009

After the publication of "Race-Mixing: Not Just for Losers Anymore?" a friend sent me a link to a *Yahoo* article on interracial dating. The article, written by an Asian man who actually snared a white woman, contains useful statistics about interracial marriage that confirms one of the points in my article, namely that Asian males and black females are the big losers in interracial dating and mating.

(1) In 2006, there were 286,000 couples with a black husband and a white wife. Given black males' aversion to marriage, we can infer that the amount of cohabitation with white women is much higher. There were 117,000 couples with a white husband and a black wife. Frankly, even this number seems shockingly high. It would be interesting to know just how much white ancestry these black women need to have to be acceptable mates to white men. I would guess that it is well above the average white ancestry for American blacks.

(2) In 2006, there were 530,000 couples with a white husband and an Asian wife. There were 174,000 couples with a white wife and an Asian husband.

Since White Nationalists are nowhere near being able to ban race-mixing outright (not yet), it is imperative that we do everything in our power today to prevent it as much as possible. We need as many arguments as possible, from as many different angles as possible, to persuade people that race-mixing is bad.

A good place to start is to circulate the meme that *"Everyone* thinks that whites who date outside their race are somehow defective. If you don't *look* defective, then people will just assume that you have some hidden physical, ahem, shortcoming, or a psychological problem. If you don't want people thinking you are somehow defective, then don't date a non-white."

One likely question you will hear is: "But even if that is true

99 percent of the time, what about the 1 percent that are not defective?"

Here is my answer: "The tragedy of interracial dating is that the non-defective few will always be lumped in with the defective many. If you want to avoid that tragedy, don't date a non-white."

And if you don't think that everyone *already* believes that white race-mixers are defective, then get to work spreading the idea around, and eventually everyone *will*.

"Trevor Lynch," *TOQ Online*, June 7, 2009

MALE GENITAL MUTILATION
& JEWISH POWER

Female Genital Mutilation describes three basic practices: (1) clitoridectomy (the partial or total removal of the clitoris) and/or the prepuce (clitoral hood); (2) the partial or total removal of the labia minora, which sometimes accompanies clitoridectomy and/or removal of the prepuce; (3) infibulation, meaning the partial sewing up of the vaginal orifice, which can also involve the other procedures. (Such practices as genital piercing and tattooing, although technically forms of genital mutilation, are generally considered a different issue.) Amnesty International, which regards Female Genital Mutilation as an abuse of human rights, estimates that 135 million women world-wide have been subjected to Female Genital Mutilation, and 2 million women and girls undergo it every year.

Female Genital Mutilation takes place primarily in Africa and the Near East, but it also exists in Southeast Asia and among the aboriginal peoples of Australia and South America. Female Genital Mutilation is hallowed by tradition and religion, including Islamic legal works, which specifically command the removal of the prepuce. The vast majority of women who undergo Female Genital Mutilation are Muslim.

The main rationale for Female Genital Mutilation appears to be the desire to reduce sexual pleasure, so as to encourage female chastity and fidelity. Because Female Genital Mutilation is seen as a tool to assure male dominance, Western-style feminists oppose it and have worked to outlaw and suppress it globally. Female Genital Mutilation is also opposed on human rights grounds, because it is seldom voluntary, and on public health grounds, because it is often performed without anesthesia and antisepsis and frequently leads to serious infections and death.

The United Nations has declared February 6th as the "International Day of Zero Tolerance to Female Genital Mutilation." Although Female Genital Mutilation used to be confined to the non-white world, massive non-white immigration into traditionally white lands has introduced a host of new problems, including Female Genital Mutilation. Thus, in 1996, the United States passed a federal law banning Female Genital Mutilation on human rights grounds. It is also banned in the United Kingdom, France, Italy, Sweden, Norway, New Zealand, Australia, the Netherlands, Spain, Canada, and Australia.

Male Genital Mutilation primarily means circumcision, the removal of the foreskin, although it also technically includes piercing and tattooing. I will be use "Male Genital Mutilation" to mean circumcision alone.

Amnesty International keeps data on Female Genital Mutilation, which it regards as a human rights violation, but it does not keep date on Male Genital Mutilation, which Amnesty International does not recognize as a human rights problem, even though the vast majority of men who are subjected to Male Genital Mutilation have no choice in the matter, which is the very reason why Female Genital Mutilation is treated as a human rights issue.

The World Health Organization estimates that 30% of males worldwide are circumcised, 68% of whom are Muslims. This is a more than one billion males, meaning that Male Genital Mutilation is more than seven times more widespread than Female Genital Mutilation.

Male Genital Mutilation was practiced by the Ancient Egyptians for reasons unknown. It was also practiced by some ancient Semitic peoples, but not all of them. But the effective source of Male Genital Mutilation in the world today is the Old Testament, in which circumcision is allegedly commanded by God as a sign of his covenant with Abraham and his seed.

The rationale, if any, behind this religious commandment is debated. Male Genital Mutilation may have been a substitute for the infant sacrifices that were also common among the ancient Semitic peoples. Instead of buying God's favors with a whole firstborn son from time to time, the Jews decided it was more advantageous to make him work for tips. Male Genital Mutilation may also have been adopted because it reduces sexual pleasure for both males and females.

Whatever the Jewish rationale for Male Genital Mutilation, the practice was abandoned by Christians who believed that their religion superseded God's covenant with Abraham. Moreover, many of the new converts to Christianity were Greeks and Romans who abhorred Male Genital Mutilation.

Islam maintained Male Genital Mutilation, both because it was a pre-existing practice among the Semitic tribes and because Islam maintains both the legalistic nature and many of the laws of Judaism.

Male Genital Mutilation is primarily confined to Israel and the Muslim world, but it is also found wherever Jewish and Muslim colonies are found. In Europe, Male Genital Mutilation is confined almost entirely to Jews and Muslims. But in the United States, Male Genital Mutilation became widespread beginning in the 20th century. About 75% American males — the vast bulk of them non-Jewish and non-Muslim — are circumcised today, but the practice has been steadily declining over the past few decades. In 2005, about 55% of American boys were circumcised. Part of the reason for the decline is increased awareness about the barbarous nature of Male Genital Mutilation. But a large part of the decline is probably due to the increasing population of Latin American Mestizos, who do not usually practice Male Genital Mutilation. Male Genital Mutilation is also more widespread in other Anglo-colonial societies like Canada (30%) and Australia (58.7%), although in England it is almost unheard of outside the Jewish and Muslim communities.

The rise of Male Genital Mutilation in the United States is a complicated matter. Although the whole practice is rooted in the Old Testament, it was supported and practiced by the medical profession on supposedly scientific grounds. But the "problem" it was supposed to solve, namely masturbation, is a problem only because of Old Testament beliefs.

Christian America was probably highly susceptible to Male Genital Mutilation because of the "Judaizing" Old Testament tendencies of the Puritans and other Protestant sects that settled America in large numbers. The same factor probably encouraged the rise of Male Genital Mutilation in Canada and Australia.

The likely reason that Male Genital Mutilation did not catch on in the mother country itself is that she exported most of her religious extremists to the colonies. The reason that Male Genital Mutilation did not become as prominent in Canada is probably Catholic Quebec and the fact that Canada was more Anglican, Tory, and Loyalist than the colonies that became the United States.

The basic pattern of advancing religious practices and values under the guise of science continues today, as circumcision is now alleged to prevent the transmission of HIV.

The arguments against Male and Female Genital Mutilation are essentially the same.

1. The presumption should always be on the side of maintaining the integrity of the body. Removing or altering a healthy part of the body is mutilation. If it ain't broke, don't fix it.
2. Genital Mutilation is almost always imposed by adults upon infants and children who are not old enough to make such decisions on their own. Individuals should be given a choice about permanent alterations of healthy parts of their bodies.
3. Genital Mutilation reduces sexual pleasure for both sexes.
4. Genital Mutilation sometimes goes wrong, producing more disfigurement than planned, causing infections, and even leading to death. (A good step toward banning Male Genital Mutilation would be to pass federal legislation creating a national database on Male Genital Mutilation mishaps, illnesses, and deaths.)
5. Genital Mutilation on grounds of religious freedom should not be tolerated any more than any other violation of human rights for religious purposes. Human sacrifice on religious grounds is illegal. So too should be Genital Mutilation.

Yet the United Nations has not declared a world-wide day

of "Zero Tolerance for Male Genital Mutilation." Female Genital Mutilation a federal crime in the United States, while Male Genital Mutilation is legal. Indeed, recently Brad Sherman, a Jewish California state representative, has proposed state legislation *against* local bans on Male Genital Mutilation. Why the double standard? Several factors are relevant here.

First, Female Genital Mutilation is a relatively new and foreign evil, while Male Genital Mutilation is an old and familiar evil. Many people do not even see the analogy between Male and Female Genital Mutilation.

Second, Men make most laws, and men love their penises, cut or uncut. Thus there is deep psychological resistance among victims of Male Genital Mutilation to acknowledging that anything important could have been lost. The fact of loss, moreover, makes it psychologically difficult to admit that the loss was for nothing. (This is why disastrous wars often provide arguments for their own continuation, since ending them requires admitting that the losses were in vain.) Protecting women from genital mutilation, on the other hand, appeals to instinctive male gallantry.

Third, American politics and culture are overwhelmingly dominated by Jews and express Jewish sensibilities and agendas. Female Genital Mutilation is primarily practiced by Muslims, who are presently the most active enemies of Jews worldwide. Banning Female Genital Mutilation, which was spearheaded by the Jewish-dominated feminist movement, serves the overall Jewish agenda of heightening tensions between white Americans and Muslims, which is a necessary condition for continued American subservience to Jewish political and military ambitions in the Middle East.

Male Genital Mutilation, however, is a paradigmatically Jewish practice, even though the majority of its victims are not Jews. Male Genital Mutilation became widespread in the United States long before Jews assumed their current political and cultural hegemony, although Male Genital Mutilation is ultimately rooted in the power of Jewish religious teachings among American Protestants. But although the current Jewish hegemony is not the cause of widespread Male Genital Mutilation, it is certainly the main impediment to legislation against it. This is true even though among Jews in the United States and Israel, there is significant and growing opposition to Male Genital Mutilation.

Every time a circumcised man looks at his penis, he should see a sign of Jewish power carved into his own flesh before he was even self-conscious. And the mainstream of the organized Jewish community is committed to ensuring that Male Genital Mutilation is perpetuated for Jews and non-Jews alike.

In light of Jewish cultural and political power, anti-Male Genital Mutilation advocates ("intactivists") tend to go to great lengths to avoid the charge of "anti-Semitism," including spotlighting their Jewish allies. According to the Intactivists website, "Intactivists' *only* issue with Judaism is circumcision. A significant proportion of Intactivists are Jews. Several of its founders and leading lights are Jewish—Edward Wallerstein, Ronald Goldman, Leonard Glick, Mark Reiss."[1]

San Diego-based intactivist Matthew Hess played by these Semitically-correct rules. But he discovered that such self-imposed restraints did not prevent Jews from targeting him. Hess wrote a bill to ban Male Genital Mutilation and sought a state legislator somewhere in the country who would sponsor it. In 2010, Massachusetts State Senator Michael Morrissey championed the bill, but it was killed in committee. (It would be interesting to know who was whispering in the committeemen's ears.) Hess also authored a measure to ban Male Genital Mutilation in the city of Santa Monica, but it was dropped when Jena Troutman, its principal backer, was charged with anti-Semitism by Jewish advocates.[2] Another Hess-written ban is on the ballot in San Francisco in November of 2011. It too has come under attack from the organized Jewish community.

This might throw some light on Hess' *Foreskin Man* comic book, specifically issue no. 2, "Monster Mohel," which has garnered national media coverage and foaming denunciations from leading Jews and their tools for its *Der Stürmer*-esque aes-

---

[1] http://www.circumstitions.com/FAQ.html#intactivism
[2] http://www.nytimes.com/2011/06/08/us/08circumcise.html

thetics.[3] Did Hess reason that, since his legislation could just as well be killed softly with a Jewish whisper campaign, it might be more advantageous and instructive to goad his highly-strung and hyper-aggressive opponents into a public temper tantrum? Is Hess calculating that his enemies might empower him through free publicity as they defeat themselves through hubris and hysteria? If so, he is rediscovering the playbook of another publisher of edifying comic-books, George Lincoln Rockwell. Whatever the outcome in November, many previously slumbering Californians will learn lessons that will not easily be forgotten. White Nationalists grappling with strategies to challenge Jewish power should pay special attention.

Counter-Currents/*North American New Right*
June 11, 2011

---

[3] http://www.counter-currents.com/2011/06/jews-menaced-by-comic-book/

LAWYERS & SEX CRIMES:
FURTHER THOUGHTS ON
COVINGTON'S NORTHWEST QUARTET

The following ended up on the cutting room floor as I prepared "Birth of a Nation," my review of Harold Covington's Northwest Quartet, for publication.[1] I decided to cut it for lack of space, and also because I thought that even serious criticisms seemed petty when considered alongside the Quartet's towering virtues. I came across these words while tidying up my files, and I decided to publish them as a free-standing essay because they echo and reinforce some very wise comments on Occidental Dissent by one of my favorite commentators, who goes by the name Trainspotter.

The most problematic feature of the Northwest Quartet, like *The Turner Diaries*, is the author's penchant for genocidal fantasies, directed not just at non-whites, but at white people as well. The most famous such passage in *The Turner Diaries* tells of the "day of the rope" in which white race-traitors, particularly those who engaged in interracial sex, are lynched by the thousands.

Covington makes clear that the creation of a white homeland would not, and indeed could not, require the mass killing of non-whites, even though moral qualms about mass murder of civilians tend to be set aside during warfare. Such killing would be logistically impossible for a small guerrilla army, and it would be unnecessary, since Covington thinks that most non-whites could be induced to flee simply by destroying their economic and social support networks through targeted killings, beatings, and property destruction, mostly aimed at the whites

---

[1] Greg Johnson, "Birth of a Nation: Harold Covington's Northwest Quartet," *The Occidental Quarterly*, vol. 9, no. 1 (2009): 107–119. Available online at: http://www.counter-currents.com/2010/07/birth-of-a-nation/

who profit from and facilitate their presence.

He is less surgical and discerning in choosing his white victims, both during the war of liberation and the subsequent "cleanup." Covington's death list contains not just white operatives and allies of the regime, but three whole categories of individuals: lawyers, race-mixers (meaning anyone who has had interracial sex, regardless of issue), and homosexuals. This is problematic, because if white nationalism begins making progress in the Northwest, these views will be broadcast far and wide to scare white people away from White Nationalism and into conformity with the system that is killing us. Beyond that, these lapses are at odds with the generally rational and pragmatic character of Covington's political thought.

First, spare the lawyers. Although killing lawyers has the authority of the Bard, and everyone enjoys a good lawyer joke, among White Nationalists of my acquaintance, lawyers are the best represented profession. Thus it seems foolish to treat all lawyers as enemies, since this will drive otherwise sympathetic and useful individuals into the arms of the system for protection.

Second, it is easy to understand why White Nationalists see homosexuals as enemies, since the organized homosexual community is an integral part of the anti-white governing coalition. Beyond that, White Nationalism is steeped in a Right-wing, conservative subculture with strong currents of anti-homosexual sentiment, which are constantly stoked by the organized homosexual community.

But Covington's stated rationale for murdering homosexuals is that homosexuality is a mental illness. I think that homosexuality is neither a sin (an offense against the God of the Jews) nor an illness, but rather it is something that might be called a "natural suboptimal condition," like baldness or myopia or a propensity to pack on pounds.

But let's just grant Covington's premise for the sake of argument. So what about all the other mental illnesses? Covington does not mention if melancholics, manic depressives, schizophrenics, paranoiacs, compulsive liars, kleptomaniacs, alcoholics, and other sufferers of mental maladies will be marked for death.

The reason for this is obvious: homosexuals are marked for death not because they suffer from a mental illness, but because the Bible — the Jewish Torah — tells us so. This is probably the source of the extreme animus toward race-mixers as well. It is, to put it mildly, a rather astonishing lapse. It makes it all too easy to parody White Nationalists as Bible-thumping hayseeds and hillbilly psychopaths.

It also serves to drive otherwise sympathetic and useful individuals — who might be guilty of nothing more than an experimental homosexual or interracial dalliance while in college or the military, where such experimentation is common — into the arms of the system for protection.

What would Aryan reason, as opposed to Jewish superstition, dictate in dealing with homosexuals and race-mixers?

First, it is no policy or solution to postulate that when a White Nationalist state is founded it will simply chase away or kill the homosexuals on its territory, for inevitably new homosexuals will appear (it does not matter whether by nature or nurture or both). Furthermore, these individuals will manifestly not be "one of them" (the anti-white ruling coalition) but "one of us" (a racially-conscious white person, raised in a racially homogenous and self-conscious society).

On Covington's premise, the policy a rational society adopts to homosexuality is an instance of the larger policy it should adopt toward mental illness. The appropriate attitude toward mental illness is not hatred but pity and compassion. It is reasonable to fear the unknown, but unreasonable to persist in one's ignorance. The idea that homosexuality should be treated as a crime is a relic of benighted times when people thought that other mental illnesses were evidence of witchcraft or demonic possession and should be "treated" by torture and burning at the stake.

Mental illness is not a crime. If mentally ill people commit crimes, we punish the crimes, not the illness. Thus it would be inhuman to exile or kill our relatives simply because they suffer from manic depression or paranoia. It would be arbitrary to treat homosexuality any differently. If homosexuality is a mental illness, not a crime, then it should be treated as an illness. If it can be cured, then cure it. If it cannot be cured but can be lived with, then live with it. If it is genetically determined, then screen for it and try to decrease its representation in the next generation. (If homosexuality has a genetic component, then homosexuals should not be encouraged to "pass" as straight and pass on their genes to their children, but to live as homosexuals and take their genes out of the next generation.)

In a healthy society, people should, of course, be free to associate with or avoid homosexuals just as they are free to associate with or avoid people who suffer from other mental maladies. But to determine rational policies and attitudes toward homosexuality, one would have to compare it to other such illnesses. One would have to determine whether homosexuals are more or less reliable friends, colleagues, and comrades than, say, manic depressives, alcoholics, or compulsive liars.

Of course there would be no problems excluding homosexuals from the pup tents of boy scouts, the locker rooms of schoolchildren, or the barracks of the military. There would be no nonsense about homosexuals marrying or adopting children, which seeks to erase the distinction between the normal and the abnormal. Should society also be expected to provide everyone who thinks himself Napoleon a coronation and everyone who thinks himself Jesus a crucifixion?

The question of race-mixing is more complicated. First, the problem is not interracial sex or marriage *per se*. The problem is interracial *babies*. Of course there are no interracial babies without interracial sex, but not all interracial sex produces babies. The problem with multiracial societies is that interracial sex is inevitable, because it is perfectly natural and normal for people to take advantage of a wider range of possible mates and sexual partners.

Many racialists claim that they are immune to interracial attractions, that they have some sort of genetic aversion. This may well be true of a tiny percentage of people, but it is surely not true of most. There may well be an instinct for mating with one's kind, but there is no reason to think that this instinct will always trump the other instincts under certain circumstances, particularly given the power of the sex drive.

For instance, the person who had the single greatest influence on my awakening on race and the Jewish question obviously had a great deal of instinctive feeling for his own kind. But that feeling was insufficient to trump his conflicting desires for a home and a family with a woman who has not corrupted by feminism and American junk culture. So he ended up marrying a woman from the Philippines. The marriage was without issue, thank goodness, and it did not last. Now he is married to a white woman who has given him three children. Yes, he made a potentially terrible mistake, but the idea that this man has committed a capital offense is ludicrous.

Interracial sex is not only inevitable in a multiracial society, it is being relentlessly promoted by every organ of the establishment. (The same is true of the normalization of homosexuality.) The propaganda is particularly intense on college campuses, where sexual experimentation has always been more common. The number of college students who have had interracial dalliances is already quite high, and if present conditions continue, it will rapidly reach the point of saturation. (We will soon have a better idea if some are genetically immune to the lure of exotic flesh.)

But the percentage of these dalliances that turn into long-term interracial relationships, much less marriage and child-rearing, is still small. Indeed, some such encounters may be the first steps down the road to a full racial awakening. (This is true of one young woman of my acquaintance, who was raped by her black boyfriend.) Again, the idea that these people have committed not just a mistake but a capital crime is offensive to reason. These people are victims of our present regime, not criminals.

What then should be the attitude of a White Nationalist regime to race-mixers? First, all whites who produce offspring with members of other races have, in effect, left our race for another. One cannot mix one's blood without mixing one's loyalties. We cannot reasonably expect that such people will be more loyal to their extended racial family than to their mixed-race children, and no White Nationalist would ask them to.

They could not, therefore, be citizens of a white ethnostate (much less would-be white nationalist leaders). Whites who have married non-whites without offspring or prospects of offspring clearly belong to a different category, but it is not clear that a different policy should apply.

As for whites who have had sexual relations with non-whites, or who married but then divorced non-whites without producing children: they should be able to become citizens of a white ethnostate without penalty. But this would not be possible without somehow addressing the irrational yet powerful antipathy they arouse in some racialists.

For the offenders, there needs to be a process of confession, contrition, cleansing, and atonement to incorporate them into a self-conscious white nation. Ideally, such a truth and reconciliation process should be modeled on a religious ceremony (how about a bath, for starters) rather than a legal proceeding, if the atonement it produces is to be heartfelt and enduring.

But racialists need to change too. There is a larger principle here that applies to more than just sexual matters. A healthy new society can be made only by and from the products of today's sick society. White Nationalists are not an Elect, chosen by genes or by God to be immune to the corruptions of our age, thus licensing us to smugly look down upon and condemn the rest of humanity.

If there is any hope for our people at all, then most of them are capable of seeing the light, and the only thing that sets today's White Nationalists apart from them is . . . time. We saw first, but we will never be saved until they see as well.

This means that there is no room for self-righteousness and much room for compassion. Indeed, the leaders of any revolution are likely to be *worse* rather than better than the average person in important respects. Not only are they imperfect to begin with, but given the dark necessities of revolution, they are likely to be monsters in the end. They may be creating a better world — *but not for themselves.*

Covington shows that he understands this in many subtle and funny ways. For instance, in *The Hill of the Ravens*, he remarks on how the veterans who created the Northwest American Republic shock their own grandchildren with the vulgar language and tastes inherited from Amurrica. Also, Covington's self-portrait as "the Old Man" is hardly flattering and shows that he too is out of place in the republic he helped create.

Until we breed a race of flawless Nietzschean Supermen, we will have to muddle through with people who have a short list of essential virtues (honesty, courage, intelligence, loyalty, good judgment, initiative) and a rather longer list of inessential flaws and past mistakes. No, I am not recommending that we try to get mileage out of creeps and kooks. Just virtuous, talented, committed, imperfect people.

Within the movement, we need to be willing to tolerate inessential flaws and past mistakes *on the condition that people are honest and transparent about them*. One can build with flawed materials, but only if one knows where the flaws are. We don't want to put the guy who is hiding his dyslexia in charge of editing, the guy who is hiding his agoraphobia out distributing literature, an insecure buffoon in charge of picking up a VIP, or a creepy compulsive womanizer among the wives and daughters of comrades, etc.

A weakness is compounded by concealment. It does not become a virtue by being flaunted. But when one is willing to acknowledge one's flaws, that is the first step toward rising above them. It is an opportunity for moral growth, a way of strengthening one's character. Thus we have to penalize concealment and reward transparency.

For a White Nationalist revolution to have any moral authority, its leaders must not just lead us to regaining control of our racial destiny. They must also lead us in self-criticism, self-purification, and atonement with the greater racial body.

TOQ Online, March 18, 2010

HOMOSEXUALITY &
WHITE NATIONALISM

I must protest Andrew Westphal's "Homosexuality Ain't Cool" and other examples of queer-bashing on VNN. I have two arguments for why this is misguided and for why tolerance is a good thing for the White Nationalist movement.

FIRST, HOMOSEXUALITY IS BESIDE THE POINT.

Because of the distorting lens of the Jewish media, it is easy to think that all homosexuals are promoters of the Jewish agenda. And Leftist gays really are repulsive. So it is tempting to make disparaging comments about them just because it is so politically incorrect and because it pisses off the right people. But this is a serious tactical mistake.

White Nationalism should be a one-issue political outlook. White Nationalism is for the interests of whites and against the interests of our racial enemies. Period. Anything else is beside the point. That means that White Nationalists must work to unite all whites into a self-conscious racial community, rallying around our common racial interests. White Nationalism has only one message for homosexuals: white homosexuals have more important interests in common with other whites than they do with non-white homosexuals. We have to resist falling for any form of the divide and conquer strategy used by our enemies to destroy our solidarity as a prelude to destroying our race. Battles between gays and straights, men and women, pagans and Christians, Nordics and Mediterraneans, Celts and WASPs, Germans and Slavs, etc. have no place in the White Nationalist movement. These will always be used by our enemies to divide and subvert us.

Intolerance of homosexuality does not just divide the white population, it divides the White Nationalist movement. Ernst Röhm was not the last homosexual to be attracted to White Nationalism. I have met a number of homosexuals in the contemporary White Nationalist movement, and I have my suspicions about a few others. All of these people, however, are intelligent and accomplished. They are real assets to the movement. Those without families are freer to speak their minds because they give fewer hostages to fortune. They also have more free time and more disposable income to devote to the cause. Quite a number of homosexual men do not fit the effeminate stereotype. They are masculine, and appreciate masculine things like facts, logic, and forthright action. And even effeminate gay men can make a real contribution. Pim Fortuyn was ideologically a mixed-bag, but he had the potential to move the Netherlands significantly to the right, and his fruity persona only helped his cause. The media found it difficult to paint a flamboyant old fop who fussed over floral arrangements and doted over his lapdogs as the next Hitler.

A unified White Nationalist movement does not require that all the different White Nationalist subgroups follow the same strategy. That would be counterproductive. The more different strategies pursued, the more chance that someone will hit on a winner. It does not require that all groups co-operate with one another either. It does not require that they like one another. It does not require that gays and straights share pup tents and take showers together. The minimum requirement for white unity is simply this: we all must focus our energies on pursuing our common goal by whatever path we choose, and we must resist wasting our time and energy on squabbles that divide us.

SECOND, INTOLERANCE OF HOMOSEXUALITY IS JEWISH.

Westphal is apparently a Christian. If you ask Christians why they think homosexuality is a sin, they cannot point to any saying of Jesus. Jesus saw fit to condemn divorce but not sodomy. Christians have to turn to the Old Testament, to the record of the Jews and their wanderings, crimes, superstitions, and hatreds. There we find homosexuality condemned as a capital crime. Why? The whole aim of the Jewish law is to set Jews apart from the rest of humanity. The Jews condemned buggery because they and all their neighbors were engaging in it. Homosexual pederasty, which still remains a taboo in our culture, was widely practiced by the ancient Aryan peoples of the Mediterranean world. The Persians, Greeks, and Romans all practiced it, including some of the manliest men in history and legend, like Achilles and Alexander the Great.

Technically, the Greeks and others were not pedophiles, who pursue children, for they focused their attention on young men who were well past puberty and ready to begin military training. The ancients regarded homosexual relationships as completely consistent with marriage and family life, and they frowned upon men who formed exclusively homosexual relationships. Homosexual relationships were also bound by a host of rules and taboos. There was nothing of the modern amoral free-for-all. But there is no question that homosexual behavior was not only tolerated by ancient Aryan peoples, it was considered normal, in some cases even ideal. It was ascribed to the gods (Zeus and Ganymede) and lauded by poets, philosophers, and historians. It is hard to maintain hateful Jewish attitudes toward homosexuality if one really understands and appreciates the greatness of classical pagan civilization.

As poisonous as the Old Testament's moral condemnation of homosexuality may be, it is based on a realistic conception of human nature. Judeo-Christianity condemns homosexuality as a sin. A sin is a matter of choice. And nobody is immune to sin. If a heterosexual is a person who is immune to homosexual attractions, then the Judeo-Christian viewpoint implies that there is no such thing as a heterosexual. If a homosexual is a person who cannot help but be attracted to people of the same sex and has no choice in the matter, then the Judeo-Christian viewpoint implies that there is no such thing as a homosexual either. There are just people, all of whom have the capacity to be tempted by homosexual attractions and to choose heterosexual attractions. Thus there is no room for moral self-righteousness.

Matters became worse in the late 19th century, when psychologists—some but not all of them Jews—created a new paradigm for understanding sexuality. There were no longer homosexual and heterosexual desires, which can be found in all people and can be controlled by our faculty of choice. There were now homosexual and heterosexual people, and what made a person one or the other was generally thought to lie outside of our choice and control. One's sexual proclivities suddenly became a whole "lifestyle," a whole "identity," giving sex an inflated importance in the scheme of things. It was not long before Freud started speculating that the whole soul can be understood in terms of sexuality. This new and false conception of sexuality has caused immense suffering and damage to our race.

First of all, it has created a great deal of anxiety for men and women who experience homosexual attractions at one time or another. In pagan societies, these desires could be acknowledged, understood, and even expressed if one chose to. In Judeo-Christian society, such desires were repressed, but their mere presence said nothing more about one's identity than one is a sinner and subject to temptation—just like everybody else. Today, homosexual desires cause great anxiety and psychological anguish. People worry if they fall into a small and stigmatized sexual subspecies, totally different from the rest of humanity. A young man gets aroused wrestling with a friend and suddenly has a psychological crisis on his hands. He wonders if he is sick. He feels alienated from his family and peers. He wonders if he will have to move to the city and buy a feather boa.

Second, this anxiety has chilled same-sex friendships and male bonding, and it is the bonded male group, the *Männerbund*, that is the foundation of all higher forms of civilization, particularly Aryan civilizations. It is amazing to read accounts of male friendships from earlier centuries, for example in Augustine's *Confessions* or Montaigne's *Essays*. It was possible for men to frankly express their love for one another without fearing the stigma of homosexuality, because that was an identity that simply did not exist before the late 19th century. (Today, these expressions of affection are read through the distorting lens of "queer theory," and Augustine and Montaigne and countless other figures have been "outed.")

Third, those who decide that they do not merely have homosexual desires, but are "homosexuals" are trapped by this self-concept into an exclusively homosexual lifestyle, which not only carries health risks, but also prevents them from affirming whatever heterosexual desires they might also have. It cuts them off from marriage and family life, which could be combined with homosexual relationships openly in pagan societies and on the sly in Judeo-Christian societies.

Fourth, it has created the heterosexual, who thinks he is immune from same-sex attractions. This allows some heterosexuals to fuse Jewish intolerance with self-righteousness, turning them into queer-bashing bullies.

All these destructive consequences could be alleviated if we freed our minds from the legacy of Jewish hatred and intolerance. Queer-bashers are in the grip of Jewry without even knowing it. White Nationalism requires that we de-Jew our thinking, but many White Nationalists have no idea of just what a radical change of outlook that requires.

"F. C. I. Clarke," *Vanguard News Network,* June 28, 2002

THE COMING PEDOPHILE
RAPE EPIDEMIC

I first drafted this essay back in June of 2012 after reading an article on CNN by a Jewish homosexual named James Cantor entitled "Do Pedophiles Deserve Sympathy?"[1] In it, Cantor argues that pedophiles should not be morally condemned as people who fail to do the right thing, but pitied as people who are born with abnormal brains.

Pedophilia is not, however, simply a sexual preference, just one more kinky thing that consenting adults might do behind closed doors.

Pedophiles by definition are not attracted to adults, and non-adults by definition cannot consent to sex. Therefore, pedophilia is by its nature a desire to rape, and rape is a crime.

Of course Cantor points out that being inclined toward pedophilia is not the same thing as actually molesting children, which is true. So trying to set aside the emotional revulsion and moral stigma attached to pedophilia, and instead looking at it as a mental illness, is not necessarily a bad thing. Indeed, it might help us find treatments for pedophilia, which might actually save children from being raped. It all sounds so sweetly reasonable. And in a well-ordered society, it might actually be a humane and workable policy.

But then a cold chill of horror went through me when I realized that, on the contrary, Cantor was actually laying the groundwork for a pedophile rape epidemic. Sympathy for pedophiles will lead to an epidemic of child rape *merely by becoming a politically correct liberal cause*. All that is required for an epidemic of rape is for a particularly rape-prone class of people to become a protected politically correct victim group. And pedophiles are by their nature rape-prone. For once the liberal mind decides that a particular cause is morally imperative, it is will-

---

[1] http://www.cnn.com/2012/06/21/opinion/cantor-pedophila-sandusky/index.html

ing to evade reality, to lie, and to defame, censor, and even per-
secute truth tellers when confronted with the negative consequences of its policies.

I never finished the first draft, however, because the argument became complicated. Racial egalitarianism is *the* great
moral crusade in modern America. And its consequences are a
catastrophe that beggars imagination when one begins to add
up the enormous increase in crime and social alienation, the
destruction of great cities, the collapse of education, and the
sheer amount of lying, corruption, and hypocrisy required to
maintain the fiction of racial equality.

Political correctness is nothing more than lying and injustice. The basic lie is that people are equal, and the injustice follows from the lie: false excuses for the guilty, false blame upon
the innocent, penalizing those who did nothing to compensate
those who suffered nothing, etc. But it does not stop with mere
rent-seeking. For political correctness demands that whites accept predatory non-whites into their societies and then covers
up the inevitable consequences: tension, hatred, and violence,
in which whites are disproportionately the victims. When liberals lie, people die.

But my argument was specifically about rape. I needed a
historical example of a rape epidemic caused and protected by
liberal political correctness. Of course we know that the
amount of interracial rape, specifically black men raping white
women, has gone up considerably over the last 100 years, from
the time when such a crime would often trigger the swift and
deadly deterrent of a lynch mob and when the only people
who had any sympathy for black rapists were Communists trying to stir the pot—to the present day when blacks mingle
freely with whites, when white girls are programmed to suppress their feelings of caution around black men lest they seem
"racist," and in which the media works to conceal black crime
and describes hulking black thugs and rapists as "gentle giants," lest people start thinking that integration is a mistake.

Raping white women has not been legalized. But it has
been massively enabled nonetheless, simply because blacks
are a politically correct protected group. But statistics sup-

porting this argument are hard to come by. In 2007, Laurence Auster cited some shocking 2005 statistics about the massive disparity of black-on-white and white-on-black rapes and sexual assaults.[2] But I could find no statistics to illustrate rape levels before and after desegregation. So I set the draft aside and went on to other things.

Then, much to my horror, an eloquent proof of my thesis that political correctness leads to mass rape appeared just last year: Rotherham, a town of 250,000 in Sheffield, England in which 1,400 girls were raped, prostituted, and otherwise sexually exploited during a 16-year period between 1997 and 2013.[3] The victims were mostly white. The perpetrators were mostly Pakistani.

Of course the police were informed of these crimes, but parents who objected to the rape of their daughters were treated as potential racists. Reports on the rape epidemic in 2002, 2003, and 2006 were suppressed by the local police and government, who judged that it was better that English girls continue to be raped by non-whites than the English to feel fear and hatred toward outsiders.

When the story went public in 2014, what happened? Did the streets of Rotherham run with "rivers of blood" as Englishmen avenged their daughters and punished gangs of rapists and the police and bureaucrats who covered up and enabled their crimes? Of course not. Some of the criminals have been punished, but none of the police and bureaucrats have been arrested.

Furthermore, since the same causes give rise to the same effects, there is nothing unique about Rotherham. Thus wherever Pakistani men have access to white girls, we have to conclude that systematic rape and sexual abuse are taking place. This is, in short, a national crisis. There are many more than 1,400 victims. And the crimes will continue until their racial, religious, and cultural roots are address rather than obscured and evaded.

---

[2] http://archive.frontpagemag.com/readArticle.aspx?ARTID=26368

[3] http://www.counter-currents.com/2014/09/rotherham/

From start to finish England's Muslim pedophile rape epidemic is the product of liberal political correctness. Pakistanis are in Europe because of multiculturalism; they mix freely with the local population because of multiculturalism; the locals were taught not to fear and shun them lest they commit the sin of "racism"; and when the pattern of rape first emerged, it would have been widely publicized and ruthlessly suppressed were it not for the overriding PC imperative of white race replacement.

Pedophile rape was not made legal in England. All that was required for a pedophile rape epidemic is for the rape-prone Paki population to become a politically-correct victim group. Then a networks of liars, excuse-makers, and crime concealers embedded in the press, academia, and bureaucracy sprang into action. Liberals lie, and your children are raped. Then they lie to cover it up, and still more children are raped.

And now the same evil bastards are at work trying to make pedophiles into a PC protected group. In the last couple of years, there has been a flurry of articles in the American press, the message of which is summed up in the title of Margot (((Kaplan's))) *New York Times* article, "Pedophilia: A Disorder, not a Crime."[4] *Salon.com*, however, has become the flagship publication for pedophile advocacy. (Evidently, journalists fear no blow-back from whites. Only Muslims pull a *Charlie Hebdo*.)

But the same causes produce the same effects. The Left is now extending its protection from Pakistani pedophiles to the whole pedophile population. Not every town has Pakis, but every town has pedophiles. Thus the movement to make pedophiles the objects of PC pity will make every town a Rotherham.

Counter-Currents/*North American New Right,*
November 13, 2015

---

[4] http://www.nytimes.com/2014/10/06/opinion/pedophilia-a-disorder-not-a-crime.html?_r=0

DRUG LEGALIZATION IN THE WHITE REPUBLIC

I'd do it. I'd push the button.

If there were a button that would instantly and painlessly annihilate alcohol, nicotine, marijuana, and all other addictive recreational drugs, I would push it, simply because nothing has done more damage to the people I love, including my race as a whole.

I do not think that our enemies could have pushed the destruction of the white race to this point if we were not so prone to turn our anger inward and numb ourselves with drink and drugs. Without them, white people would be a whole lot meaner and harder to push around, and that would be a good thing.

I would push the button, even though I am not immune to the pleasures of alcohol. In fact I love it, albeit in moderation. Some of my friends call me a teetotaler and a killjoy, but that is only because they are alcoholics.

But let's wrench ourselves away from such a utopian vision and turn our attention to *Realpolitik*. When a white homeland is established in North America, its founders will eventually get around to the issue of drug laws.

I think that a white ethnostate should consider junking most of America's drug laws. I think we should consider making alcohol, nicotine, marijuana, cocaine, opiates, psychedelics, uppers, downers, and the like available for purchase without special taxes and restrictions, save two: first, to buy and use such drugs, one must be a responsible adult (18 or over and of sound mind), and second, there should be strict penalties for those who become addicted to drugs and thus cannot fulfill their familial and social responsibilities.

Why do I favor such sweeping liberties regarding drug use? Let me first make it clear that I am not a libertarian. I don't believe that human beings have some sort of natural "rights" to the maximum amount of liberty possible, consistent with the equal liberty of others. Nor do I believe that the sole legitimate function of the state is to ensure the freedom of social atoms to pursue their individual goals.

I am not an individualist, but a racial collectivist, a racial communitarian. For me, political philosophy begins with the question of what institutions, laws, and customs are necessary for the survival and flourishing of race. It just so happens that a good deal of individual liberty makes sense in the context of a white society.

In particular, I believe that today's drug laws just would not make sense in a healthy and homogeneous white society, simply because such a society would lack the two main reasons why present-day drug laws exist: (1) a culture that encourages selfishness, hedonism, irresponsibility, and prolonged adolescence, and (2) the presence of non-white groups with strong genetic predispositions to drug and alcohol abuse and inferior capacities to control their appetites and impulses.

Individual liberty makes sense only if people are responsible enough not to abuse it. Today's white Americans—from the boomers on—are perhaps the most immature and irresponsible generations in our history. Liberty is not just wasted on us; it is an actual danger. So all talk of drug legalization in the present context is grossly irresponsible. It would just make a bad situation worse.

But this rampant hedonism and irresponsibility is largely artificial. It is the typical product of cultural decadence, in this case a decadence engineered by cultural aliens out to destroy us. But one does not have to go back too many generations to find white men and women who were mature and responsible enough to start businesses and begin families before today's kids are even allowed to graduate from High School.

In a White Republic, adolescence would not be prolonged, and hedonism and selfishness would not be encouraged. Men and women would be ready to assume adult responsibilities by the age of 18, including decisions about using alcohol and other recreational drugs. A White Republic would be all about empowering youth: about giving them what they need so that they can begin independent and productive lives as soon as it is possible.

But what if some of them develop problems? Then society would intervene, on the grounds that individuals are not mere atoms and their problems are not merely private. Drug abuse — whether of drugs that are legal or illegal in today's society — interferes with the ability of individuals to fulfill their responsibilities to their families, to their race, and even to themselves. Addicts would be forcibly dried out and barred from buying drugs. Repeat offenders should probably be sterilized.

But, by the same token, a society that seeks to cultivate personal responsibility should not deny *everyone* access to certain substances merely because *some* people abuse them.

Drug legalization advocates love to point out that many drug laws were racially motivated, and this is true. Laws against opiates were directed at the Chinese. Laws against marijuana and cocaine were directed at blacks.

A homogeneously white society would have no need to use drug laws to target non-white populations. There may, of course, be other reasons to ban such drugs. But at the very least, a homogeneously white society should look for *good reasons* rather than uncritically carry over laws that are artifacts of the multiracial societies we are struggling to leave behind.

Some people will dismiss such talk because drug legalization is "liberal" and they are "conservatives." Of course, if one turns the clock back far enough, one will find an America without drug laws and other aspects of the nanny state. So why not conserve that America? Today's conservatives are often just clinging to the consequences of yesterday's liberalism.

Others simply have silly racial prejudices about drugs. Alcohol is for white men. Pot is for blacks. But if that is the case, then a society which outlaws blacks will have no need to outlaw pot as well.

Such discussions are, of course, a bit premature. But we will never get from here to there unless we have a pretty clear image of what "there" will look like. Thus there is a place for speculation about the possible laws and institutions of a White Nationalist society.

Although nobody knows how to have fun better than some

White Nationalists I know, our enemies have successfully established the image of White Nationalists as dour jackbooted totalitarians. Many of our friends have helped them, truth be told. Thus it is useful to emphasize anything that conflicts with that stereotype.

I submit that there is a lot of appeal to the image of a society in which children of the sun are equipped with the independence and responsibility of adulthood in the full bloom of youth, so that they can enjoy the freedom to explore, create, and celebrate life. Jackboots optional.

That said, since alcohol is already a major problem in today's White Nationalist movement, the last thing we need is an influx of drug enthusiasts. Thus, although I favor drug legalization in the White Republic, as far as the White Nationalist *movement* is concerned, I am all for Harold Covington's General Order #10: Nobody working for a white homeland may use drugs or alcohol for the duration of the struggle.

Let's save the toasting for the white homeland, comrades. Or for Valhalla.

TOQ Online, April 14, 2010

AGAINST POT

Put your bongs down people and listen to me for a few minutes. I want to explain why I think marijuana is one of the most insidious substances known to man from the point of view of long-term self-actualization.

I fell in with some stoners my first year of college. Naturally, they tried to share their vice. But it did nothing for me, and I hated smoking of any kind, so I never got into it.

Years later, though, after I had my Ph.D. and a teaching job, a friend came to visit me and asked where he could get some pot. I said, "There's a sign down by the record store that says 'Drug Free Zone.' I bet you can buy some there." So we walked to the store. I went inside and bought a Marianne Faithfull CD, and by the time I came out, he had scored some pot. We walked back to my place, and I decided to try it.

Obviously marijuana had become increasingly potent and hallucinogenic over the years, because this time it had a profound effect. We were watching an episode of *Alias*, and during a commercial, I had an extraordinary experience. I felt that the commercial had expanded into a whole world in which an utterly compelling drama was unfolding. I completely sympathized with our heroine's struggle to get a whiter-than-white wash. Her pain was my pain. A 30-second commercial had just moved me as much as an epic drama. "I've got to try this again," I thought.

I had symphony tickets the next day, so my friend and I partook some more, then had dinner at my favorite restaurant. It was the tastiest meal I'd ever had. Then we heard *Ein Heldenleben* (*A Hero's Life*), Richard Strauss's musical autobiography, with sections on his art, his romance and marriage, his battles with the critics, and his peaceful retirement from the world. It was the most profound musical experience I had ever had. I was completely inside the music. I lived, felt, and understood the meaning of every theme. I particularly got into the romance section, with its musical flirtation, bickering, and lovemaking. I wanted to do a whole *Ring* cycle on drugs.

On the way home, though, I had the same profound musical experience listening to an utterly insipid pop song on the radio. And before we got home, I wanted to get a snack, so we stopped at a convenience store, and I got a box of crusty, day-old donuts. They were every bit as delicious as the meal we had earlier.

At that point, it dawned on me why the potheads I knew seemed perfectly content to sit around in their pajamas eating Captain Crunch and watching daytime television. If Britney Spears is as profound a musical experience as Richard Strauss, why go through the trouble of appreciating Strauss? If TV commercials can be as dramatically profound as Sophocles and Shakespeare, why strain your brain? If day-old donuts and cold cereal are just as delicious as a skillful chef's creation, why bother with cooking? If masturbation can be just as enjoyable as sex, then who needs other people? If being a slacker is just as pleasurable as accomplishing something in one's life, why even get out of bed?

I realized that marijuana had the power to totally destroy my ability to create and grow as a human being. It has the power to turn men into sensuous, swinish philistines. It also robbed me of sleep by inducing fevered, racing thoughts at bedtime. It had completely lost its charms.

Now, I am willing to grant that your mileage may vary. I know couple of highly accomplished people who regularly smoke pot. But these are outliers. I have known far more un-ambitious slugs. I have also known two people who have de-stroyed businesses and friendships and their own dignity as human beings through pot-induced paranoia.

I also know there are legitimate medical uses of marijuana, although I would wager that 95% of medical marijuana users are just malingering stoners gaming the system.

Why are so many adults today seemingly frozen at juve-nile levels of maturity and taste? The main reason is the domi-nance of selfish, hedonistic individualism. At the age of 14 or 16 or 18, some people decide that henceforth they are going to satisfy rather than transcend themselves. Thus they seek out only those social relations that affirm rather than challenge their initial preferences. And as long as you can pay, some capitalist will cater to you in your comfort zone. (Bad credit? No credit? No problem!) Hedonistic individualism and capitalism thus make it possible for more and more people to reach 40 or 50 or 60 with their teenage selves still intact.

Marijuana is just hedonistic individualism in herbal form. Self-actualization requires pain and struggle. Virtue is hard not easy. But why worry about that, when marijuana can make you perfectly content with whatever level of ignorance, immaturity, and bad taste that you happen to be at when you take your first hit?

Counter-Currents/*North American New Right*
May 22, 2015

FORCED TO BE FREE:
THE CASE FOR PATERNALISM

Paternalism means treating people like children. Children lack the maturity and wisdom to make their own decisions. Thus they need parents — or people playing the paternal role — to tell them what to do and, on occasion, to force them to do it.

Most people have no problem with paternalism when dealing with actual children, as well as the retarded, the senile, and the insane. But normal adults bristle at paternalism, even though we all act like children from time to time. Paternalism, they think, is incompatible with freedom.

I wish to argue, however, that there is no conflict between paternalism and freedom, provided that both terms are properly understood.

First of all, real paternalism has to be "for your own good," i.e., in the actual interest of its object. People might claim to be abridging the liberty of others to help them, when in reality they are concerned to benefit only themselves. But that is fake rather than real paternalism. Real paternalism must be in the interest of its objects. Real paternalism is a kindness. Fake paternalism is merely a crime.

Second, there are true and false forms of freedom as well. Most people will agree that freedom is doing what you want to do. But what do we want to do? On this matter, I follow Plato and Aristotle, who argued that we all want basically one thing: the good life, happiness, self-actualization, or well-being (*eudaimonia*). That is the ultimate aim of every particular action. Every choice, whether we know it or not, is made in pursuit of the good life as we see it.

Thus if freedom is doing what we really want, and we all really want a good life, then *living a good life is freedom*. This implies that if we choose to do things that are not conducive to the good life, we are not acting freely, for doing things we don't really want to do is unfreedom.

In other words, not every *voluntary* act is a *free* one. We are free when we pursue the good life (what we really want). We are unfree when we fail to pursue the good life (which we don't really want to do).

There are two basic causes of unfreedom. First, there is ignorance of what is really conducive to happiness. We might think that smoking 20 cigarettes a day will make us happy, but it won't. Second, there are occasions when we know perfectly well what will make us happy but we fail to do it because we are overcome by our emotions. We fear doing the right thing, or we find doing the wrong thing too pleasurable to resist.

We might *choose* to act out of ignorance or passion. We might even *feel* free when doing so. But if such actions are not conducive to the good life, they are not free, they are a form of bondage. Paternalism, therefore, can restore freedom by forcing us to stop throwing away our happiness out of ignorance or passion. Since freedom is doing what we really want, and we can be forced back onto that path, man can be *forced to be free*, as Jean-Jacques Rousseau put it so memorably.

This means that libertarianism, which claims that freedom is incompatible with paternalism, and that force is always the opposite of freedom, is simply wrong. If you really care about freedom, then the state should, in principle, have the power to paternalistically intervene when people are throwing away their freedom out of lack of knowledge or excess of feeling. One can debate the grounds and scope of such paternalistic interventions. But the principle is clear: paternalism is not an enemy of real freedom but one of its necessary guardians.

Counter-Currents/*North American New Right*
May 25, 2015

REDNECK ROUSSEAU:
JIM GOAD'S *SHIT MAGNET*

Jim Goad
Shit Magnet:
One Man's Miraculous Ability to Absorb the World's Guilt
Los Angeles: Feral House, 2002

Jim Goad is a brilliant stylist, satirist, and social commentator. His first book, *The Redneck Manifesto* (New York: Simon and Schuster, 1997) not only contains more insights about society and politics than a dozen dry academic tomes, it is compulsively readable and downright hilarious.

Goad seems to know the score on race and the Jews, but refuses to identify himself as a white racist. Ultimately, I think that he is too self-centered, too irresponsible, and too alienated from any community, much less a racial one. And for all his transgressive posturing, he is just too conventional to cross that line. This is a major disappointment, because it would be great to have a satirist of Goad's talent on our side. But *The Redneck Manifesto* still has much to offer to White Nationalists.

Goad's new book *Shit Magnet* is disappointing. The style, as usual, is brilliant, and the satire is cutting. But Goad is in a rut, and that rut is named Jim Goad. The book is all about Jim Goad, Jim Goad, Jim Goad. We learn about Jim's abusive parents, the abusive nuns at Catholic school, his teenage cocksucking, his nose job, his hair implants, his every fist-fight and black eye, the birth of his infamous 'zine *ANSWER Me!* and the associated controversies.

He shares all the details of his twelve hellish years with Debbie, a neurotic Jewish bitch with an IQ of 86, now mercifully dead of cancer, and his one hellish year with Ann, the psychotic white trash who sent him to prison, including every scratch he received and every black eye he inflicted in his fights with both women. His tiresome rants addressed to both women (Debbie is dead, Jim) indicate, amazingly, that he still has not gotten over them.

Goad shares every little detail of his arrest, his plea-bargain, and his two-and-a-half years in prison. We learn that prisoners always suffer more than their victims. That apparently applies to the various serial killers he met behind bars. We also get to share every little tear Jim cried along the way. And for all his skills at satire, he's deadly serious.

Why does Jim insist on sharing all this with us? Has he no shame? Is he not embarrassed to share episodes like the following with perfect strangers?

> *Some skinny black kid with glasses paid me five bucks for the privilege of letting him suck my cock on the concrete stairwell to a fluorescent-lit Norristown subterranean parking lot, and he had his eyes closed all worshipfully slobbering all over it and said I could fuck him if I wanted to but I said no, and the way he fawned over my bone was the same way Ardea that fat cloth-ing-industry fag hag knelt down and prayed to it and said it tastes great when she swallowed and she'd be cute if she lost a hundred pounds, and I've never had a steady girlfriend or any-one tell me they love me and thinking about all this makes me want to put a bullet in my head. Or someone else's.* (p. 46)
> (Italics in original)

Goad also writes about consorting with black female prosti-tutes in his puerile, pornographic online 'zine *Exotic*.

Jim may well have some shame, but he has another motive that always overwhelms it: the desire to justify himself. To whom? Why, to any and all of us. To the vast, anonymous herd of strangers he pretends to despise. To the morons to whom he insists he is so superior. We have to like him, you see, or he cannot like himself.

Goad's strategies of self-justification change as the book plods on. At first, he takes a standard Jean-Jacques Rous-seau/Karl Marx/Oprah Winfrey line: all men are naturally good. Every baby is naturally innocent. There is a little rosebud of sweetness in every heart. What makes us bad? Why, other people make us bad. Society makes us bad. This is why we have to hear about Jim's abuse at the hands of his parents, teachers, and peers. The only reason he grew up violent with others is that others were violent with him first. The only reason he made such rotten romantic choices is that other people didn't give him the right kind of love.

Near the end of the book, however, he changes his tune. However innocent he once was, he is thoroughly fucked up now. It is not his fault of course. But fucked up as he is, he is better than the rest of us. Why? Because we are all fucked up too. We are all guilty. We all deserve to go to prison. But we are in denial about it, and Jim is honest about it, so Jim is better than us. He has no illusions, and we do. That is why Jim was sent to prison: not for his crimes, but for ours. He is no more deserving of prison than the rest of us. We sent him to prison to silence his brutal honesty and avoid facing the fact that we are just as bad as he is (and, presumably, the child rapists and serial killers with whom he was incarcerated).

Well, Jim, it does not wash. I do not believe in original sin, but I do not believe in Rousseau's "natural goodness of man" either. I do believe that character is destiny, and that more of our characters than we like to admit is shaped by purely genetic factors. And Jim, from your own description of your family, you really are white trash. That means that you are from the shallow, stupid, violent, alcoholic, emotionally unstable end of the white gene pool. You were not just from a bad seed, you were from a bad egg and a bad sperm. Through some genetic kink, you are smart white trash, but white trash nonetheless. And in my book that pretty much explains everything about you. Like attracts like, Jim. That's why you're a *Shit Magnet*.

And as for this "we're all guilty but I have the guts to admit it" crap: I know a lot of people, and not one of them is as fucked up as you are. For all my faults, I'm better than you, and for all their faults, so are all my friends. You went to prison for repeatedly punching the psychotic bitch you insisted on returning to again and again. You went because of your deeds, not your words. For your brutality, not your honesty. For your guilt, not mine.

If I had to describe my political philosophy, I would say:

"Libertarianism now, fascism later." We need to preserve our civil liberties now in order to take them away from the morons later, when we create a healthy white society: an organic state with no parties, no elections, no demagoguery, and no politicians—a society where the best rule for the good of all—a society that takes eugenic measures to drain the Goad end of the gene pool forever—a society where the degrading filth of Judeo-Afro-Cholo-Homo-Pomo popular culture is rolled up by a giant dung beetle and plopped into the bottomless pit of oblivion. (Thanks for that last image, Mr. Tsun.) And when that day comes, I am afraid that Goad's 'zine *ANSWER Me!*, with its special issues on suicide and serial killers and rape, and his webzine *Exotic* will have to go too.

Thus I feel conflicted when I read Goad's chapters on the controversies surrounding *ANSWER Me!*: the obscenity trial in Washington state because some dizzy broad somehow imagined that "Let's Hear It for Violence Against Women" might promote violence against women, the unwelcome publicity he received when White House shooter Martin Duran was "linked" to *ANSWER Me!* like Tim McVeigh to *The Turner Diaries* by a quote scrawled on a sheet of paper, and the further unwanted publicity when three brilliant but depressed English neo-Nazis who committed suicide were also linked to the suicide issue of *ANSWER Me!* On the one hand, I want to maintain civil liberties. But on the other hand, I applaud the healthy instincts of my fellow citizens and think that maybe we should speed up the clock and let the cleansing begin.

It is amusing to see the hard, transgressive, Devil-may-care Jim Goad ducking and weaving to maintain his innocence amid all the 'zine scandals. After all (gulp) some stranger might think ill of him. It is amusing to see the brutally frank Jim Goad hide behind the pretense that he bears no responsibility when he markets magazines glorifying rape, serial murder, and suicide to mentally unstable, marginalized people, and then those same mentally unstable, marginalized people leave a trail of broken, violated, dead bodies in their wake.

Perhaps the most repulsive episode in *Shit Magnet* is when Jim tells us of the tears he cried over Jane Greenhow, the gifted but depressed English neo-Nazi who put a bullet in her brain after mailing all of her money to Jim with a note saying that he only writes about suicide, but she is going him one better by actually killing herself. In my book, Schopenhauer ranks as a greater psychologist than Freud for proving that every tear we cry is a tear of self-pity. So I'm sorry Jim, but your tears do not absolve you of your guilt, they convict you. You obviously nudged her over the edge. Perhaps if you had recommended pumping depressed brains with Prozac instead of lead, Jane Greenhow would be alive and loving Hitler and playing her cello today.

Shit Magnet is the most repulsive exercise in self-pity and self-justification by a narcissistic, borderline personality since Rousseau's *Confessions*, and from a literary standpoint it is almost as brilliant. Much as I loathe Christianity, books like *Shit Magnet* demonstrate that it is still far better than its secular replacements. There is something infinitely more manly and psychologically realistic about Augustine's *Confessions*. The man believes in original sin. He believes he is guilty and rotten by nature. He believes that he deserves hell, not heaven. He believes that forgiveness is a gift of God, not an entitlement. This is a lot of metaphysical cant, but it is far more conducive to intellectual honesty and personal responsibility and genuine repentance for one's crimes than Rousseau's (or Goad's) aggrieved sense of innocence and pouting sense of entitlement to the good opinion, not of someone exalted like God, but of the perfect strangers who read his books.

Most artists are narcissistic. And, as Alex Linder pointed out to me, there seems to be a law that when an artist receives attention for his work, he begins to fixate on himself as well. The narcissism takes over, and he ceases to develop as an artist. This is exactly what happened to Goad. *Shit Magnet* was written in prison. Since his parole, even his best essays have been marred by a juvenile smuttiness that seems positively Jewish. Work on your scat jokes Jim and you could be writing for Hollywitz as well as *Hustler*.

For all its flaws, *Shit Magnet* does have something noble about it. It is a secular search for the redemption of a failed life.

But you don't cleanse yourself by crawling inside your own colon then turning it inside out for all the world to see. You cleanse yourself by dedicating your life to something bigger and better than yourself in the hope that some of that bigness and goodness will rub off. Until then Jim, you'll not be just a *Shit Magnet*. You'll be a shit factory.

"J. P. Nash," *Vanguard News Network*, 2002

IT'S TIME TO STOP
SHOPPING FOR CHRISTMAS

Even though I am an unbeliever, the Christmas season is my favorite time of the year. Christmas, like dogs, brings out the best in people. It awakens a desire to beautify one's world and adorn one's soul with good deeds.

The worst kind of evil is not merely harming people, but harming people by exploiting their goodness. A pickpocket merely steals your money. A con artist who steals your money by saying that he is collecting donations for a good cause also penalizes virtue and undermines the trust that is the foundation of civilized society.

That is why I despise the commercialization of Christmas. There is a whole economy of "fourth quarter" industries that depend on Christmas giving. Advertisers whip us into materialistic frenzies, so we rack up huge credit card debts. Traditionally, Christmas shopping begins after Thanksgiving. But recently, it has been creeping back toward Halloween. If capitalists had their way, of course, we would be listening to Christmas muzak and pushing shopping carts in midsummer.

But there is a limit to when Christmas shopping can begin. If religion had anything to do with it, the absolute limit would be Easter. But economics is the deciding factor here. And in economic terms, Christmas shopping cannot begin until consumers have paid off their credit card debts from the previous Christmas.

The Friday after Thanksgiving is now called "Black Friday." Traditionally, a Black Friday marks a massacre or disaster, and for consumers, I suppose it is. Merchants may be in the black, but consumers end up in the red.

It is too soon for White Nationalist politics in the United States. But racially conscious people still want to "do something." The best thing we can do is make ourselves strong as a community. And the best way to do that is to become as independent as possible from the existing political and economic system. The Christmas season is the best time to begin that process, because it is the time when we spend the most money on the dumbest things in the dumbest way in the least amount of time.

So it is time to STOP shopping for Christmas.

Take a holiday from holiday shopping.

Stop running yourself ragged running up debts.

1. DON'T GO INTO DEBT.

Freeze your credit cards. Literally. Go to the kitchen, fill a container with water, put your credit cards in it, and stick it in the freezer. Don't even think about thawing them out until January. And when January comes, resist the temptation and see just how long you can go without them.

2. GIVE THE GIFT OF FREEDOM.

Make a list of the people with whom you exchange gifts. If you have enough ties, enough sweaters, enough useless "novelty" items and your friends do as well, call them up and propose that you let one another off the hook.

3. REGIFT.

Admit it, the thought has crossed your mind. I have done it countless times, usually with sweaters. A lot of people buy gifts just to buy gifts. What are the chances that they know you well enough and have the time and the taste to find you the perfect gift? This means that the first time around, many gifts do not reach the right recipient and end up unappreciated. Regifting is a way of helping them find the right home, at no additional cost and with the added benefit of reducing clutter. I start thinking about regifting well in advance (on Christmas day, truth be told), whereas many people choose gifts at the last minute.

4. CREATE, REUSE, REFURBISH.

Can you make your own Christmas cards, wreaths, and ornaments? Do it. Were your garden and fruit trees unusually productive? Consider giving preserves or pies for Christmas. If you have a particular talent for making bread or brewing beer or bottling wine, give those for Christmas. Old furniture is usually better made than new stuff. Learn to refinish and reupholster. Do you bind books? Offer to rebind a friend's favorite book. Do you sew, knit, crochet? Make something. Between now and Christmas, you have plenty of time to do any of these things. You even have time to pick up new skills.

5. TEACH, ENCOURAGE, EMPOWER.

Do you have talents and skills you can teach your friends? Give them "gift certificates" (handmade, of course) entitling them to lessons. Do you play the piano? Offer the children of your friends some introductory lessons. Do you know how to maintain and repair your car, your air conditioner, your bicycle, your appliances, your plumbing, your lawnmower? Well, most of your friends don't. They spend hundreds of dollars every year repairing or replacing items that they have not maintained properly. Give them lessons, and you will help them save money and become more independent. Are you a great cook? Give your friends cooking lessons. People spend enormous amounts of money eating out. When they can make better food cheaper at home, they will not need or want to.

6. IF YOU MUST BUY GIFTS . . .

If you still have gifts to give after running through the above list and you are *compelled* to go shopping, consider the following rules of thumb.

- ❖ Buy from local, small businesses, not big chains.
- ❖ Buy goods made by white people around the world, not non-whites.
- ❖ Patronize artists and craftsmen, not mass producers of plastic junk.

7. KEEP YOUR MONEY IN THE RACIALLY CONSCIOUS COMMUNITY.

Buy from racially conscious publishers, booksellers, and other merchandisers.

No, I am not Scrooge. I am not the Grinch. I am not trying to steal your Christmas. I am merely suggesting that we celebrate Christmas intelligently and creatively, in ways that enrich us as a community rather than impoverish us, in ways that empower rather than weaken us. Decommercializing Christmas and reconnecting it with family and community will actually make it more meaningful and fun than ever.

Happy Thanksgiving and Merry Christmas from everyone at Counter-Currents/*North American New Right*!

Counter-Currents/*North American New Right*,
November 25, 2010

PLASTIC CHRISTMAS

My whole adult life, I have had my own Christmas tree on only two occasions. The reason is simple: I always spent Christmas at home or with the family of a friend. But even so, I love Christmas trees. So every year, I bought three or four ornaments, which I would bestow upon my hosts and other friends.

I put a great deal of time and discernment into buying ornaments, but seldom much money. My shopping would begin with the after-Christmas clearance sales, but it would extend year round. I would buy from museum stores, thrift and antique shops, ethnic festivals and arts and craft fairs, and souvenir and gift shops when I traveled. (The best places were in Munich and Nuremberg.) I was particularly pleased when I could buy something handcrafted in Germany or Scandinavia.

But I never kept any ornaments for myself. Thus, when I had my first Christmas tree in Atlanta, it was a last-minute thing, and a friend loaned me some ornaments, including a large selection of glass fruits and vegetables. (I still wonder where she got glass asparagus and pea pod Christmas ornaments. Her only answer was cryptic: "We were from California.")

This year, I decided to stay home in anticipation of a move. And the last thing I wanted before moving was to accumulate new things. But then the Christmas spirit got into me. So on Saturday, we braved crowds, traffic, and cold winds and rain to get a Christmas tree. We also needed to buy ornaments, since I had exactly four: one that had been given to me, and three that I had bought as gifts for a friend who died a couple of years ago.

The first stop was the Target store in Serramonte, south of San Francisco. I figured I could get some simple, cheap red and gold glass ornaments and a couple of strings of lights. It was the nightmare before Christmas! I always tell people in Middle America who pooh-pooh my concerns about white demographic displacement to take a trip to the future in a time machine. By that, I mean buy a plane ticket to California, where America's future is now. The Serramonte Target store should be their first stop. The store was gridlocked with a vast, sluggish tide of brown people chattering in every language except English. In the background, I heard a remarkably insipid song, pitched to the tastes of toddlers, Teletubbies, and Toltecs, wishing us all a "Feliz Navidad!"

The Christmas ornaments were pretty much cleaned out. The only ones that were untouched were decorated with the silhouettes of bears, elk, foxes, and moose. There was also a box of cardinals. As I put one set of each in my basket, I wondered why they had been overlooked. Then it occurred to me that none of the shoppers I had seen could relate to such creatures, even as food. I imagined that the vast empty shelves had been stocked with festive Christmas armadillos, peccaries, burros, and chupacabras.

Tucked away at the back of one shelf were a couple of boxes of old-fashioned Christmas balls in red, green, gold, and silver. Noting only that they were labeled "shatter resistant," I grabbed them and headed for the endless queues at the registers, where I lined up behind the only other white people there: a brother and sister, both tall and blonde, which at one time was considered quintessentially "California." (I had passed two other white men as I came in, both dorks in tow of their "submissive" Asian girlfriends.)

But I know that I was not the only one in that store who felt like he was in a foreign country. The place was foreign to everyone. But the alienation of whites is even worse, because every non-white in that store had a homeland somewhere in the world. But whites no longer have homelands anywhere. White countries are for everyone.

Then it was off to buy the tree. A sour old white woman in Santa hat presided over a lot filled with fir trees and lawn ornaments. Her little helpers were Mexican mestizos. Communicating in sign language and painfully mangled English, one of them helped us pick out a tree, then he trimmed its branches and netted it.

As we checked out, the woman asked him "Noble or Douglas fir?" His response was "Nobless." "Douglas?" "No, nobless!" "Douglas?" she asked again, in evident annoyance, adding, "That looks like a noble fir." Feeling that I was in a *Fawlty Towers* episode, I cut in and said, "Noble. He is saying 'nobless.'" Without a word, she rang me up, and her little helper carried the tree to the car.

We offered him bungee cords to tie it to the roof, and he refused, using twine. "I been working here 30 years," he said, in his first sentence of (almost) correct English. Thirty years, I thought, and he can barely speak English, even to communicate the most basic vocabulary connected to his job. "Feliz Navidad!" he said cheerfully. Naturally, I replied, "Merry Christmas."

Sunday, I went out to get some lights for the tree. More torrential rains and surging non-white crowds. I like *Blade Runner* plenty, but I never thought I would be living in it.

When it was finally time to trim the tree, I discovered, first off, that although the tree was grown in the United States, everything else I bought was made in China. The instructions for the lights were written in Chinglish.

The three glass cardinals came with red cloth loops to hang them on the branches. One of the cardinals did not have eyes painted on it. (Perhaps the Chinese slave who created it was sent off for organ harvesting before she was finished.)

None of the other ornaments had hangers. Or, to be more precise, they did not have little metal hooks. Instead, they had bits of gold string that I was expected to thread through the top of each ornament and tie into loops. I tried it once, but the thread was so thin that I could barely see what I was doing and so slick that the knot did not hold. As soon as I hung it on the branch, the ornament fell to the floor. Fortunately, it was "shatterproof," which, I discovered, means "plastic."

I was horrified: Christmas ornaments should not be shatterproof, like engine parts. They should be made of glass, metal, and wood (and what I refer to, somewhat desperately, as "the better kind of resin"). They should be beautiful, fragile, and exquisitely crafted. They should be carefully displayed, then

carefully stored away until next year. But under no circum-
stance should they be plastic.

Thoroughly disgusted and just wanting to get it over with, I
resorted to hanging the ornaments with twist ties, which actually worked quite well. I could not find a star for the tree, so I
used a large package bow. By this point, I saw no reason not to
yield to the sheer farce of it all, so I tossed on a couple of Hindu
religious symbols that I bought in Varanasi in 2004 (also made
of plastic).

Then I stood back to judge my handiwork. It actually *looked*
good. But I knew that this Christmas tree, like America as a
whole, is just a cheap, hollowed out, globalized plastic simula-
crum of something real, something that I grew to love as a
child but now, I fear, is gone forever.

Well, at least the tree is made of wood.

Counter-Currents/*North American New Right*
December 24, 2012

Merry Christmas, Infidels!

It was about twenty years ago when I first noticed that "Merry Christmas" was being replaced by the bland, neutral "Season's Greetings" and "Happy Holidays."

I asked a schoolteacher of my acquaintance, a benighted liberal who is an infallible barometer of the latest currents of political correctness, why this was happening. I was answered with another question: "If you were Jewish, wouldn't you feel offended if someone wished you a Merry Christmas?" The tone communicated that this was self-evident, that we must avoid giving such offense at all costs, and that I was stupid for even asking. Obviously she had spent too much time talking down to students.

I thought to myself, "I would not be offended if a Jew wished me a Happy Hanukkah. That would be small-minded. So why should a Jew be offended if I wished him a Merry Christmas? What makes Jews different? Why do people cater to such small-mindedness?"

I also thought to myself, "Wouldn't a pluralistic, liberal attitude imply many different holiday greetings, rather than one bland, characterless, homogeneous one?"

I also began to notice the proliferation of the abbreviation "X-mas," even in greetings cards, store displays, and advertisements. Abbreviations are perfectly OK in hand-scrawled notes and e-mails. But they are gauche in more formal contexts, so I wondered what was driving this lapse in taste and style. Why are people literally "X"ing "Christ" out of "Christmas"? Is it merely another symptom of the secularization and commercialization of Christmas? But who is behind that trend? And is there some anti-Christian malice at work here?

In recent years, there has been a proliferation of news stories about the destruction of Christmas in England and the US to cater to the tastes of anti-Christian minorities. For instance, in 2002 in Mobile, Alabama, the annual Christmas parade, celebrated since 1945, was to be renamed "The Jolly Holiday" parade.

According to the organizers, "They said they wanted a name that was more inclusive, since the parade this year would include Hanukkah and Kwanzaa floats along with the usual Christmas fair [*sic*]."

Are we losing Christmas to pander to celebrators of Kwanzaa? The answer is no.

Kwanzaa is the ersatz African holiday invented in 1966 by an American Negro who goes by the name of Maulana Ron Karenga. Kwanzaa is supposed to be a Negro alternative to Christmas. It is a seven-day feast, celebrated from December 26 to January 1. Each day of Kwanzaa commemorates a different concept: unity (not diversity; unity is for them, diversity for us), self-determination, collective work and responsibility, cooperative economics, purpose, creativity, and faith.

Up to this point, most people will give Kwanzaa a respectful hearing. But wait: to commemorate each day of Kwanzaa, a candle is lit in a seven-branch candelabrum called the "Kinara." Now "Kinara" is supposed to sound like "Menorah," but with a "k" for Kwanzaa. Get it? (I know, you thought that the Kinara was a rank in the Ku Klux Klan, like a Kleagle and a Kligrapp.) The Kinara reveals just how infantile, contrived, and derivative Kwanzaa really is. Even the most patronizing liberals roll their eyes.

But stupidity is no bar to advancement in today's America, so Kwanzaa is slowly on the rise. In 1997 the US Post Office released a Kwanzaa stamp. Merchandisers see the potential for Kwanzaa profits, and so do politicians. Bill Clinton began issuing annual Kwanzaa proclamations, a practice continued by "conservative" president George W. Bush.

But Kwanzaa is not destroying Christmas. Most Americans still have never heard of it, and no white American can think of it without embarrassment. Even white liberals probably prefer not to think of it at all, so it is not likely to be in the back of their minds when they wish you a hearty "Happy Holidays!" Besides, most blacks who celebrate Kwanzaa probably celebrate Christmas too, so it is unlikely that they would bristle to the defense of Kwanzaa if wished a "Merry Christmas!"

No, it is the Jews who stole Christmas. Kwanzaa merely

apes Hanukkah. Hanukkah is a minor Jewish holiday that cele-brates, like most Jewish holidays, the massacre of tribal ene-mies. It is primarily in the US that Hanukkah has been promot-ed as a Jewish rival to Christmas.

The motives for this are unclear. One may be crypsis, the desire of some Jews to blend in among their host populations. Crypsis is certainly a motive in Reform Judaism. Reform syna-gogues have even adopted stained-glass windows and organ music to give the impression that Judaism is just another "Judeo-Christian" denomination.

Another motive may be rivalry: Jews recognize the appeal of Christmas, and want to keep their children busy doing some-thing else during the Christmas season.

Malice probably also plays a role.

First, there is the resentment of the eternal outsider trying to make himself feel comfortable by breaking down the distinc-tion between inside and outside. To do this, he has to efface the host culture's defining symbols. A Jew feels outside when you say "Merry Christmas," but he feels comfortable when you say "Happy Holidays." Indeed, he feels pleased with this concrete token of his cultural and political power.

Then there is the particular resentment that Jews nurse to-ward Christianity. There are at least three reasons for this. First, Jesus was an apostate Jew, and nobody likes an apostate. Sec-ond, Jesus rejected Judaism for its tribalism, inhumanity, and intellectual dishonesty, and the truth hurts, so Jews hate Jesus as a bearer of bad news. Third, although today Islam is the re-ligion most resistant to Jews and Christianity the most embar-rassingly apologetic and subservient, this has been the case primarily since the foundation of the state of Israel. Before that, Jews lived securely in Muslim lands while they were being ex-pelled from virtually every Christian country in Europe. Chap-ter 5 of Israel Shahak's *Jewish History, Jewish Religion: The Weight of Three Thousand Years* contains an eye-opening discussion of Jewish attitudes toward non-Jews, including a comparison of Jewish attitudes toward Christians and Muslims.

The Jew Philip Roth is the author of dreadful novels that are nonetheless extremely revealing of the operations of the Jewish mind. In *Operation Shylock: A Confession*, he gloats:

> God gave Moses the Ten Commandments and then he
> gave Irving Berlin "Easter Parade" and "White Christ-
> mas," the two holidays that celebrate the divinity of
> Christ—and what does Irving Berlin do? He de-Christs
> them both! Easter turns into a fashion show and Christ-
> mas into a holiday about snow.

So how do we take back Christmas? First, let me say something about my motives. I was raised a Christian, but it never
took. I would prefer to keep Christianity out of politics, and I
would hate to live in an intolerant Christian society. Frankly, I
wish that our ancestors had held onto their old pagan religions.
Indeed, Christmas incorporates many old European pagan elements, but note that multiculturalists make no attempt to cater
to the celebrants of Yule, Saturnalia, and the birthday of Mith-
ras. Nothing white is promoted by the multiculturalists.

But, still, I like Christmas a lot. When the days grow short
and the weather gets bad, it is nice to create an environment of
cheer and good will. At bottom, my objection is not religious,
but cultural. I hate to see the homogenizing, secularizing, leveling forces of modernity at work, even on a religion that I do not
profess.

So what is to be done? First, although Jews are the driving
force behind the destruction of Christmas, they are a tiny minority, unlovable and unloved, and all the pushiness in the
world would not have triumphed if whites were not such
pushovers. Second, the Mobile "Jolly Holiday Parade" incident
is instructive. The gentiles pushed back:

> . . . citing e-mail and telephone threats from residents
> opposed to a parade without the word Christmas in its
> title... Mobile Christmas Parade Inc.... announced there
> would be no parade this year. . . . Three hours later, vol-
> unteers with Main Street Mobile, a city-staffed organiza-
> tion formed to promote downtown, announced that a
> parade will roll. . . . It will be called the Mobile Christ-

mas Holiday Parade.

This year, I have been pushing back in a subtle but steady way. Every chance I get, I wish people a "Merry Christmas," most pointedly when I am wished "Happy Holidays." I have even been wishing a "Merry Christmas" to the atheists and Odinists I know.

So, with that long preface in mind: from one infidel to another, "Merry Christmas!"

"T. C. Lynch," *Vanguard News Network*, December 25, 2003

ALAN WATTS AT 100

Alan Watts is one of my favorite writers. Today is his 100th birthday.

Born in Chislehurst, Kent, England, Watts was raised an Anglican, but became a Buddhist at age 15. In 1941, while Watts was living in New York City, his first wife Eleanor had a mystical vision of Jesus. This led him to return to Anglicanism.

Watts skipped undergraduate study, but later earned an MA in theology and a doctorate in divinity and was ordained an Anglican priest in 1945. For several years, he was the Anglican chaplain at Northwestern University, renowned for his accessibility and innovative rituals. In 1950, he left the priesthood, primarily due to the breakup of his first marriage. (Watts had a recognized gift for "ritual magic," which he continued to perform as a shaman once he was finished being a priest.)

In 1951, he moved to San Francisco, where he joined the faculty of the American Academy of Asian Studies. He was based in the Bay Area for the rest of his life.

In the mid-1950s, he left the Academy for the life of an independent scholar and writer. Watts became world-famous as an interpreter of Buddhism, Vedanta, and Taoism. During his lifetime, Watts published 24 books and countless articles. Another 25 volumes, plus numerous lecture recordings and videos have appeared posthumously.

Watts' writings fall into four periods. First are his early Buddhist works: *The Spirit of Zen* (1936), written when Watts was only 19; *The Legacy of Asia and Western Man: A Study of the Middle Way* (1937); and *The Meaning of Happiness: The Quest for Freedom of the Spirit in Modern Psychology and the Wisdom of the East* (1940).

Then there are his Anglican works, where he tries to synthesize Christianity and Eastern thought. The high points are *Behold the Spirit: A Study in the Necessity of Mystical Religion* (1948) and *The Supreme Identity: An Essay on Oriental Metaphysic and the Christian Religion* (1950).

Watts' third period commences with *The Wisdom of Insecurity* (1951). He abandoned Christianity as a framework and focused on Buddhism, Vedanta, and Taoism. Works from this period include *The Way of Zen* (1957), *Nature, Man and Woman* (1958), *Beat Zen, Square Zen, and Zen* (1959), *"This Is It" and Other Essays on Zen and Spiritual Experience* (1960), *Psychotherapy East and West,* (1961) *The Joyous Cosmology: Adventures in the Chemistry of Consciousness* (1962), and *The Two Hands of God: The Myths of Polarity* (1963), culminating in his most brilliant works, *Beyond Theology: The Art of Godmanship* (1964), in which Christianity is situated within the Vedantic context as a mode of *maya,* and *The Book: On the Taboo Against Knowing Who You Are* (1966), a *summa* of Vedantic non-dualism.

With each new work, Watts' presentation became fresher and more original, less "scholarly." Pedants of course dismissed him as a "popularizer," but in truth Watts had evolved beyond mere scholarship. It takes far greater insight and talent to thoroughly internalize a philosophy and then to restate it in completely fresh language. But Watts went beyond popularization as well to insightful comparison, creative synthesis, fruitful application, and genuinely new insights. He was, in short, a philosopher in his own right.

Finally, I discern a fourth period in Watts' writings, in which systematic thought is replaced by essayistic and poetic play. This period commences with *Nonsense* (1967) a book of whimsical doggerel, and it includes *Does It Matter?: Essays on Man's Relation to Materiality* (1971), as well as *In My Own Way: An Autobiography, 1915–1965* (1972), *Cloud-hidden, Whereabouts Unknown: A Mountain Journal* (1973), and the posthumously published *Tao: The Watercourse Way* (1975). These writings are sheer delight, characterized by effortless grace, playful humor, and dazzling metaphors.

In 1973, Alan Watts died at the age of 58, at the height of his powers.

The best sources of information on Watts' life are his autobiography, *In My Own Way* and Monica Furlong's biography *Zen Effects: The Life of Alan Watts* (also published under the title *A Genuine Fake*). *In My Own Way* is pure pleasure to read. Furlong's biography depends heavily on *In My Own Way,* especially in the first half, but she also did some original research, particularly about topics Watts found too embarrassing to discuss himself. Most of this research is found from page 91 on.

Watts was the primary interpreter of Asian philosophy to the beatniks of the 1950s and the hippies of the 1960s. His interpretation of Asian thought was uniquely suited to a self-indulgent and hedonistic age, but this is no reason to dismiss it, for it is actually consistent with both Eastern and Western orthodoxy and individually verifiable spiritual experience, not to mention the fact that we actually do live in the Kali Yuga, the age of chaos and disintegration in which dark forces must be harnessed for spiritual attainment (the so-called Left-Hand Path).

According to Watts, the aim of religion is a mystical experience of unity with the active, creative, eternal energy of the cosmos (being, Brahman, God). But Watts argued that this experience of identity is not an "attainment" of ego-directed ascetic discipline, but rather a "realization" of a pre-existing identity; one awakens to the fact that one always-already was God, a fact hidden by our identification with our egos and their projects, secular or ascetic.

Indeed, Watts argued that this oblivion of our true nature is actually reinforced by ego-directed ascetic religion, and only way in which asceticism can lead to authentic spiritual realization is by exhausting the ego to the point when one lets go of striving for attainment . . . and realizes that one was already what one aspired to be, that one was already where one wanted to go.

Watts argues that the Christian distinction between salvation by means of human works as opposed to divine grace is found in Asian philosophy as well. Buddhists, Hindus, and Taoists have created formidable systems of asceticism and monasticism. But they also recognize the possibility of spontaneous and effortless spiritual realization, so-called "instant Zen."

Watts was a great advocate of hanging loose, letting go, tuning in, turning on, and dropping out as spiritual pathways. He experimented with psychedelic drugs and argued that LSD and mescaline produce genuine mystical experiences.

In his personal life, Watts was anything but an ascetic. In his autobiography, Watts writes:

I am an unrepentant sensualist. I am an immoderate lover
of women and the delights of sexuality, of the greatest
French, Chinese, and Japanese cuisine, of wines and spir-
ituous drinks, of smoking cigars and pipes, of gardens,
forests, and oceans, of jewels and paintings, of colorful
clothes, and of finely bound and printed books. (*In My
Own Way*, p. 47)

Watts was a genuine aesthete and dandy, a man of refined
tastes and sensibilities, a mystic who knew how to live in the
material world.

But there was a dark side to his sensualism: a dimension of
compulsion and addiction. Watts married three times, divorced
twice, and fathered seven children. But as a family man, he was
a success only in the most minimal Darwinian sense. He was a
compulsive womanizer and a neglectful father, which caused his
wives and children much pain. Like many products of the British Public School system, with its repulsive traditions of beatings
and bullying, Watts had a streak of sexual masochism. He began
smoking as a child and never stopped. He was also a serious alcoholic. Watts' father lived into his 90s, thus it was a very real
possibility that Alan Watts could have celebrated his 100th
birthday with us today, with 50 more books to his name, had he
been just a bit of an ascetic, had he controlled his sensualism rather than letting it control him.

Politically, Watts was a man of the Right. In his youth, he was
a follower of the mysterious Serbian guru and operator Dimitrije
Mitrinovic, an advocate of such quasi-fascistic ideas as Guild
Socialism, Social Credit, and European Unity (as long as it
wasn't Hitler who was doing the unifying). Watts also claimed
that he returned to Anglicanism largely out of conservative motives, searching for tradition and security in a world in disarray.
In *The Supreme Identity*, he offers an absolutely withering Traditionalist critique of the basic premises of liberalism.

Watts' main problem with Christianity is that it chafed
against his emerging sexual libertinism. But there were intellectual reasons as well. In the late 1940s, he began reading the Traditionalist writings of René Guénon and Ananda Coomaraswa-

my, who assimilated Christianity — along with Taoism, Buddhism, and Vedanta — to the universal Tradition, undermining the Church's claim to exclusive truth. (There is, by the way, no evidence that Watts ever read Julius Evola.)

Finally, the Traditionalists convinced Watts that we are living in the Kali Yuga, and he explicitly claimed that he left the church to find a spiritual life more in keeping with the age.

In his later years, Watts preached the Traditional doctrine of decline and the folly of all projects of progressive world-improvement even when he had become a guru to the Leftist counter-culture.

Watts' most Traditionalist book is *The Supreme Identity* (1950), a beautifully written but very dense and rigorously argued synthesis of Traditionalism, with a special reference to Christian theology, which is logical given his background and audience. Watts' next book, *The Wisdom of Insecurity* (1951), is a much more "popular" work, but it still uses the Traditionalist language of "realizing" (as opposed to knowing) the ultimate identity of self, world soul, and being.

Although Watts found Traditionalism useful in liberating his mind from Christianity, he ultimately rejected it. In the Preface to *Beyond Theology*, he explains his reason. Traditionalists claim that Christianity is just an exoteric expression of the one primordial tradition which is the inner truth of all religions. But Watts points out that there is no evidence that the founders of Christianity thought that way. Instead, Christianity has always insisted on what Jan Assmann calls the "Mosaic distinction" between true and false religions. Christianity is the one true religion, and all others are simply false. Thus in *The Supreme Identity*, Watts treats Christianity as an expression of primordial truth, but in *Beyond Theology*, he treats it as a mode of illusion.

Why remember Alan Watts' centennial on a New Right/Traditionalist website? A more telling question is why Watts' centennial seems to have been forgotten virtually everywhere else. Perhaps because he died before he found his true audience.

Counter-Currents/*North American New Right*,
January 6, 2015

THE SPIRITUAL MATERIALISM
OF ALAN WATTS

Alan Watts
Does it Matter?
Essays on Man's Relation to Materiality
New York: Vintage, 1971

Does it Matter? is one of my favorite Alan Watts books, to which I have returned again and again. It is also an excellent introduction to Watts' work. Thus I was delighted to discover that, at long last, it has been reprinted, hence this review.

The theme of *Does it Matter?* is material existence. The book begins with five long essays. "Wealth versus Money" deals with economics; "Murder in the Kitchen" deals with ecology and home design as well as cooking. (Both were originally published in *Playboy.*) "Clothes—On and Off," "The Spirit of Violence and the Matter of Peace," and "Psychedelics and Religious Experience" have self-explanatory titles.

Images of Gandhi's hunger strikes, skeletal yogis in dirty dishrags, and onion-headed monks with begging bowls (not to mention the occasional kerosene and Zippo self-immolation) have fostered the impression that Eastern philosophy and religion are entirely "spiritual" and world-denying. Similarly, images of the America's sprawling cities, bustling superhighways, luxurious homes, and consumerist cornucopias have fostered the impression that our civilization is materialistic and this-worldly.

Watts argues, however, that in some respects the opposite is actually true.

For instance, Watts claims that if Americans were true materialists, we would not build such ugly cities and eat such beastly food. He argues that the ugliness of urban America and the insipidness of the typical diet are actually expressions of a kind of Gnostic or Cartesian dualism, a spiritualistic discomfort with the material world that leads to a crude, unrefined materialism that prizes quantity over quality. Watts argues that the French are more genuinely materialistic than Americans, which is why French cities are more beautiful and French food is so superior. I think this is brilliantly insightful, and there is something like it on every page—indeed in every paragraph—of *Does it Matter?*

Watts also argues that Eastern philosophy and religion are not necessarily spiritual and world-denying. For instance, the non-dualistic interpretation of Vedanta (the philosophy of the Upanishads) implies a kind of pantheism. The divine is identical with the material universe and with each individual being.

The goal of religion is the mystical experience of our oneness with the divine/cosmos. This experience may require asceticism and contemplation. But it can just as well be spontaneous and effortless. It can hit you in the marketplace, on the battlefield, or in your turnip patch.

Mahayana Buddhism, moreover, stresses the unity of *samsara* and *nirvana*. Nirvana is not blissful annihilation, but a change of attitude in this life that allows freedom and detachment in the whirl and rush of material existence. Such philosophies foster attitudes of freedom, detachment, and aesthetic playfulness in relation to material life. They are conducive to artistic creativity and the refinement of taste.

"Wealth versus Money" proposes a utopian economy. Wouldn't it be lovely, Watts asks, if machines put us all out of work? Watts envisions a *Star Trek* economy where high technology and cheap energy abolish scarcity and the money economy, providing free sustenance for all. Would everybody run hog-wild accumulating things? Well, what would be the point of that? People hoard only when there is scarcity, and scarcity is precisely what is being abolished. Would people vegetate? What would be the point of that, given that people vegetate only between bouts of work, and work is being abolished?

Watts argues that instead, people would adopt lives of material simplicity and that a new economy would emerge to occupy people's leisure. Since any quantity of manufactured goods would be free, people would value quality and uniqueness. This would give rise to a new appreciation of craftsmanship. Old and unique objects would be highly prized and new and unique objects would be created. Art, craft, literature, and scholarship would flourish. So would games and sports. Tastes would be increasingly refined and exquisite. Life would be playful, ritualistic, and beautiful.

Watts does not mention it, but such a society would benefit from a gentle program of eugenic selection that would decrease the representation in each further generation of people who could not benefit from or contribute to such a society — people whose idle hands would be occupied solely with the Devil's work.

To most readers, the theory of "Wealth versus Money" seems both amazingly original and astonishingly naïve. But that is because Watts is concealing his sources. In fact, the foundation of his proposals is merely a version of C. H. Douglas' Social Credit theory. Of course Watts had good reason not to mention Douglas in the pages of *Playboy* in 1968: Social Credit was the economic system favored by Anglophone fascists like Ezra Pound. Watts was known to be a quiet man of the Right, but it is high time that scholars determine just how far to the Right he was. Watts tries to reach out to the '60s counter-culture in *Does it Matter?*, but at the same time he makes it clear that he accepts the Traditional idea of historical decline and rejects all progressivism and cause-mongering.

"Murder in the Kitchen" is really an essay about ecology at its deepest, about man's embeddedness in — our oneness with — nature and what this implies for daily life, from the food we eat to the houses we inhabit. Watts also deftly shows the connection between Western Gnostic and Cartesian mind-body dualism and such phenomena as Velveeta, Wonder bread, and Tang; factory farms; drab, clinical kitchens; air-conditioned hells (of the stationary and wheeled varieties); and suburban sprawl.

One of Watts' most surprising and refreshing positions is his critique of vegetarianism. For Watts, vegetarianism is simply an attempt to evade the fact that life feeds on life, that the universe is a vast web of creation and destruction. A vegetarian is just a person who spares his own feelings by killing creatures that can't scream. Vegetarianism is an attempt to remove man from nature, rather than to embrace nature and plunge into it. As such, vegetarianism can be part of an ascetic retreat from life. But Watts will have none of that.

Once we own up to the fact that we live by killing, we should make sure that we do not kill needlessly or cruelly. Beyond that, it is far more important to ensure animals have good lives rather than merely good deaths.[1] This means no more factory farms and feedlots and milk-fed calves. Furthermore, an animal that is badly cooked has died in vain. Finally, the place where we properly honor the creatures upon which we feed is a well-appointed kitchen, a kitchen that expresses a full commitment to the refinement and perfection of material existence.

Watts' descriptions of ideal kitchens, living spaces, and foods—and their typical American antipodes—are vivid and charming. His description of modern bread is genuinely hilarious. (It is clear that there has been a lot of real progress on the food front since the late '60s.) Yes, there is much personal opinion here—unapologetically offered as such—but there is much truth, goodness, and beauty too.

Watts' essay on clothes is less successful. He has a prejudice against Western clothing, particularly British, and a penchant for Oriental dhotis, sarongs, and kimonos. But instead of owning up to his preferences, he tries to deduce them (rather implausibly) from Vedanta. But if the cosmos is the gods at play, trying on every possible mask, acting out every possible scenario, then Chanel is as legitimate as a sari, a Prussian uniform as legitimate as samurai armor, a corset as legitimate as a lotus foot (and far less destructive).

Western clothes, Watts says, are uncomfortable, which only proves he did not know his correct size or a good tailor. Properly fitted and seasonally appropriate Western clothes are as comfortable as any Asiatic loincloth and usually far more flattering. (But I will admit that I have a prejudice for the English look.)

---

[1] Watts anticipates Finnish Deep Ecologist Pentti Linkola's critique of vegetarianism. See Pentti Linkola, *Can Life Prevail? A Radical Approach to the Environmental Crisis* (Aarhus, Denmark: Integral Tradition Publishing, 2009), especially chapter 3, "Animals."

Besides, comfort is so "bourgeois," ruled by the realm of necessity. Fashion is the realm of freedom. It is always better to look good than to feel good. And that is where the true gist of Watts' argument points. Watts offers a defense of dandyism as a rebellion against modern democratic leveling and conformism, as well as uptight and aggressive relations to one another and the natural world. He might also add Puritanical Gnosticism. There is no reason why the playful and refined embrace of material existence should not allow some room for male vanity. "Human beings the whole world over need to relax, become *gentle*men, take themselves lightly, and 'come off it.' Easy, gracious, and colorful clothing might well be a beginning" (p. 68). But Watts also needs to "come off it" and admit that military uniforms, along with priestly vestments, are one of the great Western bastions of dandyism.

Which bring us to the next essay, "The Spirit of War and the Matter of Peace," which blames war on dualistic alienation from the material world. This may be true of wars fought by alienated dualists, but it certainly does not capture the essence of all war. Historically, most wars have not been fought over ideologies at all, much less metaphysical dualism, but over honor and gain. Thus Watts tends to gross oversimplification. Moreover, he has a clear prejudice against war, which is at variance with Hindu tradition, which regards war as one of the darker games the gods play, and as such a necessary part of the whole which must be affirmed, indeed sacralized, and carried out as a solemn duty of the warrior caste.

Watts' essay "Psychedelics and Religious Experience" is superb. Dualists like R. C. Zaehner cannot grasp how a material substance like a psychedelic drug can be the basis of a genuinely "spiritual" — i.e., mystical — experience.[2]

But pantheism — which is essentially how Watts interprets Vedanta, Buddhism, and Taoism — rejects such dualism and understands the mystical problem as overcoming a false con-

---

[2] R. C. Zaehner, *Mysticism, Sacred and Profane: An Inquiry into Some Varieties of Praeternatural Experience* (New York: Oxford University Press, 1961).

sciousness of ourselves as isolated, mortal, suffering individuals. Dualism adds another layer to this false consciousness by insisting that we are cut off from the divine because of our material embodiment. The truth is that we are one with the active, eternal energy of the cosmos because our body is part of the body of the cosmos, which is divine.

The mind is as material as the cosmos. The cosmos is as spiritual as the mind. Thus there is no metaphysical difference whether we attain cosmic consciousness at the end of a long ascetic and meditative approach—or spontaneously and instantaneously (so-called "instant Zen") triggered by a random event: looking at a bee gathering pollen or the gleam in a pewter vessel—or chemically, through mescaline or LSD. The use of psychedelics is usually likened to instant Zen because of its relative effortlessness, but it is also analogous to asceticism, because it is a deliberate, self-initiated transformation of consciousness, rather than something random and triggered by external conditions.

Watts' descriptions of his psychedelic experiences are fascinating:

> I was amazed and somewhat embarrassed to find myself going through states of consciousness which corresponded precisely with every description of major mystical experiences I had ever read. Furthermore, they exceeded both in depth and in a peculiar quality of unexpectedness the three "natural and spontaneous" experiences of this kind which I had had in previous years. (p. 81)

Watts describes four traits of psychedelic experience that precisely correspond with mystical experiences. (They correspond, of course, because they are the same.)

First, time seems to slow down and the present seems to expand.

Second, one rises above opposites, realizing that they are just polarities in an underlying unity. Self and other, good and evil, God and the devil, all seem one, and there is an affirmation of the whole—an experience of identification with it—that lies beyond all distinctions of good and evil.

Third, there is an experience of the identity of all selves with a cosmic all-self, as well as a sense that all the lights of consciousness that flicker on and off, all the little worlds that expand and collapse, are manifestations and "masks" of this all-self.

Fourth, there is the experience of the identity of the self with the eternal energy of the cosmos. One no longer sees oneself as a finite being who merely suffers, but as one with the infinite, active energy of the cosmos.

Here the fear of death ceases, for although the individual ego suffers and dies, the true self is eternally active and creative. And isn't the fear of death the main reason why people never really live fully actualized lives in this world?

Does it Matter? concludes with seven small, jewel-like essays, each a few pages long, dealing with religion, art, Aldous Huxley, and D. T. Suzuki. In "The Basic Myth," Watts encapsulates Indian religion and philosophy in four pages.

Alan Watts is an obligatory thinker for those who would combine Traditionalist spirituality, aesthetic attunement, and world-embracing power. *Does it Matter?* is not just the perfect introduction to Watts' philosophy. It is also a great introduction to philosophy as such, for everyone who first comes to philosophy wonders "Does it matter? Does it matter at all? Does it matter to me?" Watts shows that the answer to all these questions is a resounding "Yes!"

Counter-Currents/*North American New Right*,
December 11, 2010

DEFEATING THE LEFT:
VOX DAY'S *SJWS ALWAYS LIE*

Vox Day
SJWs Always Lie:
Taking Down the Thought Police
Foreword by Milo Yiannopolous
Castalia House, 2015

At the risk of sounding like the Oprah of the New Right, I want every one of you to buy and read this book. Vox Day has written an indispensable manual for resisting the politically correct witch-hunts of so-called "Social Justice Warriors." Day gives advice to individuals who are being targeted on how to fight back. He also details two remarkably successful and inspiring popular resistance campaigns against SJWs, GamerGate and Sad Puppy. Finally, he concludes the book with nothing less than a plan to destroy Leftist power root and branch.

If I seem a bit breathless and effusive, it is because my world has been dramatically expanded in the space of an afternoon (all it takes to read this slender volume). I had never heard of Vox Day until Ann Sterzinger's review of this book at Counter-Currents.[1] Nor had I heard of Larry Correia, Sad Puppy, and Castalia House publishing. And I knew virtually nothing about GamerGate except a vague recollection that something called *Gawker* (which I don't think I have ever read, unless it covered Charles Krafft) had gotten in trouble for publishing an article praising bullying of gamers.

None of it was on my radar, simply because I long ago decided that the Left needs to be totally discredited, disempowered, and silenced, and I don't need daily reminders; because the only Leftists I read are serious intellectuals who write books, not shrieking, purple-haired, PC harpies who blog and tweet; because my only experience of gaming was watching

---

[1] http://www.counter-currents.com/2015/09/is-god-the-new-yoda/

someone play Pac Man for five minutes, getting bored, then going and reading a book; and because the most recent piece of science fiction I read was *Chapterhouse: Dune* (1985; pretty disappointing).

Vox Day is the the pen name of Theodore Beale, a 47-year-old American who claims to be of mixed White and Amerindian ancestry. He is a political conservative and an Evangelical Christian. He is a musician, video game designer, essayist, and science fiction and fantasy novelist. Judging from this work alone, Day is highly intelligent, witty, and brave. I plan to read more of his work.

Although Day's work is useful for White Nationalists, he is not one; he hints at knowledge of biological race differences (who are those immigrants lowering Europe's IQs?); he does not mention the Jewish question, but he does offer the following epigraph for chapter 6, on SJW entryism:

"You belong to your father, the devil, and you want to carry out your father's desires. He was a murderer from the beginning, not holding to the truth, for there is no truth in him. When he lies, he speaks his native language, for he is a liar and the father of lies." — John 8: 44

Chapter 1, "An Introduction to the SJW," briefly lists their basic values (equality and diversity) and basic goals (imposing these values through soft totalitarian speech codes, employment discrimination and denial, and the persecution of dissenters).

Chapter 2, "The Three Laws of the SJW" lays out their basic operating system, offering detailed examples from Day's own experiences with SJW sci-fi writer and blogger Joe Scalzi.

The first law is that *SJWs always lie*. This makes sense, because their worldview is premised on lies: Humans are equal. Apparent human differences like race and "gender" are merely "social constructs." Inequality is the result of social injustice. Diversity is a strength. The non-white, non-male, and subnormal are never responsible for their failings. Instead, whites are at fault, particularly white men.

A worldview premised on lies of course requires more lies to advance it. But Day goes further: SJW's don't just lie about politics. They lie habitually and compulsively about *everything*, always to put themselves in a flattering light. In fact, it may be the case that SJWs are merely weak and botched people who adopt their worldview just because it puts them in a more flattering light: it blames other people for their failings, and it lets them play the role of warriors for justice while in fact they are merely cowardly, mendacious drama queens and bullies.

People who lie to cast themselves in a flattering light, including blaming their failures on others, suffer from malignant narcissism. What M. Scott Peck calls "evil."

The second law, *SJWs always double down*, refers to what happens when they are caught in lies, which fits with the malignant narcissist profile, since admitting wrong and losing face are not possible for them.

The third law, *SJWs always project*, namely they accuse you of the evils they do themselves, is also a characteristic of malignant narcissism, which can suffer no negative judgments, so when a particularly apposite one is hovering around the edge of their consciousness, they naturally try to fob it off on their enemies instead. Day also mentions that many SJWs talk quite openly about their mental health problems, most commonly depression.

Chapter 3, "When SJWs Attack," describes how SJWs have hounded prominent people like Nobel Laureate James Watson, Nobel Laureate Tim Hunt, and Mozilla CEO Brendan Eich out of their jobs for politically incorrect statements—a process that has been repeated hundreds if not thousands of times with less well-known individuals. The basic strategy was outlined by Jewish radical Saul Alinsky in his *Rules for Radicals*. Day lays out and illustrates 8 steps, most of which are self-explanatory:

1. Locate or create a violation of the PC Narrative
2. Point and shriek
3. Isolate and swarm
4. Reject and transform, which refers to the futility of apologies, which simply are used as evidence for in-

tensified attacks

5. Press for surrender, which refers to the tendency of
    SJWs to press their targets to resign, which allows
    them to hypocritically deny any responsibility for
    their mark's destruction
6. Appeal to amenable authority, which means the
    SJWs' search for the weakest link in their target's
    employment or social status
7. Show trial
8. Victory parade

This chapter is a very helpful road map of what happens, and what comes next, when SJWs attack. Unfortunately, for most people, the result is the same: social ostracism and the loss of employment and reputation. But there is hope, because people have successfully fought back, which Day discusses in the subsequent chapters.

Chapter 4, "Counterattack," is the story of GamerGate, the populist uprising of gaming enthusiasts against arrogant SJW journalists. GamerGate was a leaderless, viral resistance which turned the tables on SJW bullies, exposing their hypocrisy and corruption and mocking them viciously. Gamergate got some SJWs fired, prompted others to ragequit, and went after the advertisers of SJW periodicals like *Gawker*, which is now in dire financial straits. And every moment the SJWs spend on defense is a moment they cannot spend harming another innocent dissident.

Chapter 5, "Release the Hounds," deals with the campaigns of Day and fellow conservative sci-fi writer Larry Correia against the SJW lock on science fiction and fantasy journalism and awards. The "hounds" in the title refers to the Correia's Sad Puppy campaign to nominate non-PC writers for the Hugo Awards and Day's Rabid Puppies campaign, based on the GamerGate model.

Due to the hounding of the Puppies, the Hugo Awards was forced to adopt new nomination rules that make them less under the control of SJW cabals. But the dogs are not done yet. They are pushing for the firing of leading SJW editors. They are also picking off the weakest members of the SJW herd, who fall silent due to demoralization and depression. Better them than us.

These campaigns, GamerGate in particular, are part of the stirring in the *Zeitgeist* that gave us the cuckservative meme and has been filling the sails of Donald Trump's campaign, which has made immigration restriction, economic nationalism, and the rejection of political correctness live political issues again.

Chapter 6. "The SJW Next Door," describes how SJWs infiltrate and subvert institutions, focusing on Human Resources Departments and the creation of vague, elastic PC codes of conduct which can be used to stigmatize and purge dissidents. Ever wonder why, despite your expensive education, extensive experience, and meticulously crafted resumes, cover letters, and Linkedin profiles, you just don't seem to have any job prospects, White Man? Because corporate choke points are occupied by people like Eve T. Braun of Barclays, the British bank. This is what Braun posted on the London Ruby User's Group mailing list "explaining how she had successfully prevented the hiring of straight white men and other presumed non-SJWs":

> Two other things we implemented which aided the recruitment process: We followed advice which is quickly becoming the industry norm. Never look at someone's Github profile until you have made the decision to hire or not hire them and do not let it influence you. Github profiles tend to favor CIS White men over most minorities in a number of ways. CIS white men often have more spare time or chose to pursue building up an impressive portfolio of code rather than women or minorities who have to deal with things like raising children or institutionalised racism. Some in the SocJus community have even said that technically companies could possibly even be breaking discriminatory law by allowing peoples github profiles and publicly available code to influence their hiring decisions — watch this space. We used Randi

Harper's blockbot to assess applicants twitter profiles for problematic or toxic viewpoints. This may sound a bit extreme but some of the staff here suffer from Aspergers & PTSD and our top priority is to ensure that they don't get put in triggering situations. Making a wrong hire could present a scenario where the employee could be triggered on a daily basis by another employee with an oppressive viewpoint. Other than from a diversity standpoint, from a business standpoint these sorts of negative interactions can cost a company a huge amount of time & money in employees taking off sick days. When all the employees are on the same page the synergy in the office aids productivity.

Remember this whenever you feel an impulse to take a tolerant, live-and-let-live attitude toward SJWs.

Chapter 7, "What to Do When SJWs Attack," is practical advice for individuals under fire:

1. Recognize the attack, remain calm, and realize that very few friends and coworkers will help you.
2. Don't try to reason with them: you are not dealing with rational people, but with raving beasts who will take every gesture of good will as a sign of weakness and will use everything you say against you.
3. Do not apologize: apologies are treated as evidence of guilt and invite intensified attacks.
4. Accept your fate: try to adopt a Stoic attitude of indifference about outcomes; focus simply on doing the right thing, which is to fight.
5. Document their every word and action: most organizations have rules for firing or disciplining people; know the rules; demand that they be followed; admit nothing; demand the accusers do all the work; get everything in writing, and get it signed.
6. Do not resign! Don't do the enemy's work for them.
7. Make the rubble bounce: basically, this means counter-attack; do everything you can to raise the price of

attacking you for your enemies and your employer. This is worth quoting at length: "Whether you survive the attempted purge or whether you don't, it's very important to observe who has defined himself as an ally, an enemy, or a neutral party during the process. The choices people make will pleasantly surprise you about as often as they disappoint you. Once everyone's choices have been made clear, your task is simple. Target the enemy at every opportunity. Hit them wherever they show themselves vulnerable. Play as dirty as your conscience will permit. Undermine them, sabotage them, and discredit them. Be ruthless and show them absolutely no mercy. This is not the time for Christian forgiveness because these are people who have not repented, these are people who are trying to destroy you and are quite willing to harm your family and your children in the process. Take them down and take them out without hesitation. If you have any SJWs working under you, fire them. If you have an SJW relying upon you for something, play dumb and assure him that he'll get it on time, then fail to deliver, all the while promising that it's going to be done next week. Above all, understand that the normal rules of live and let live are no longer in effect. The more you disrupt their activities and their daily routine, the more difficult they will find it to purge you. Assume that you are on your way out—if you've followed the previous advice given, you should already have your landing zone prepared and are only waiting for the right moment to exit— and salt the earth. Leave devastation in your wake so that it will take weeks or even months for them to try to recover from the damage of your purging."

8. Start nothing, finish everything: basically, don't act out of anger; don't initiate attacks, but when attacked, respond with disproportionate, overwhelming force.

Chapter 8, "Striking Back at the Thought Police" and Chapter 9, "Winning the Social Justice War," are the most exciting parts of the book, for Day makes it clear that he is not content with just fending off the Left, but on rolling it back completely. This is what sets him miles apart from mainstream conservatism, which has never conserved anything from the Left, much less taken back lost ground. I will just deal with the highlights of these chapters.

Day's first strategic principle is to know oneself and one's enemy, and act accordingly. Day points out that the Right has a systematic advantage over the Left, because the Left is based on lies; Leftists do not understand themselves or their enemies, but we do.

One of Day's most important principles is to reject the ideals of SJWs: equality, diversity, tolerance, and progress. Day flatly rejects equality as a fact or a moral ideal. He flatly rejects the daft notion that diversity is a strength. He does not measure progress in terms of equality and diversity, but in terms of science and technology, and points out that these forms of progress are incompatible with the first two ideals. He dismisses tolerance as "little more than a cloak for SJW entryism," noting that SJWs always demand it but never practice it.

Day simply denies the Left the moral standing to judge the Right. He dismisses them as followers of false ideals that lead to injustice and tyranny. For Day, the values of the Right are Truth, Liberty, and Justice. (I prefer Truth, Justice, and a Nice White Country. I think individual liberty is fine, but not when it conflicts with the common good.)

Day believes that SJW types must be purged from all institutions of society, and safeguards must be created to prevent any new entryism. We must begin with institutions we control, then seek to extend our control to the whole of society, completely uprooting Leftist power. He frankly states that "the single most important principle to adopt is a ruthless intolerance for anyone expressing even a modicum of sympathy for social justice ideals. While this may sound too paranoid or detail-oriented for you, rest assured that if you do not go to the trouble of aggressively keeping out the SJWs, they will invade your organization and they will do their best to take it over."

Day urges us to defund and destroy the Left's propaganda centers: the educational system and the mass media/popular culture. The best way to do that is to create our own alternative educational system and media, until we can take over the mainstream ones.

Day also recommends that we create organizations and livelihoods that are "antifragile"—resilient to SJW attacks and subversion. Self-employment is probably the single most important guarantee of independence from SJW attacks.

Day stresses the importance of morale for both our forces and our enemy. SJWs tend to be mentally ill; thus they are easily demoralized if one stands up to them and then counterattacks. He recommends fine-grained attacks on SJW activists, who must be targeted, doxxed, and denied employment and a public voice. He even recommends that we counter SJW ideas whenever we encounter them in face-to-face interactions. Since SJWs are generally ineducable though, he recommends that we do not argue with them, but simply communicate verbally and subverbally that we find their ideas silly and boring. In short, Day calls for full-spectrum resistance, from face-to-face encounters to revolutionizing social institutions.

A final point has to do with solidarity. Day is quite frank that this battle can be lonely. Society is full of moderates who will split the difference between truth and lies, innocence and guilt, good and evil, rather than take sides. Thus we need to cultivate allies, even if we do not fully agree with them. For instance, Day, an Evangelical Christian, is allied with pick up artist Roosh V. in battling political correctness.

We also need to prepare ourselves to be disappointed by the cowardice of our colleagues and friends and even families. But apologizing and surrendering will change nothing. So if you have slipped up and spoken an unacceptable truth, don't think about the friends you might be losing. Because they weren't real friends anyway, and you won't get them back by caving in. Think of the friends you will be gaining by standing firm.

But that only works if one actually gains friends, if people actually come to your aid. So I want each and every reader to pledge that you will place a copy of this book into the hands of anyone in your community — mighty or humble — who is targeted for destruction simply for speaking the truth. If more people stand firm for the truth, others will be emboldened to stand with them, and around them a new nation might be born.

Don't let the silly cover and flippant title fool you: *SJWs Always Lie* is one of the most radical Right-wing manifestos of the post-War era. Buy it and read it today.

Counter-Currents/*North American New Right*
September 4, 2015

MAKING IDEAS VIRULENT:
MALCOLM GLADWELL'S *THE TIPPING POINT*

Malcolm Gladwell
The Tipping Point:
How Little Things Can Make a Big Difference
New York: Little, Brown, 2000

The son of an English father and a Jamaican mother, Malcom Gladwell is the author of five books and countless articles, many of them published in *The New Yorker*, where he is a staff writer. *The Tipping Point* is a highly readable blend of popularized psychology, epidemiology, and case histories from the business world which I am placing on the required reading list of White Nationalists who are serious about creating a revolution. For although our movement today is very small, Gladwell explains how little things—including lone, often unknown individuals— can make a big difference.

The enemy's tired old script is that White Nationalists are always "spewing" what they call "virulent" ideas or just "hate." "Virulence," of course, refers to the propagation of a disease. This is more than just an insult, however. They may liken us to rats and our ideas to the plague. But like a plague, unfashionable ideas can reach a "tipping point" and suddenly "go viral," spreading geometrically and sweeping through large populations. And that is what the enemy fears. So let's give them something to be afraid of. Let's make our ideas genuinely virulent, so we can heal the world.

The viral changes Gladwell discusses have three chief traits. First, they are *contagious*. They spread from person to person. They are not radiated outward from a central hub to isolated recipients, like a television broadcast. Second, *little changes often have huge effects* by being multiplied or amplified geometrically rather than arithmetically. Finally, once these processes are afoot, widespread changes can happen *very quickly*.

The distinction between arithmetic and geometric changes is

crucial. Imagine that you make a pledge to convert one other person to White Nationalism each year. That is not such a difficult goal to imagine. At the end of the first year, there will be two of you. At the end of the second year, there will be three. At the end of ten years, there will be eleven of you. This is an arithmetic progression, and it is a slow process. At that rate, you would need a million years to convert a million people to White Nationalism.

Now imagine that, in addition to converting one person a year, you also convert them to the idea of converting one other person per year, and get each new convert to do the same. So you are communicating not just White Nationalism, but White Nationalism with a multiplier effect, White Nationalism plus a mission to convert others to White Nationalism. At the end of the first year, there will be two of you, as before. But at the end of the second year, there will be four. At the end of the third year, there will be eight. The progression looks like this:

Year 1: 2 White Nationalists
Year 2: 4
Year 3: 8
Year 4: 16
Year 5: 32
Year 6: 64
Year 7: 128
Year 8: 256
Year 9: 512
Year 10: 1024

Remember, after 10 years of arithmetic growth, there will be only 11 of you, whereas after 10 years of geometric growth, there will be 1,024. I have been a White Nationalist for 15 years now. And if I had started this conversion process 15 years ago, there would be 32,768 of us, and none of it would have happened unless I made the *individual effort to start the process.*

How much longer would it take to get to 1 million White Nationalists by this process? *Only five more years.* After 20 years of geometric growth, the number would be 1,048,576—a number that we could not reach in a million years of arithmetic growth. Five more years after that, and we would top 33 million converts. And five years after that, we would pass the *one billion* mark.

And bear in mind that this process presupposes only that we convert one person per year. At the end of 20 years, I individually would have converted only 20 other people. Now, I will wager that that is a goal that even the most tongue-tied and introverted amongst us can imagine attaining. Each one of us already knows 20 people whom we might be able to convert if we had an entire year to bring each one around.

So imagine the changes that could be brought about by a really charismatic individual with a particularly persuasive statement of our position and the means to deliver that message. Such a person could convert hundreds or thousands or tens of thousands of people a year, and impart the same mission to his converts. Such a person could set the world aright.

The transformative potential of moderate individual efforts if they are geometrically compounded is astonishing. But it puts the existing movement in a perhaps unfairly unflattering light. For instance, in the 8 years I have focused on activism, have I converted even a measly 256 people? Maybe I have, but I have no way of actually knowing. What I know for certain that my senior colleagues, who can boast of 20 years of activism have not converted more than a million. Those who have been at it for 25 years have not converted more than 33 million. And those who can boast of 30 years of activism fall far short of the one billion mark that simple geometric progression yields. And remember, all any of these long-time movement veterans would have had to do to reach a billion converts today is convert 30 people over 30 years, and get each of them to do the same.

So we have to conclude that the White Nationalist movement has not quite found the right people, formulated the right message, and created the right means of propagating it. Not yet, anyway. But we're trying. And Gladwell can help.

In chapter 1, "The Three Rules of Epidemics," Gladwell offers three principles of viral propagation. First, there is the *Law of the Few*. Economists talk about the 80/20 Principle, which holds that in any given situation, roughly 80 percent of the effect will be caused by 20 percent of the individuals involved:

> In most societies, 20 percent of criminals commit 80 percent of crimes. Twenty percent of motorists cause 80 percent of all accidents. Twenty percent of beer drinkers drink 80 percent of all beer. When it comes to epidemics, though, this disproportionality becomes even more extreme: a tiny percentage of people do the majority of the work. (p. 19)

Second, there is the *Stickiness Factor*. In epidemics, a virus spreads more the longer it sticks around in a carrier's system. A virus that is easy to cure, or that is immediately fatal, will therefore spread less than one that is hard to cure but does not kill its carrier immediately. Likewise, ideas that stick in one's head are more likely to be passed on than ones that are easily forgotten.

Finally, there is the importance of *Context*, which can affect the spread of a disease or an idea in unanticipated ways.

I found chapter 2, "The Law of the Few," the most exciting part of the book. Here Gladwell discusses three types of individuals who are highly influential in the spread of ideas: *Connectors*, *Mavens*, and *Salesmen*. All of these individuals are involved in person-to-person interactions, which is how contagious ideas are spread. Again, we are not talking about ideas being diffused to separate individuals from a common hub, which is how the system controls our minds, but about person-to-person interactions, which can do an end run around top down control. This chapter deserves careful study, because communicating ideas is our business. Gladwell holds up a mirror, in which we can see both our strengths and our shortcomings.

In further pieces on Gladwell, I will discuss his analyses of Connectors, Mavens, and Salesmen, as well as some contextual factors that may prove useful to White Nationalists.

CONNECTORS VS. POLARIZERS

In his book *The Tipping Point*, Malcolm Gladwell talks about the importance of people he calls Connectors, Mavens, and Salesmen in the viral propagation of ideas. Connectors are people who have a gift for making friends and acquaintances. Gladwell attributes this knack to "some combination of curiosity, self-confidence, sociability, and energy" (p. 49).

Although he does not talk about introversion and extroversion, his examples indicate that good connectors are extroverts, who are energized rather than drained by social interactions.

Good connectors are people who have a foot in many different social worlds and thus can bring them together. Interestingly, in terms of finding new information and opportunities, most advantageous connections are often weak ties of acquaintance. This makes sense, because your close friends are all in the same social world, so it stands to reason that acquaintances would expand your connections to other realms.

Connectors are extremely valuable for the spread of ideas through word of mouth, simply because they know more people in more social realms.

In my experience, the best connectors are not just people who reach out, but who are approachable and responsive when others reach out to them. That is half of how connections are made. Once made, such connections have to be maintained as well. This is why Facebook is such a boon to us. Although it is fashionable to deride social media, what differentiates it from the other media is that it facilitates person-to-person connections, particularly the loose, tenuous, and far-flung ones that are actually the most world-expanding.

Many movement people deride the internet in favor of the real world. Of course the real world is where politics happens. But before politics comes metapolitics: sharing ideas and building networks. And the internet is great for that. I would wager that 95% of White Nationalists under 50 would not be with us were it not for the internet.

The most important principle of movement connectivity I know is what I call the Fight Club principle: *everybody gets to choose his own level of explicitness and involvement, and everybody else has to respect that decision.* Since every society, regardless of its ideology, is ruled by better than average people, we need to recruit better than average people to our cause. But the people who have the most skills, resources, and connections also have the most to lose. Such people will not involve themselves in a dissident movement unless they have a reasonable assurance that we will respect their privacy. People who rant at and browbeat people who do not wish to become open advocates set off alarm bells. They are not to be trusted. They may eventually "out" people. Thus prudent people will not and should not have anything to do with them. If you want people to connect to you, they need to know that you understand and respect their decisions about their level of involvement.

The best connector I know in the White Nationalist world is Jez Turner of the London Forum, which is one reason why the London Forum is such a success, putting on veritable movement summit conferences multiple times a year. Given the bitter factionalism and difficult personalities in the movement, this level of success requires a lot of good humor and excellent diplomacy. The reason that there are not London Forum type events in every major European city is that good connectors are in short supply.

One of the weaknesses of depending on connectors is that once they are gone, the network is destroyed. That is what happened when my friend Beryl Cheetham, who was an important connector, died in June of 2015. Once she was gone, I had no way of contacting the people I knew through her. But there was enough redundancy in our network that I could reestablish those ties, and the most helpful person for doing turned out to be Jez Turner.

Because of my role as Editor of Counter-Currents, I am a *de facto* connector. But I'm just not good at it. Psychologically, I am introverted (INTJ, to be exact), so it is a stretch for me. At a certain point, I just can't deal with one more social interaction and shut down, which is why I am often a tardy correspondent. Nor am I good at multitasking or remembering names. Ideally, I would have an assistant who is extroverted and good at multitasking (women are typically better at that than men).

Gladwell does not talk about the opposite of a connector, which is a polarizer: a person who sows distrust and discord. Connectors build up the social capital of the movement. Polarizers tear it apart. I have encountered two kinds of polarizers.

The first group are polarizers on principle: they openly announce that their strategy is to subject anyone who is closer to the mainstream to relentless attack, both ideological and *ad hominem*, on the theory that this will split off people and win them over to their vanguardist groupuscule. I don't deny that such an approach might appeal to some types of people, primarily masochists with inferiority complexes or under-fathered "lost boys"—the kinds of people who wanted to join the Marine Corps after watching *Full Metal Jacket*, for instance. But, as I argue in my essay "The Smartest Guy in the Room,"[1] it only appeals to people who are inferior to whoever is issuing the harangue, which is no way to put the movement on an upward path toward attracting better and better people. Superior people simply ignore such polarizers, or want to crush them like bugs. I suspect that polarizers on principle are simply trying to make a virtue out of indulging their own prickly narcissism and tendencies toward paranoia and embitterment.

The most insidious polarizers actually pose as connectors. Like genuine connectors, they like to be at the center of things. But their dominant drive is ego gratification, and whenever that conflicts with the needs of the movement, the movement always loses. I have had dealings with two such people over the years. Both of them pose as connectors and uniters of different camps and factions. But I began to notice problems.

First, despite their pose as uniters, the trend of their thinking always pulls toward the negative. They are gossips, gatekeepers, well-poisoners, purgers, and shunners.

Second, they prefer the Star Chamber and the whispering campaign to open discussions, so the accused cannot defend

---

[1] In *Truth, Justice, & a Nice White Country.*

themselves.

Third, they always insisted on remaining middlemen. They would not just put people in touch and let them take it from there, because at that point they were no longer needed.

Fourth, they would tell me stories designed to alienate me from people I did know.

In both cases, however, it turned out that these people were pathological liars. And their lies served only one purpose: to stir up drama and intrigue around themselves, which apparently satisfied a neurotic need for attention and a desire to feel powerful. There is really no calculating how much damage such drama queens have done to the movement, since the people they drive apart seldom ever compare notes and realize how they have been deceived.

Gladwell's discussion of connectors brings a very important phenomenon into focus. Connectors are extremely valuable and extremely rare. If we want our message to go viral, we need to find and cultivate connectors whose tendrils reach out into as many different worlds as possible.

Polarizers, by contrast, are a plague. Open polarizers are easy to spot and are generally ignored, because the better sort of people don't want to work with jerks. Drama queen stealth polarizers are a much bigger problem, but now you know how to spot them.

Counter-Currents/*North American New Right*
September 8, 2015

MAVENS & SALESMEN

According to Malcolm Gladwell's *The Tipping Point*, Connectors — people with friends and acquaintances in many different social worlds — are crucial in making information go viral. But where do they get their information? To answer this, Gladwell introduces the concept of Mavens. Mavens are collectors of information. In the economic realm, Mavens are people who collect information on prices and products. They are an inexhaustible source of comparisons, rankings, and tips. Mavens are the kinds of people who type out 1,000 word reviews of pillows on Amazon.com. If you are buying a computer, talk to a computer Maven. If you are buying a car, talk to a car Maven.

Being a market Maven naturally has economic advantages. But that is seldom their primary motivation. Mavens generally collect this sort of information simply because it interests them, and they share it simply because they want to help. And because they are not paid pitchmen, their recommendations carry a great deal of weight.

Gladwell's focus is on market Mavens, but the same motives and personality traits are present in scholars, especially academic researchers, who pursue often highly specialized knowledge as an end in itself, but whose efforts often have wide-ranging practical consequences. Although Gladwell does not mention the autism spectrum, the Maven's intense and disinterested pursuit of fine-grained knowledge points in that direction.

There are many Mavens on the Right, and they play an important role. They are the people who compile quotes, links, and concrete illustrations. They are the people who like to crunch numbers. But Mavens are often underappreciated. Activist types dismiss them as pimply-faced nerds lacking a sense of political utility and urgency. But right now we are in a war of ideas, and Mavens collect and deliver ideas that we can weaponize.

Although sincerity and disinterestedness count for a lot, Mavens are not the ideal people to deliver ideas. They tend to be spammers. They tend to be myopic. They often deliver too much information. They sometimes lose sight of the big picture. But when I need information, I turn to Mavens. I can keep track of the big picture myself. I can filter and prioritize information myself. So I actually prefer Mavens to collect and deliver as much raw and disorganized information as possible.

The more Mavens the New Right attracts, and the happier we make them, the stronger our movement will be. But to find and cultivate Mavens, we have to understand them, which is why Gladwell is so helpful.

Gladwell's discussion of Connectors and Mavens also turns out to be a discussion of Jews. The Connectors and Mavens profiled by Gladwell all seem to be Jews. When he offers a way to rate your connectedness by counting the number of people you know whose surnames match randomly chosen names from the New York City telephone directory, the test obviously has a pro-Jewish bias. I am a highly connected person, but I make it a point of *not* knowing people named Alpern, Aran, Arnstein, Ballout, Bamberger, Blau, Bohen, Borsuk, Brendle, Cohen, Cohn, Eastman, Fermin, Finkelstein, Farber, Falkin, Feinman, Friedman, etc. (to choose from the first dozen lines). Gladwell even mentions that the word "Maven" comes from "the Yiddish." Since Gladwell lives in New York City and works for *The New Yorker*, one might dismiss the judeo-centrism of his analysis as simple sampling bias. But the more interesting possibility is that a propensity to being Connectors and Mavens contributes to Jewish success and social dominance. Which recommends his analysis to other groups that aim for social dominance.

Information and connections alone are not enough to make ideas go viral, however. The third essential component is action. People must be persuaded to actually buy a product or an idea. Hence Gladwell's discussion of Salesmen, whose main traits turn out to be *weaponized information* and *charisma* (these are my terms).

Salesmen have to command information. But it has to be weaponized. The best salesmen have a vast repertoire of facts and arguments to answer every objection. Talking points, in other words, and the ability to deliver them.

Charisma is a form of charm and attractiveness that makes people want to look at you, listen to you, agree with you, even obey you. Charisma is a non-rational form of persuasiveness. It is a non-violent form of coercion. It is "force of personality." It can lead to action without appeal to reason or force. Charisma is a mysterious phenomenon, but Gladwell cites a couple of scientific studies that throw some light on it.

First, it turns out that people are very attuned to non-verbal forms of communication, such as gestures and expressions. Second, certain gestures and expressions can be contagious. If I yawn, for example, you are more likely to yawn. If I smile, you are more likely to smile. Third, the causal connection between emotions and expressions goes two ways. We smile because we are happy, but we can also make ourselves happy by smiling.

Charismatic people are exceptionally good at communicating their inner states not just verbally but also through sub-verbal cues. If these become contagious, they can change our way of thinking. A salesman who smiles can make us smile. A salesman who nods can make us nod. And if we smile, we are more likely to feel happy. If we nod, we are more likely to agree with what is being said. When this form of non-rational persuasion is wedded with facts and well-delivered arguments it has the power to change the world.

The Stickiness Factor refers to the fact that ideas that stick in our minds are more likely to spread. Therefore, if you want to make ideas viral, make them memorable. Make them simple, state them elegantly, make them concise, make them rhyme, associate them with striking images, etc. Gladwell's discussion deals mostly with children's television, which is not really relevant to politics, although it illustrates the idea that sometimes tinkering on the margins can dramatically transform the stickiness of a message. The most important lesson of the chapter is that information becomes stickier if it is accompanied by an opportunity to act on it immediately. (Which, for one thing, has given me some ideas for tweaking the design of the Counter-Currents site.)

The most important element of Gladwell's discussion of Context deals with the critical role of groups as the incubators of viral ideas. This illustrates nicely the harmony of the two branches of metapolitics: propagating ideas and building communities. If you want ideas to become sticky, discuss, practice, and embody them in a group. Groups also amplify the connectivity of ideas, for each member is connected to a different set of people.

Gladwell cites interesting research on the ideal scale of groups. Given the limits of the human mind to keep track of individuals and relationships, we can maintain genuine personal social interactions with a maximum of 150 people, which is why Hutterite colonies split when they reach 150 members. Larger groups require impersonal, mediated forms of organization, which can scale to encompass billions. The law of 150 is worth remembering for those who wish to organize White Nationalist tribes and fraternal orders. Such groups are not a substitute for civilization, but they can be vehicles for preserving Western Civilization in a battle with invaders and parasite tribes.

I highly recommend *The Tipping Point*. I have only been able to hit the highlights in my discussion. Gladwell offers many useful analyses and case studies of how ideas and products go viral. But he makes it clear that these processes also depend upon countless contingencies, which make it impossible to plan, predict, and control them. The good news is that the same contingencies make it impossible to *suppress* viral ideas as well.

The role of chance also means that each and every one of us may be the last straw, the one who tips the balance. That fact is empowering, so long as we recognize that these processes cannot be planned or controlled. So we should detach ourselves from the outcomes and look for *intrinsic* rewards in the struggle. We should regard it as a moral duty, and we should also try to have as much fun with it as possible. And if enough of us dutifully and joyfully muck around, creating memes and real-world relationships, we might luck out and change the world.

Counter-Currents/*North American New Right*
September 11, 2015

INDEX

This index lists all occurrences of proper names plus definitions and discussions of important concepts and issues. Numbers in bold refer to a whole chapter or section devoted to a particular topic.

About the Author

GREG JOHNSON, Ph.D. is Editor-in-Chief of Counter-Currents Publishing Ltd., as well as Editor of *North American New Right*, its webzine (http://www.counter-currents.com/) and occasional print journal.

He is the author of *New Right vs. Old Right* (San Francisco: Counter-Currents, 2013) and *Truth, Justice, & a Nice White Country* (San Francisco: Counter-Currents, 2015). Under the pen name Trevor Lynch, he is the author of *Trevor Lynch's White Nationalist Guide to the Movies* (San Francisco: Counter-Currents, 2012) and *Son of Trevor Lynch's White Nationalist Guide to the Movies* (San Francisco: Counter-Currents, 2015).

He is editor of many books, including Alain de Benoist, *On Being a Pagan*, trans. Jon Graham (Atlanta: Ultra, 2004); Michael O'Meara, *Toward the White Republic* (San Francisco: Counter-Currents, 2010); Michael J. Polignano, *Taking Our Own Side* (San Francisco: Counter-Currents, 2010); Collin Cleary, *Summoning the Gods: Essays on Paganism in a God-Forsaken World* (San Francisco: Counter-Currents, 2011); Irmin Vinson, *Some Thoughts on Hitler and Other Essays* (San Francisco: Counter-Currents, 2011); *North American New Right*, vol. 1 (San Francisco: Counter-Currents, 2012); Kerry Bolton, *Artists of the Right: Resisting Decadence* (San Francisco: Counter-Currents, 2012); James J. O'Meara, *The Homo and the Negro: Masculinist Meditations on Politics and Popular Culture* (San Francisco: Counter-Currents, 2012); Jonathan Bowden, *Pulp Fascism: Right-Wing Themes in Comics, Graphic Novels, and Popular Literature* (San Francisco: Counter-Currents, 2013); James J. O'Meara, *The Eldritch Evola . . . & Others: Traditionalist Meditations on Literature, Art, & Culture* (San Francisco: Counter-Currents, 2014); Jonathan Bowden, *Western Civilization Bites Back* (San Francisco: Counter-Currents, 2014); Collin Cleary, *What is a Rune? & Other Essays* (San Francisco: Counter-Currents, 2015); and James J. O'Meara, *Green Nazis in Space! New Essays on Literature, Art, & Culture* (San Francisco: Counter-Currents, 2015).

His writings have been translated into Czech, Danish, Dutch, Estonian, French, German, Greek, Hungarian, Norwegian, Polish, Portuguese, Russian, Slovak, Spanish, Swedish, and Ukrainian.

www.ingramcontent.com/pod-product-compliance
Lightning Source LLC
Chambersburg PA
CBHW031427270326
41930CB00007B/597